Great Chefs® of HAWAII

Hele mai a'i –

"Come here and eat"

Great Chefs® of HAWAII

Companion to the International Television Series
Great Chefs® of Hawaii

By
Kaui Philpotts

GREAT CHEFS® Publishing

Other Great Chefs®
companion cookbooks
available:

Great Chefs of New Orleans I
Great Chefs of New Orleans II
Great Chefs of San Francisco
Great Chefs of Chicago
Southwest Tastes
Great Chefs: the Louisiana new Garde
Great Chefs of the East
Great Chefs–Great Cities
Great Chefs Cook American
Great Chefs Cook Italian

All series now available on home video, including
Great Chefs of Hawaii

Additional home videos available:

Great Chefs: Appetizers	*Great Outdoor Cooking*
Oriental Obsessions	*Great Chefs, Great BBQ*
A New Orleans Jazz Brunch	*Great French Fest*
Great Chefs: Chocolate Passion	*Down Home Cookin'*
Great Women Chefs	*Great Chefs Cook American*
Great Chefs: Seafood Sampler	*Great Chefs Cook Italian*
Great Chefs: Desserts	*Great Chefs Halloween Treat*
Mexican Madness	*Great American Inns*
Great Chefs: Chocolate Edition	*A Southwest Thanksgiving Feast*
Great Southern Barbecue	*An International Holiday Table*

Published by
Great Chefs® Publishing
G.S.I., Inc.
P.O. Box 56757
New Orleans, LA 70156
1-800-321-1499

Printed in China.

First Printing 1996

Library of Congress Cataloguing-in-Publication Data

Kaui Philpotts
Great Chefs® of Hawaii

Library of Congress Catalogue Card Number 96-076710
Includes index
     1. Cooking in America
        I. Great Chefs of Hawaii
        II. Title
ISBN   Hardbound 0-929714-73-3
           Softbound 0-929714-72-5
UPC   Hardbound 0-490092-733-1-0
           Softbound 0-490092-725-1-5

CONTENTS

Great Chefs® of HAWAII

The Chefs

The spirit of aloha is a spirit of welcome and sharing. These outstanding Hawaiian chefs contributed the more than 400 recipes which comprise the 124 creative dishes contained in this book.

Hawaii

Kauai

Oahu

All chefs and restaurants are listed in this book as they were taped for television.
Chefs and restaurants do change; if you wish to dine with a particular chef or restaurant,
Great Chefs suggests you call the restaurant when planning your trip.

Acknowledgements

I feel fortunate to have been involved with many of the chefs represented in this book from the beginning. In less than a decade they have taken an island cuisine that was not much more than sliced pineapple and frozen mahimahi, and catapulted it into another dimension.

Thanks to them we can now dine on strawberries from the slopes of Haleakala crater, shrimp from the ponds of Kahuku, and fresh greens from the farms of Waimanalo. Hawaii's great chefs have taken our mixed heritage and melded it into one cuisine. The result is glorious.

Thanks to John Shoup for hiring me on the spot—while he watched the sun go down from the lanai of the Outrigger Canoe Club on Waikiki Beach. And to my New Orleans connection, Linda Nix, for her patience, organization, and humor on deadline.

Carolyn Miller in San Franciso, a diligent and exacting editor, helped make everything I said sound better and made sure the recipes of so many different chefs were clear and user-friendly for you at home.

Many thanks to Tad Sewell, Conard Steiner, and Tyna Millacci of Calabash Occasions in Honolulu, and Judy Furtado on Maui, for testing all of the recipes.

And especially to my husband, Doug, who listened to sighs coming from my office off the kitchen. He knew enough to take me to dinner when, after a day of writing about food, the thought of actually cooking it was simply too much.

Kaui Philpotts

Preface

Aloha. Welcome to a taste of paradise.

There is a Hawaiian welcoming song, which says — *e komo mai, e noho mai, e 'ai a e wala'au* — come in, come sit, eat, and talk. This is our spirit of aloha, the spirit of sharing. The sharing of food has always been an important part of our traditions, and I am delighted to share with you some of the best Hawaii has to offer.

The great variety of Hawaii's cuisine reflects our heritage from many lands. It also showcases our development over the past decade as a truly great place for fine food. Hawaii's chefs turned to our farmers and fishing industry for the best foods from our lands and sea, and a whole new industry blossomed. During my two terms as governor, we were proud of this development, reaching all segments of the economy. We are especially pleased to be able to share our cuisine with you, both in this book and on television, through Great Chefs.

Enjoy *Great Chefs of Hawaii.* You now have over 400 new reasons to visit. Aloha.

John Waihee
Former Governor, State of Hawaii
1986-1994

Foreword

When I began writing about food in Hawaii a dozen years ago, I had no idea I'd been assigned to cover the hottest breaking story in the Islands. I'd booked a front-row table just in time for the revolution.

Half a generation ago there was good food in the Islands, but you had to look to find it. It could be found in little ethnic restaurants with unpronounceable names and Formica-topped tables. Or at lunch wagons that sold a cross-cultural mix of entrees on paper plates. Or at private parties and luaus where the buffet table might offer Hawaiian kalua pig and lomilomi salmon, Chinese duck and noodles with char siu, Japanese teriyaki, tonkatsu and sushi, Vietnamese spring rolls, Filipino lumpia, Korean kalbi and kim chee, Thai curry and green papaya salad.

This was not fashionable food. It was just food we liked, and shared among ourselves. It certainly wasn't the food we ordered in white-tablecloth restaurants. And it was definitely not the food we served to visitors.

We served visitors what we thought they liked—French onion soup, Caesar salad, chateaubriand, duck à l'orange, chocolate mousse. Surrounded by an ocean teeming with fish, we flew in frozen sole and served sole almondine. We even served visitors food they thought was Hawaiian, but wasn't. We covered chicken with sliced pineapple, sprinkled macadamia nuts on imported fish.

But then, at first slowly, things began to change.

From France, from the Mainland, from Japan, the new resorts brought in highly creative young chefs. Hawaii began to develop more homegrown talent—chefs with Hawaiian or Asian or mixed backgrounds who went to school, absorbed the craft, and had the advantage of knowing the territory. It occurred to these young chefs that they would never become truly great unless they exploited the fresh ingredients around them.

And what ingredients they found. The ocean teemed with some of the best seafood in the world—ahi, mahimahi, opah, opakapaka, shutome. An infant aquaculture industry provided freshwater prawns and cold water lobster.

Warm and sunny, Hawaii could grow virtually anything, not just sugar and pineapple. The chefs began talking to the farmers. You began to hear about fresh herbs on Molokai. Chocolate on the Big Island. Strawberries, onions, and blue potatoes on the slopes of Upcountry Maui. Baby lettuces, watercress, and lemongrass just a 20 minute drive from downtown Honolulu. The alliance between chefs and farmers created a rapidly evolving regional cuisine. Hawaii was America's only tropical state. It burst forth with flavors no other part of the country could provide.

And Hawaii had one other crucial ingredient—a resident population already accustomed to mixing and matching a multitude of Polynesian, Eastern, and Western flavors. It was an audience who responded enthusiastically when a few daring chefs began charring ahi with Japanese spices and serving it with a lilikoi sauce. Or filling a taro basket with Peking duck and wild mushrooms. Or steaming local fish in a combination of Provençal herbs and Hawaiian-style seaweeds.

All the tastes we had cultivated all those years in secret were out of the closet. Better yet, they were on the restaurant table—done with the precision and power of skilled chefs.

Hawaii went food crazy. New restaurants sprang up. Menus changed daily. Going out for dinner grew into an adventure. Dozens of chefs, emboldened, cooked up their own versions of Hawaiian regional cuisine. Their contributions were hotly debated, analyzed, and enjoyed. Overnight small farmers became celebrities, the cutting edge of agriculture. And everyone who took pleasure in great food profited—including visitors to the Islands, who turned out not to have wanted sole almondine after all.

Great Chefs has done a tremendous job, first of finding this culinary revolution in the middle of the Pacific, and then of documenting it so beautifully. And I have to salute my friend Kaui Philpotts, who 10 years ago first introduced me to the blue potatoes and Ulupalakua strawberries of Upcountry Maui. It's no surprise to anyone who knows her that Kaui has written such a useful and enjoyable book.

Even reading the lists of ingredients, the names of the dishes, you can feel the warm sun, hear the tradewinds rustling through the palm fronds, and almost taste paradise.

Aloha. Enjoy.
John Heckathorn
Editor
HONOLULU Magazine

For the past 12 years John Heckathorn has covered the Island restaurant scene for *HONOLULU* Magazine, winning both the Hawaii Publishers Association award and the national William Allen White award for his food criticism. He has written more than 120 articles on food and wine, and, in addition, serves as the magazine's editor. He was the consulting editor for the *Berlitz Guide to Hawaii*, and managing editor in Hawaii for the Gault Millau *"Best of Hawaii"* guide.

Oheloberry Dessert in Tulip Cookies; Peter Chilla, Coast Grill, Hapuna Beach Prince Hotel, Mauna Kea Resort, Kamuela, Hawaii

Hawaiian Food:
From Native Culture to the New Cuisine

Think Hawaiian food, and you may conjure up a dish with a sticky-sweet pineapple sauce worthy of a fifties cookbook. Or even worse, you may recall a tale of culinary horror from a neighbor who attended a luau for tourists at a Waikiki resort hotel. But there's a lot more to Hawaiian food than these sad examples. A revolution that is nothing short of phenomenal has occurred in island cuisine in the past decade, led by young chefs working with fresh foods from Asia, Hawaii, and California.

The first Hawaiians were Polynesians who arrived in two groups, the first from the Marquesas somewhere around 300 A.D. and another from Tahiti around 900 A.D. In their seaworthy voyaging canoes they brought all their staples: kalo (taro root), rock salt, ulu (breadfruit), 'uala (sweet potato), pua'a (pigs), moa (chicken), ilio (dogs), kukui (candlenut tree), coconuts, and bananas.

The water was sweet in these isolated islands in the middle of the Pacific. Fish were abundant in the sea, as were limu (seaweed) and opihi (shellfish) close to shore. To their diet the Hawaiians added the hoio fern, the spinachlike leaves of the taro root (luau) and the taro's crimson stalks (haha). As the society and culture developed, the men became the preparers of food, building fire pits lined with hot volcanic rock called imu, while the women made the family's clothing from kapa cloth (the pounded bark of the wauke, or mulberry tree). Religious significance was placed on certain foods, such as bananas, coconuts, pork, and shark's meat, and women were forbidden to eat them, on the threat of death. Men and women dined separately, and many other strict rules of conduct directed their lives. It was not until 1819, when the great Queen Kaahumanu, regent and widow of Kamehameha I, sat down with his badly shaken young son and heir Liholiho and ate a meal with him in public, that the old kapu (tabu) against men and women eating at the same table was thrown out.

In March 1820, Hawaiian spiritual life underwent a radical change with the arrival of the first Protestant missionaries from New England aboard the *Thaddeus*. In the years between the "discovery" by Captain James Cook in 1778 of what he called the Sandwich Islands and the arrival of the missionaries, Hawaiians had been introduced to hard tack, salt-cured salmon, and beef from ships headed for China to trade furs from the American Northwest. These merchant sailors also brought with them liquor and a bawdy lifestyle.

The New England missionaries and other early merchant settlers from England, Scotland, France, and Germany combined the imported foods of their homelands with what was fresh and available locally. Many of the earliest adventurers married Hawaiian women and stayed in the islands, further blending dietary habits.

By the middle of the nineteenth century, a need for cheap field labor developed due to the planting of sugar cane and pineapple. The native Hawaiian population had declined in alarming numbers because of disease and dissipation, and the Hawaiian temperament, while hardworking and good-natured, was not suited to the grueling labor patterns imposed by the plantation owners.

Waves of immigrants came from Asia, first from China, then from Japan, Korea, and the Philippines. Later in the century, workers were imported from the Portuguese islands of Madeira and the Azores, as well as Puerto Rico. With them came their cuisines.

Plantation families imported what they could from back home, and adapted traditional recipes to what was available or could be grown in Hawaii. Every plantation home had a small vegetable garden, and on weekends families went to the ocean to gather limu (seaweed), opihi (limpets), and fish from the shore. Net and shore fishing was popular.

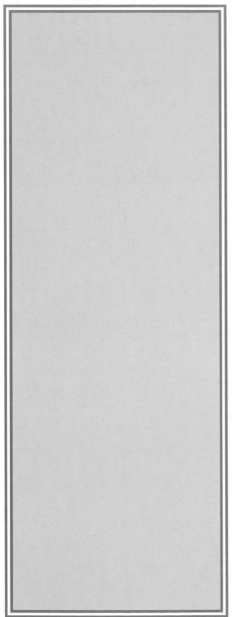

All plantation camps had shady mango trees, small lime trees, and aloe cactus for burns and rashes. The Chinese planted lychee trees and juicy sweet star fruit (carambola). The Japanese made sure they had turnips (daikon) for their pickles. The Koreans planted cabbage and small red chilies for their kim chee. From the Portuguese came backyard stone ovens for bread making, and fragrant vegetable and bean soups as well as pungent vinegar-laced roasts called vinha d'alhos.

By the 1930s, a robust folk cuisine had been well established throughout the island chain. All the different nationalities, as they began intermarrying, reveled in each other's festivals and food.

Restaurants and hotels, however, ignored "local food" and served dishes that reflected the tastes of the mainland United States and Europe. At great expense, foods like fresh strawberries, beef, and lamb were flown in to be served in the best dining rooms at luxury resorts. Local food was considered too ethnic, unsophisticated, and definitely inferior.

But then things changed. Influenced by the new American cuisine movement on the mainland, the younger chefs who came to oversee the kitchens of the new resorts that popped up in the late seventies and through the eighties became interested in local ingredients. Hawaiian Regional Cuisine was nurtured by a group of seminal chefs who developed local contacts among farmers and fishermen and showcased local ingredients. The ripples of that movement spread rapidly.

The result was the kind of food featured in this book: fresh island ingredients and dishes combined with the foods and cuisines of the many cultures that have become part of today's Hawaii.

In this book we have featured recipes from Hawaii's finest restaurant and resort chefs who appear on the GREAT CHEFS OF HAWAII television series. All the recipes have been revised and tested for the home cook, and we have provided a glossary of ingredients and Hawaiian food terms indicating substitutions whenever possible. We urge you to prepare these dishes for your family and friends. We know you will be surprised and delighted. Some recipes are complicated and geared toward cooks with advanced skills, but most are well within the abilities of the home cook.

Native Hawaiians have an expression — *Hele mai a'i* — that means "Come here and eat." This greeting was traditionally extended easily and often to friends, family and even total strangers passing by.

We hope you will use this book, then call your friends and neighbors and say, "Hele mai a'i."

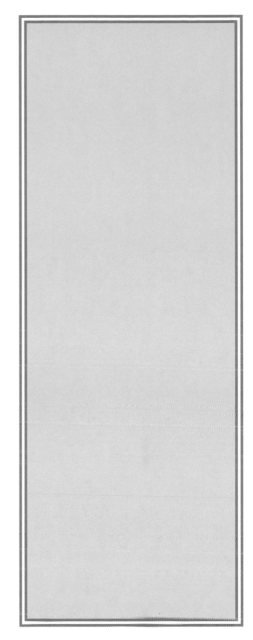

Ahi Tartare with Taro Chips; Gerard Reversade, Gerard's at the Plantation Inn, Lahaina, Maui

Appetizers

There is no better way to sample the complex flavors of Hawaiian cuisine than to graze through the appetizer courses on any island restaurant menu. The same goes for using this book. Chefs are often at their most creative in developing appetizers. Here you will find Asian sauces and dressings with miso and chilies, and smoked and seared fish with fresh fruit salsas. The dishes range in complexity from nori-wrapped peppercorn-crusted ahi tuna with mizuna, enoki mushrooms, and wasabi aïoli, to a simple torte of fresh island vegetables.

ALAN WONG

Alan Wong's Restaurant, Honolulu, Oahu

When Alan Wong opened his namesake restaurant on King Street in Honolulu in 1995, he was an instant hit. But like all "instant" stars, years of work were behind his success.

Born in Tokyo to a Japanese mother and Hawaiian-Chinese father, Wong was raised on authentic Japanese food. His paternal grandfather was a chef and often cooked Chinese food for the family, so Wong had a head start learning the cuisines of the Pacific Rim.

This chef's most creative dishes, like seared peppered ahi with ginger slaw and soy vinaigrette, and roasted duck on crispy chili-scallion tapioca chips, helped put The CanoeHouse at the Mauna Lani Bay Hotel & Bungalows on the culinary map. While at the Mauna Lani he was asked to revamp the menu and style of their fine dining restaurant, Le Soleil. Each summer he presided over a food gala called Cuisines in the Sun.

Like all proponents of new Hawaiian regional cuisine, Wong uses fresh island ingredients, Asian seasonings, and classic European techniques and presentation. When selecting island fish for his menus, he always prefers the less common varieties.

Wong's earliest training was in the two-year culinary program at Kapiolani Community College in Honolulu, where he was named Most Outstanding Student on graduation. From there he did a two-year apprenticeship program at Greenbrier in West Virginia. That led to a position as chef de partie at Lutèce in New York City. When he returned to Hawaii in 1988, Wong became an instructor at Kapiolani Community College.

He has appeared on NBC's "Today Show," been given rave reviews in *Food & Wine,* and in 1993 cooked at the James Beard House in New York City as part of their prestigious Rising Star of American Cuisine series.

Wong has received several gold medals in competitions of the American Culinary Federation, and has participated in the American Harvest Workshop at Cakebread Vineyards in California.

Ahi Cake

Alan Wong
Alan Wong's Restaurant
Honolulu, Oahu

Serves 8

A Hawaiian version of a terrine, this ahi cake combines the color and flavor of sweet Maui onion, eggplant, and seared ahi tuna.

1 garlic clove
1 teaspoon minced fresh rosemary
3 fresh thyme sprigs
1 cup olive oil
4 Maui or other sweet white onions, cut into 1/4-inch-thick crosswise slices
4 Japanese eggplants, cut into 1/4-inch-thick diagonal slices
Salt and freshly ground pepper to taste

8 ounces sashimi-grade ahi tuna, cut into 1/4-inch-thick vertical slices

4 vine-ripened tomatoes, cut into paper-thin slices
8 basil leaves

Put the garlic, rosemary, and thyme in a blender or food processor and puree. With the motor running, gradually add the oil. Set aside.

Preheat the broiler. Sprinkle the onions and eggplant on both sides with salt and pepper and place on a dish for 15 minutes to sweat. Pat the vegetables dry with paper towels. Place the vegetables on a grill pan and brush on both sides with the garlic-herb oil. Broil the vegetables 3 inches from the heat until they are lightly browned, about 2 minutes. Refrigerate.

Sprinkle the ahi with salt and pepper. Heat a large sauté pan or skillet over high heat, coat the pan with the garlic-herb oil, and sear the ahi slices for 15 seconds on each side, or until the outside is cooked and the center is still rare. Transfer the ahi to a plate and refrigerate.

To assemble: Fan half the tomato slices in a circular pattern around the bottom of a 6-cup bowl lined with plastic wrap. Layer half of the onions, basil leaves, and eggplant at the bottom of the dish. Drizzle with 1 tablespoon of the garlic-herb olive oil. Place half of the ahi slices over the vegetables. You may have to cut and piece ahi together to form an even layer. Repeat this process to make a second layer of vegetables, infused oil, and seared fish. For the last layer, fan the remaining tomatoes in a circular pattern over the top of the vegetables. Place a small plate upside down on top of the tomatoes and weight with a heavy, small dish or other object. Refrigerate for 1 hour.

To serve: Drain the juices from the ahi cake. Unmold the ahi cake, carefully slice it into 8 even portions, and serve.

Ahi Cake; Alan Wong, Alan Wong's Restaurant, Honolulu, Oahu

Ahi Carpaccio with White Truffle Vinaigrette

Jean-Marie Josselin
A Pacific Café
Kapaa, Kauai

Serves 4

Here is a simple and very good way to prepare ahi. If you can't find truffle oil, try walnut or macadamia oil instead. The garnish used here is tobiko or caviar. You can substitute gray, black, and red caviar if you prefer.

1 cup virgin olive oil
¼ cup white truffle oil
1 shallot, minced
Juice of 2 lemons
Salt and freshly ground pepper to taste
12 ounces sashimi-grade ahi tuna,
    cut into ¼-inch-thick slices

Garnish
1 teaspoon green tobiko
1 teaspoon red tobiko
1 teaspoon black tobiko
Freshly ground black pepper to taste
¼ cup finely chopped green onion
    tops
4 fresh basil sprigs

In a small bowl, combine the olive oil, truffle oil, shallot, lemon juice, salt, and pepper. Whisk until emulsified. Put the ahi in a shallow glass dish. Pour this mixture over the ahi and let sit for 2 hours in the refrigerator, or until it has turned opaque.

To serve: Arrange the thin slices of ahi tuna in an overlapping single layer on each of 4 plates. Garnish the tuna with small spoonfuls of the green, red, and black tobiko. Sprinkle with green onion and top each plate with a sprig of basil.

Ahi Carpaccio with White Truffle Vinaigrette; Jean-Marie Josselin, A Pacific Café, Kapaa, Kauai

Ahi Tartare with Taro Chips

Gerard Reversade
Gerard's at the Plantation Inn
Lahaina, Maui

Serves 2

Fresh ahi prepared in this manner is a wonderful variation of steak tartare. If taro root is not available for the chips, sweet potatoes will work just as well.

2 egg yolks
Hawaiian or kosher salt to taste
Freshly ground pepper to taste
1 teaspoon wasabi powder
2 tablespoons fresh lemon juice
1 teaspoon soy sauce
2 tablespoons extra-virgin olive oil
2 tablespoons finely chopped Maui
   or other sweet white onion
2 tablespoons finely chopped
   cornichon pickles
2 tablespoons chopped capers
2 tablespoons minced fresh herbs
   (parsley, chervil, tarragon, chives)
8 ounces ahi tuna, cut into ¼-inch dice

Taro Chips

1 taro root, peeled, sliced, and soaked
   in cold water
Peanut oil for frying
Hawaiian or kosher salt to taste

Lettuce leaves for serving

To make the tartare: Combine the egg yolks, salt, pepper, wasabi powder, lemon juice, and soy sauce in a bowl. Gradually whisk in the olive oil. Add the onion, cornichons, capers, and herbs. Just before serving, toss the diced ahi with the dressing.

To make the taro chips: Drain the taro root and pat it dry with paper towels. In a wok or deep-fryer, heat 1 inch of the oil to 375°F, or until almost smoking. Add the taro and fry for 2 to 3 minutes, turning it until it browns and is cooked through. Remove with a slotted spoon and drain on paper towels. Sprinkle with salt.

To serve: Place lettuce leaves on each plate and top with one-fourth of the ahi tartare. Serve with taro chips on the side.

Ahi Tartare with Taro Chips; Gerard Reversade, Gerard's at the Plantation Inn, Lahaina, Maui

Cassoulet of Island Opihi in Pineapple Cream with Okinawan Sweet Potatoes and Crispy Ogo; Ronald Nasuti, Roy's Poipu Bar & Grill, Poipu, Kauai

Cassoulet of Island Opihi in Pineapple Cream with Okinawan Sweet Potatoes and Crispy Ogo

Ronald Nasuti
Roy's Poipu Bar & Grill
Poipu, Kauai

Serves 4

Opihi are small limpets that can be consumed raw or marinated in a brine. Islanders love to pick them from the rocks along the coasts. Opihi are chewy and are considered a great delicacy, but they have a tendency to become tough if overcooked. If you cannot get opihi, you may substitute small mussels or scallops.

Okinawan Sweet Potato Puree
2 to 3 Okinawan sweet potatoes or
   yams, peeled and coarsely chopped
4 to 5 tablespoons milk
4 tablespoons unsalted butter
Salt and freshly ground pepper to taste

Pineapple Cream
½ cup ⅓-by-1½-inch spears fresh
   pineapple
Olive oil for coating, plus 1 tablespoon
1 teaspoon minced shallots
½ cup julienned Maui or other

sweet white onion
⅓ cup pineapple juice
½ cup heavy (whipping) cream
½ teaspoon minced fresh thyme
⅓ cup shiitake mushrooms,
   stemmed and sliced

18 to 20 small opihi
Salt and freshly ground pepper to taste

Garnish
3 tablespoons balsamic vinegar
2 ogo (seaweed) sprigs
½ cup peanut oil

To make the potatoes: Cook the potatoes in salted boiling water until tender, about 15 to 20 minutes. Drain the potatoes and force them through a ricer into a bowl. Mix in the milk, butter, salt, and pepper to make a smooth puree. Put the potatoes in a pastry bag with a star tip.

To make the pineapple cream: Coat the pineapple slices with olive oil. In a medium sauté pan or skillet over high heat, sear the pineapple slices for 2 minutes, or until golden brown on each side. Set aside.

In a sauté pan or skillet over high heat, heat the 1 tablespoon olive oil and sauté the shallots and onion until they start to brown. Add the pineapple juice and stir, then blend in the cream. Sprinkle with the thyme and cook for about 2 minutes. Add the mushrooms, then the seared pineapple. Cook over high heat until the sauce thickens. Add the opihi and cook for 1 minute, or until just warmed. Season with salt and pepper.

To make the garnish: In a small saucepan, cook the vinegar over medium heat until reduced to 1 tablespoon. Set aside. Dust the ogo sprigs with flour. In a sauté pan or skillet over high heat, heat the oil until very hot, but not smoking. Add the ogo sprigs and fry until crisp. Using a slotted spoon, transfer to paper towels to drain.

To serve: Pipe a ring of pureed potatoes around the plate. Fill the center of the ring with the opihi and pineapple cream. Drizzle the reduced balsamic vinegar over the cream. Place the ogo sprigs on top of the pineapple cream.

Charred Sichimi Ahi Coated with Japanese Spices with Lilikoi–Soy Sauce; OnJin Kim, Hanatei Bistro, Honolulu, Oahu

Charred Sichimi Ahi Coated with Japanese Spices with Lilikoi-Soy Sauce

OnJin Kim
Hanatei Bistro
Honolulu, Oahu

Serves 4

Japanese flavors predominate in a simple dish of seared ahi with greens. The lilikoi-soy sauce adds the island touch.

½ Maui or other sweet white onion, finely sliced
½ teaspoon fresh lemon juice
½ daikon, cut into julienne
½ carrot, peeled and cut into fine julienne

12 ounces ahi tuna
3 tablespoons shichimi
½ tablespoon olive oil

Lilikoi-Soy Sauce
1 cup dry white wine
¼ cup unsweetened lilikoi (passion fruit) puree or passion fruit concentrate
1 shallot, sliced
6 white peppercorns
1 bay leaf
1 tablespoon soy sauce
1 tablespoon sugar
1 cup heavy (whipping) cream
½ cup (1 stick) unsalted butter, cut into tablespoon-sized pieces

Garnish
4 shiso leaves, stemmed
4 pieces pickled ginger, drained

Toss the onion with the lemon juice. Place the daikon in cold water to crisp for 15 minutes. Drain the daikon and mix with the carrot. Set aside.

To prepare the ahi: Cut the ahi 1½ inches thick, then into rectangles about 6 inches long. Coat the fillets with shichimi. In a heavy, large sauce pan or skillet over high heat, heat the olive oil until just before smoking. Cook a batch of ahi for about 10 seconds on each side, or until seared on the outside and rare on the inside. Using a slotted spatula, transfer to paper towels. Repeat to cook the remaining ahi. Slice the ahi against the grain into ⅛-inch-thick pieces.

RONALD NASUTI
Roy's Poipu Bar & Grill, Poipu, Kauai

Ronald Nasuti was born to Italian-American parents outside of Boston, Massachusetts. By the time he was fifteen, he was running the kitchen of a small restaurant serving classic Italian cuisine. At eighteen, he became an apprentice at Les Dames d'Escoffier Society at Boston's Copley Plaza Hotel.

In 1992, Nasuti began working for pioneer Hawaii chef Roy Yamaguchi in his Hawaii Kai restaurant. After two years, like so many young Yamaguchi-trained chefs, Nasuti was given his own restaurant to run. He is currently chef at Roy's Poipu Bar & Grill on the island of Kauai, where the atmosphere is relaxed and the clientele mostly from the United States mainland. Here Nasuti relies on local fish and produce that is often less exotic than that served in Honolulu and that requires a more direct style of preparation.

To make the sauce: In a medium saucepan, combine the white wine, lilikoi puree, shallot, peppercorns, bay leaf, soy sauce, and sugar into a saucepan. If using sweetened passion fruit juice concentrate, omit the sugar.

Bring to a boil over medium heat and cook until reduced to ¼ cup. Add the cream and continue to cook to reduce to ½ cup. Remove from heat and whisk in the butter, one piece at a time. Keep warm over hot water until ready to use.

To serve: Place ½ teaspoon of the sliced onion in the middle of each plate. Mound 1 tablespoon daikon mixture on top. Place 1 shiso leaf on the top of each plate and set 1 piece of the ginger on the leaf. Ladle 2 tablespoons of sauce around the daikon on the bottom third of each plate. Lean the ahi against the daikon on top of the sauce.

MAKO SEGAWA-GONZALES
Roy's Poipu Bar & Grill, Poipu, Kauai

Mako Segawa-Gonzales was raised in a multicultural household. The child of a Japanese father and Mexican mother, he was born on the Big Island of Hawaii. While still in high school, he moved to Tucson, Arizona.

It was his international heritage that made it so easy for him to grasp the spirit of new Hawaiian regional cuisine. After graduating from the Culinary Institute of America in 1992, he joined Roy Yamaguchi's young team, assisting chef David Abella at functions at A Pacific Café on Kauai, at Mauna Lani Resort, and at the Mauna Kea Beach Hotel.

After two years with Yamaguchi, Segawa-Gonzales was given the executive chef position at the new Roy's Poipu Bar & Grill on the island of Kauai.

Crisp Nori-wrapped Shrimp with Wasabi Aïoli and Sweet Shoyu Glaze

Mako Segawa-Gonzales
Roy's Poipu Bar & Grill
Poipu, Kauai

Serves 4

Shrimp wrapped in nori stand on a bed of lightly dressed salad greens. The drizzle of sweet soy glaze and tangy wasabi aïoli make this a delightful appetizer.

Nori-wrapped Shrimp
1 tablespoon Asian sesame oil
½ cup fresh bean sprouts
¼ cup carrots, peeled and shredded
½ won bok (napa cabbage)
1 teaspoon minced garlic
1 teaspoon minced fresh ginger
½ teaspoon soy sauce
1 nori sheet
4 large shrimp, peeled and deveined
¼ cup peanut oil for frying

Wasabi Aïoli
2 tablespoons wasabi powder
½ cup mayonnaise (page 195)
1 tablespoon soy sauce
1 teaspoon plain rice wine vinegar
1 teaspoon water

Sweet Shoyu Glaze
2 cups mirin or sweet sherry
1 Hawaiian or Thai chili
1 tablespoon furikake
½ cup sugar
¼ cup soy sauce

Sesame Baby Greens
1 tablespoon Asian sesame oil
1 tablespoon mirin or sweet sherry
1 teaspoon white sesame seeds
1 tablespoon plain rice wine vinegar
2 handfuls (2 ounces) mixed baby greens
½ red bell pepper, seeded, deribbed, and finely chopped
1 cup fresh bean sprouts for garnish

To prepare the shrimp: In a wok or sauté pan over medium high heat, heat the sesame oil and sauté the bean sprouts, carrots, won bok, garlic, and ginger for 2 minutes, or until just softened. Add the soy sauce.

Cut the nori sheet into 4 triangles. Place a shrimp with the tail hanging over the long side of the triangle. Spoon about 2 tablespoons of the cooked vegetables on top of the shrimp and fold the 2 opposite ends over it. Fold the remaining end over to form a triangular package. Turn over and fold in the bottom corner. The shrimp tail will remain outside the packet.

In a wok or deep fryer, heat 1 inch of oil to 375°F, or until almost smoking. Add 1 packet and cook for 2 minutes, or until golden brown on both sides. Using a slotted spoon, transfer the packet to paper towels to drain. Repeat to cook the remaining packets. Set aside and keep warm.

To make the aïoli: Mix all the ingredients together until incorporated. Pour into a squeeze bottle and set aside.

To make the glaze: In a small saucepan, cook the mirin or sherry and chili over high heat for 2 to 3 minutes. Add the furikake and sugar and continue cooking until reduced and syrupy. Let cool until the foam subsides. Add the soy sauce. Strain and let cool completely. The glaze will thicken as it cools. Pour into a squeeze bottle and set aside.

To prepare the baby greens: In a small bowl, whisk the sesame oil, mirin or sherry, sesame seeds, and rice wine vinegar together. Toss the greens and bell pepper with the vinaigrette. Set aside.

To serve: Pile the greens in the center of each plate. Stand a packet with the shrimp tail up on the greens. Drizzle the aïoli and glaze around the edges of the plate. Sprinkle some glaze on top of the shrimp. Garnish with bean sprouts.

Crisp Nori-wrapped Shrimp with Wasabi Aïoli and Sweet Shoyu Glaze; Mako Segawa-Gonzales, Roy's Poipu Bar & Grill, Poipu, Kauai

Crispy Sea Scallops Wrapped in Shredded Phyllo

Corey Waite
Coast Grill
Hapuna Beach Prince Hotel,
Mauna Kea Resort
Kamuela, Hawaii

Serves 4

Shredded phyllo resembles a grass skirt and gives these little packets of scallops a festive look. The rich lobster sauce would be wonderful with any simple broiled seafood.

Lobster Sauce
¼ cup oil
8 ounces lobster or shrimp shells
2 shallots, minced
1 carrot, peeled and finely diced
1 onion, finely diced
1 celery stalk, finely diced
1 lemon, halved
4 white peppercorns, lightly crushed
1 bay leaf
1 tablespoon tomato paste
½ cup dry white wine
3 cups fish stock (page 200)
    or clam juice

2 tablespoons olive oil
8 sea scallops
1 tablespoon minced fresh lemongrass
    or grated lemon zest

Salt and freshly ground pepper to taste
1½ pounds fresh or thawed kataifi
    (shredded phyllo)
4 won bok (napa cabbage) leaves
    or savoy cabbage leaves (green part
    only), blanched and patted dry

Garnish
Fresh cilantro sprigs
Hawaiian or Thai chilies
Chili oil for drizzling (page 188)

To make the sauce: In a heavy, large saucepan over medium heat, heat the oil and sauté the lobster or shrimp shells. Add the shallots, carrot, onion, celery, lemon, peppercorns, and bay leaf and sauté for 4 to 5 minutes, or until cooked. Stir in the tomato paste, white wine, and fish stock or clam juice. Cook for 1½ to 2 hours, or until the sauce coats the back side of a spoon. Strain through a fine-meshed sieve and discard the solids.

To make the phyllo pouches: Preheat the oven to 350°F. In a small sauté pan or skillet over high heat, heat the oil and sauté the scallops and lemongrass or zest together for 2 minutes, or until half cooked. Season with salt and pepper. Divide the kataifi into 8 bundles. Place one bundle on a work surface. Cross it with a second bundle. Place 2 scallops on each blanched won bok leaf. Carefully wrap the scallops in the leaf. Place the bundle on 1 portion of shredded dough. Wrap the bundle with the dough. Gather at the top and secure the dough in place with a small piece of aluminum foil to form a pouch. Repeat to make 4 pouches. Place the pouches in a pie pan and bake for 20 minutes, or until browned.

To serve: Pool lobster sauce on each plate. Place a phyllo pouch on each pool of sauce. Garnish with cilantro sprigs and chilies. Drizzle chili oil over the sauce.

Crispy Sea Scallops Wrapped in Shredded Phyllo; Corey Waite, Coast Grill, Hapuna Beach Prince Hotel, Mauna Kea Resort, Kamuela, Hawaii

Eggplant Napoleon

David Paul Johnson
David Paul's Lahaina Grill
Lahaina, Maui

Serves 4

Layers of eggplant, herbs, and mozzarella cheese create a savory tower with Italian flavors. The vinaigrette is so good you'll want to make it for other salads.

Tomato-Balsamic Vinaigrette

1 large tomato, peeled, seeded, and diced (page 203)
½ cup finely chopped white onion
¼ cup chopped fresh basil
⅓ cup Dijon mustard
⅓ cup balsamic vinegar
2 tablespoons sugar
1 teaspoon ground pepper
1 teaspoon salt
1 teaspoon Worcestershire sauce
1½ cups olive oil

Chive-infused Oil

2 garlic cloves
¼ cup snipped fresh chives
Pinch of kosher salt
¾ cup olive oil

Napoleon

¼ cup olive oil
4 garlic cloves, crushed

Eggplant Napoleon; David Paul Johnson, David Paul's Lahaina Grill, Lahaina, Maui

Fried Poke with Keahole Ahi Nori; Sam Choy, Sam Choy's Restaurants of Hawaii, Kailua Kona, Hawaii

2 tablespoons minced mixed fresh herbs
2 large Italian eggplants, cut into ⅛-inch thick slices
1 pound mushrooms, thinly sliced
8 ounces smoked mozzarella cheese, thinly sliced
1 cup black olives, pitted and finely chopped
1 large Maui or other sweet white onion, finely diced
2 red bell peppers, roasted, peeled, seeded and diced (page 196)

Garnish

2 tablespoons chopped mixed fresh opal and green basil
2 tablespoons grated romano cheese

To make the vinaigrette: In a medium bowl, combine all the ingredients except the oil. Let sit for 10 minutes, then gradually whisk in the oil. If dressing is too thick, add a little cool water. Cover and refrigerate for at least 1 hour.

To make the chive oil: Put the garlic, chives, and salt in a blender or food processor and puree. With the machine running, add the olive oil in a thin stream. Strain through a fine meshed sieve and pour into a squeeze bottle.

To make the napoleon: In a small bowl, combine the olive oil, garlic, and herbs. Lightly brush the eggplant with this mixture on both sides. In a large sauté pan or skillet over high heat, sauté the eggplant for 2 minutes on each side, or until browned and crisp. Set aside to cool. Repeat the process with the mushrooms.

To serve:. Pool 2 tablespoons of vinaigrette on each salad plate. On each plate, layer ingredients in the following order: eggplant, cheese, olives, onions, bell peppers and mushrooms. Finish with the eggplant. Sprinkle each with ½ tablespoon basil and ½ tablespoon romano. Decorate the rim of each plate with chive oil from the squeeze bottle.

Fried Poke with Keahole Ahi Nori

Sam Choy
Sam Choy's Restaurants of Hawaii
Kailua Kona, Hawaii

Serves 4

Poke is a traditional Hawaiian dish usually made with cubes of freshly caught fish eaten raw and seasoned with coarse salt, chilies, and seaweed. Here it gets an update by quickly searing the fish, ahi, or skipjack tuna, until it is cooked on the outside and remains rare in the center.

Fried Poke

2 teaspoons soy sauce
½ cup finely chopped onion
2 teaspoons finely chopped green
    onion tops
½ cup ogo (seaweed)
2 teaspoons Asian sesame oil
10 ounces marlin, cut into
    1-inch cubes

Keahole Ahi Nori

Four 10-ounce ahi tuna steaks, cut into
    ½-by-3-inch sticks
Salt to taste
4 teaspoons wasabi paste
2 nori sheets
2½ cups canola oil for deep-frying

Asian Dressing

4 cups fresh orange juice
¼ cup black sesame seeds
6 tablespoons sugar
2 tablespoons salt
1 cup canola oil
6 tablespoons plain rice wine vinegar
¼ cup soy sauce

Wasabi Vinaigrette

4 cups orange juice
¼ cup black sesame seeds
6 tablespoons sugar
2 tablespoons salt
1 cup canola oil
6 tablespoons plain rice wine vinegar
¼ cup soy sauce
¼ cup wasabi paste
4 handfuls (4 ounces) mixed baby
    greens

To make the poke: In a medium bowl, combine the soy sauce, onion, green onions, ogo, and 1 teaspoon of the sesame oil. Mix well. Add the marlin and stir to coat. In a wok or skillet over high heat, heat the remaining sesame oil and sear the marlin on all sides for 1 or 2 minutes, or until the outside is opaque and the inside is rare. Transfer the marlin to a plate and set aside.

To make the ahi nori: Season the ahi sticks with salt and spread wasabi paste on one side of each stick. Cut the nori sheet in half and wrap each fish stick lengthwise. The wasabi paste and moisture from the fish help the nori to adhere. Add 1 inch of oil to a wok or large, deep skillet. Heat the oil to 365°F, or until it sizzles but does not smoke. Add the wrapped fish sticks and cook for about 15 seconds, or until nori is crisp. Using a slotted spoon, transfer the sticks to paper towels to drain.

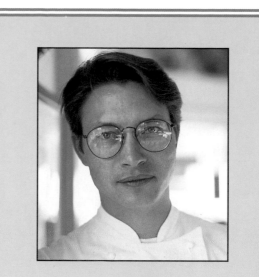

DAVID PAUL JOHNSON

David Paul's Lahaina Grill, Lahaina, Maui

When Crazy Shirts, Inc., creator Rick Ralston was searching for someone to open a stylish cafe on the ground floor of his restored Lahaina Hotel, he asked David Paul Johnson to advise him. Johnson, who was then operating David Paul's Gourmet Catering on Oahu, couldn't find anyone who was right for the job. He decided to take a look at the location himself, and the closer he looked, the more he liked the concept.

Located in the middle of the art galleries and gift shops of the nineteenth-century whaling port of Lahaina, David Paul's is a pretty, bright cafe that is deceptively simple in style. The artwork on the walls changes periodically, and Johnson's wife Michelle creates the show-stopping floral arrangements.

Johnson came to Hawaii in 1978 and went to work at the Hyatt Regency Waikiki, followed by The Lobster Tank, Chez Michel's, and The Black Orchid. In 1990 he made the move to Maui and his own restaurant.

The menu at David Paul's is a collage of flavors and techniques gathered from around the world and given his own touch. His lamb is roasted with Kona coffee. The popular island appetizer maki sushi is deep-fried in the Johnson version.

Now firmly established on Maui, and praised in such publications as *Food Arts, Bon Appétit, Esquire, GQ, Hemispheres, Condé Nast Traveler,* and *Food & Wine,* Johnson periodically hosts "Fear of Cooking 101" classes to benefit Maui nonprofit agencies. And he takes a special interest in programs that help children.

To make the Asian dressing: Combine all ingredients in a bowl and whisk until incorporated.

To make the wasabi vinaigrette: Combine all ingredients in a bowl and whisk until incorporated.

To serve: Divide the baby greens among 4 plates. Place the fried poke in the center of the greens. Slice the ahi nori into pieces and fan around the edges. Drizzle both dressings over the poke and ahi nori.

Grilled Kahuku Prawn Relleno with Puna Goat Cheese and Smoky Tomato Salsa

Jacqueline Lau
Roy's Nicolina
Kahana, Maui

Serves 4

The flavors in this appetizer owe as much to the Southwest as to Hawaii. The sharp, spicy chilies mix delightfully with island prawns and goat cheese in a dish that is fresh, smoky, and piquant all at once.

4 Anaheim chilies
4 fresh Kahuku prawns or jumbo shrimp, peeled and deveined
Olive oil for coating
Salt and freshly ground pepper to taste

Goat Cheese Filling
12 ounces Puna or other fresh white goat cheese at room temperature
¼ cup minced fresh cilantro
16 garlic cloves, roasted and mashed (page 198)

Black Beans
½ cup olive oil
1 cup cooked black beans, drained
1 Maui or other sweet white onion, cut into julienne
½ cup finely chopped green onion
1 cup julienned red bell pepper
2 ancho chilies, cut into julienne
2 tablespoons minced garlic
Salt and freshly ground pepper to taste

Smoky Tomato Salsa
¼ cup olive oil
1 tablespoon minced garlic
3 large vine-ripened tomatoes, smoked and dried (page 203)
3 tablespoons finely chopped green onion
2 tablespoons minced Maui or other sweet white onion
¼ cup minced fresh cilantro
Juice of 1 lime
Salt and freshly ground pepper to taste

Fresh cilantro sprigs for garnish

Roast the chilies over a gas burner or under a preheated broiler until charred on all sides. Place in a paper bag, close, and let cool for 10 minutes. Peel off skin. Make a slit on one side and remove the seeds. Coat the prawns or shrimp with oil and sprinkle with salt and pepper. Broil for 1 to 2 minutes on each side, or until the prawns or shrimp turn pink.

To make goat cheese filling: In a small bowl, combine all the ingredients and mix well with a spoon. Set aside.

To make the black beans: In a medium sauté pan or skillet over medium-high heat, heat the olive oil and sauté the black beans, onion, green onions, bell pepper, and ancho chili for 3 minutes, or until soft. Add the garlic and cook for about 1 to 2 minutes. Season with salt and pepper.

To make the salsa: In a large sauté pan or skillet over high heat, heat the olive oil until it smokes and sauté the garlic and tomatoes for 5 minutes. Add the green onion, Maui onion, and cilantro and sauté for 5 more minutes. Transfer to a medium bowl. Add the lime juice, salt, and pepper.

To serve: Preheat the oven to 400°F. Stuff the Anaheim chilies with the goat cheese filling. Place in a baking dish and bake for 3 minutes. Place the black bean mixture on the plates. Place the stuffed chilies on top and 1 prawn or shrimp on top of each chili. Spoon some tomato salsa on top of the prawns or shrimp and around the outside portion of the plates. Garnish with fresh cilantro.

Grilled Kahuku Prawn Relleno with Puna Goat Cheese and Smoky Tomato Salsa; Jacqueline Lau, Roy's Nicolina, Kahana, Maui

Kalua Ducklings with Mango-Tomato Relish and Chili Cream

Gary Strehl
Hawaii Prince Hotel Waikiki
Honolulu, Oahu

Serves 4

Traditional *kalua,* or ground-roasted meat, inspired this dish. The slow braising of the duck — combined with its spiciness, the sweetness of the mango, the peppery flavor of the arugula, and the crunch of the phyllo — give it excitement.

Thighs and legs of 2 ducklings
Hawaiian or kosher salt to taste
2 cups sliced stemmed shiitake
    mushrooms
1 cup finely diced peeled carrots
1 cup finely diced celery
1 cup chopped green onions, including
    some green tops
2 teaspoons minced garlic
2 teaspoons minced fresh ginger
½ cup hoisin sauce
½ cup Japanese plum sauce
½ cup Sichuan chili sauce
1 cup plum wine
½ teaspoon minced fresh thyme
8 cups duck or chicken stock
    (pages 201 or 199)
¼ teaspoon Chinese five-spice powder
4 star anise pods

Mango-Tomato Relish

1 mango, peeled, cut from the pit
    and cut into ½-inch dice
2 tomatoes, peeled, seeded, and
    cut into strips
1 Maui or other sweet white onion,
    cut into very thin slices
1 tablespoon minced fresh cilantro
1 tablespoon balsamic vinegar
2 tablespoons olive oil
Juice of 1 lime
Pinch of salt

Chili Cream

1 large green bell pepper, roasted
    (page 197)
1 cup sour cream
1 teaspoon sambal olek
Juice of 1 lime
Salt and freshly ground pepper to taste

4 sheets phyllo dough
2 cups arugula, stemmed
¼ cup walnut oil
2 tablespoons raspberry vinegar
4 fresh rosemary sprigs

To prepare the duck: Season the duck thighs and legs with the salt. In a dry large sauté pan or skillet over high heat, sear the duck, skin side down, for 4 to 5 minutes, or until very well browned. Remove the duck and drain the fat from the pan. Add the mushrooms, carrots, celery, and green onions to the pan and sauté for 5 to 6 minutes, or until they are caramelized. Add the garlic and ginger.

Return the duck to the pan and spoon the vegetables, hoisin, plum sauce, chili sauce, and plum wine over the duck, coating it heavily. Add the thyme, duck or chicken stock, five-spice powder, and star anise pods. Cover and reduce heat to low. Cook for 1½ hours, or until the meat is falling off the bone. Remove and shred the duck meat.

To make the relish: Combine all the ingredients and toss. Let sit at room temperature.

To make the chili cream: In a blender or food processor, puree the roasted pepper. In a small bowl, combine all the ingredients and whisk together. Refrigerate.

To make the phyllo cups: Preheat the oven to 300°F. Cut four 6-inch squares out of the phyllo dough. Grease large muffin cups with a small amount of butter. Press each square into a cup. The dough will rise above the rim of the cup about 3 inches. Bake for 30 minutes, or until browned. Set aside and cool.

To serve: Toss the arugula with the oil and vinegar. Place one-fourth of the arugula in each phyllo cup. Add ¾ cup shredded duck and top with 3 tablespoons mango relish. Garnish with a sprig of rosemary and drizzle chili cream over the top.

Kalua Ducklings with Mango-Tomato Relish and Chili Cream; Gary Strehl, Hawaii Prince Hotel Waikiki, Honolulu, Oahu

ROY YAMAGUCHI
Roy's Restaurant, Honolulu, Oahu

Roy Yamaguchi is synonymous with new Hawaii Regional Cuisine in the islands. Born in Tokyo and educated at the Culinary Institute of America in New York, Yamaguchi signed up for home economics class in high school just to be where the girls were. To his surprise, he loved being in the kitchen.

In 1976, after graduation, he headed for Los Angeles, where he began the chef's usual grind of twelve-hour days, seven days a week. After what he calls the "school of hard knocks" in the French kitchens of L'Escoffier, L'Ermitage, and Michael's, he eventually became executive chef at Le Serene and Le Gourmet, and soon opened his own restaurant, 385 North.

His highly personal style of blending French sauces with such Asian seasonings as wasabi, root vegetables, and chilies attracted both Hollywood foodies and critics. In 1987 the California Writers Association named him Chef of the Year.

Yamaguchi's grandparents were from Hawaii, and in 1988 he moved there to open his first restaurant in the Hawaii Kai community of East Oahu. It was an instant success and set the tone for other restaurants featuring island cuisine in an open, casual setting.

Since then Yamaguchi has been busy expanding to restaurants in Tokyo, Guam, Maui, and Kauai. His enthusiasm has helped promote other aspiring chefs in employing the fresh regional style.

He has already taped two seasons of "Hawaii Cooks with Roy Yamaguchi" for Hawaii Public Television. Praise for his cooking has also come from such publications as *Condé Nast Traveler* and *Bon Appétit.*

Kona Shrimp Lumpia with Spicy Mango Sauce

Roy Yamaguchi
Roy's Restaurant
Honolulu, Oahu

Serves 6

No appetizer has ever tasted as good as this new twist on the old-fashioned egg roll. Frozen extra-thin lumpia wrappers work well, and you won't be able to get enough of the spicy mango sauce.

Lumpia Filling
6 ounces cellophane noodles
3 ounces fresh shiitake mushrooms, stemmed and diced, or 1 ounce dried shiitakes, soaked in warm water for 30 minutes
2 tablespoons Asian sesame oil
1 cup finely chopped Chinese mustard cabbage or napa cabbage
1 teaspoon minced fresh cilantro
1 teaspoon minced fresh ginger
1 teaspoon minced garlic
1 green onion, including some of the green top, minced
3 fresh water chestnuts, finely diced
1 pound shrimp, chopped
1 to 2 tablespoons Thai fish sauce (nam pla)
5 tablespoons water
2 tablespoons cornstarch, plus cornstarch for dusting
12 lumpia wrappers

Spicy Mango Sauce
¼ cup Thai chili paste or any sweet chili paste
1 cup sake
¼ cup lilikoi (passion fruit) puree, or orange juice concentrate
¼ teaspoon minced fresh ginger
¼ teaspoon minced garlic
1 teaspoon minced shallot
1 mango, peeled, cut from the pit, and finely diced

Garnish
2 teaspoons white sesame seeds, toasted (page 196)

4 teaspoons snipped fresh chives
¼ mango, peeled, cut from the pit, and cut into julienne

To make the lumpia: In a large pot, bring salted water to a boil. Add the noodles and cook for 1 minute, or until just tender. Drain and set aside.

If using dried shiitakes, drain and squeeze them dry, reserving the soaking liquid for another use. Dice the mushrooms. In a skillet over medium-high heat, heat the sesame oil and sauté the mushrooms, cabbage, cilantro, ginger, garlic, green onion, water chestnuts, and cooked noodles for 1 minute. Let cool, then combine with the shrimp and fish sauce.

Mix the water and 2 tablespoons cornstarch in a small bowl. Lay the lumpia wrappers on a work surface and brush the edges of the wrappers with the cornstarch mixture. Place 2 tablespoons filling in a line on the front edge of each wrapper, leaving a ½-inch border. Fold the edge of the wrapper nearest you over the filling, then fold in the sides and roll the wrapper into a cylinder. Seal the ends and dust with cornstarch. In a large sauté pan or skillet over high heat, heat the oil until very hot and fry the lumpia, 4 at a time, for about 45 seconds on each side or until golden brown. Repeat with the remaining lumpia. Remove with tongs and drain on paper towels. Keep warm.

To make the mango sauce: Combine all the ingredients in a medium saucepan. Simmer over low heat for 15 minutes. Strain through a fine-meshed sieve. Set aside and keep warm.

To serve: Pool ¼ cup of the warm sauce on each of 6 salad plates. Place 2 lumpia on top of the sauce and garnish with the sesame seeds, chives, and mango.

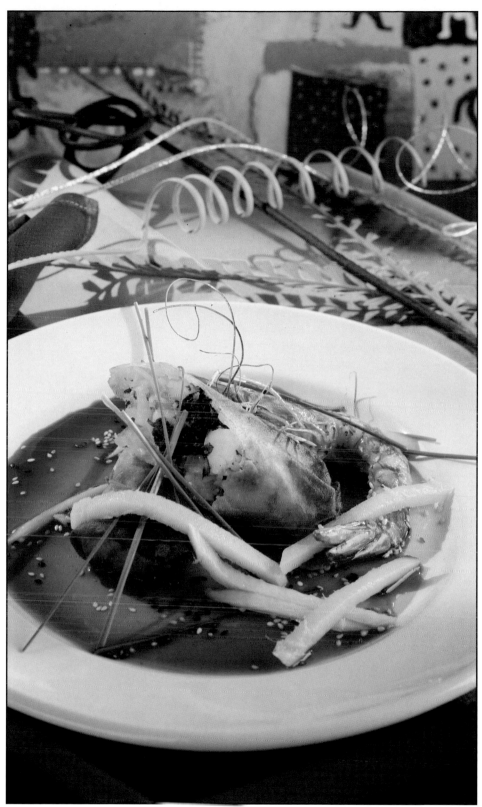

Kona Shrimp Lumpia with Spicy Mango Sauce; Roy Yamaguchi, Roy's Restaurant, Honolulu, Oahu

Kula Vegetable Torte; Beverly Gannon, Haliimaile General Store, Haliimaile, Maui

Kula Vegetable Torte

Beverly Gannon
Haliimaile General Store
Haliimaile, Maui

Serves 8

Studded with colorful carrots, beans, peppers, and broccoli and bound with ricotta cheese, the Kula vegetable torte is a delicious way to serve vegetables. This also makes a wonderful lunch.

2 cups broccoli florets
2 cups green beans
2 cups peeled sliced carrots
4 tablespoons canola oil
1 tablespoon minced fresh ginger
2 cups onions, thinly sliced
2 tablespoons white sesame seeds, toasted (page 196)
2 garlic cloves, minced
3 eggs, beaten
1 pound ricotta cheese
2 tablespoons minced fresh cilantro
Salt and freshly ground pepper to taste
2½ sheets puff pastry
2 cups peeled roasted red bell peppers (page 196)
2 tablespoons poppy seeds

Blanch the broccoli in boiling, salted water for 2 minutes; drain and plunge into a bowl of iced water to stop the cooking. Drain and set aside in a medium bowl. Blanch the green beans in boiling water for 2 minutes, or until al dente; drain and plunge into a bowl of iced water. Drain and set aside in a medium bowl. In a medium sauté pan or skillet over medium heat, sauté the carrots in 2 tablespoons of the oil for 3 to 4 minutes, or until barely tender; stir in the ginger and set aside.

In a medium sauté pan, sauté the onions in the remaining oil for 2 minutes, or until translucent. Drain any liquid from vegetables and blot them with paper towels. Toss the broccoli with the sesame seeds. Toss the green beans with the garlic. In a medium bowl, combine the eggs, ricotta, cilantro, salt, and pepper.

Line a 10-inch springform pan with 2 sheets of the puff pastry. Make 1 layer each of all of the following: carrots, onions, green beans, ricotta cheese, broccoli, and peppers, pressing each layer firmly into the pan. Cut ¼-inch strips of dough from the remaining puff pastry. Cover the top of the torte with a lattice design using the strips. Sprinkle with the poppy seeds. Refrigerate the torte for 45 minutes.

Preheat the oven to 425°F. Bake the torte for 50 minutes or until well browned. Remove from the oven and allow to cool for 2 to 3 hours. Unmold the torte from the springform pan and cut into 8 wedges.

BEVERLY GANNON
Haliimaile General Store, Haliimaile, Maui

"Feed people great food and lots of it. Make them smile — make sure they leave the table satisfied. That's the way I was raised," says Dallas native Bev Gannon.

Gannon began her career as a road manager for entertainment industry stars like Liza Minnelli, Ben Vereen, and Joey Heatherton, but she always loved to cook. When she decided to get serious about it, she flew off to attend Le Cordon Bleu in London and then to take classes from Marcella Hazan in Italy and Jacques Pepin in France.

She returned to Dallas and worked as a caterer before starting her own company in 1980. It was about this time that she met her husband and partner, Joe Gannon, an entertainment producer, director, and lighting designer for contemporary musical performers, and moved to Maui.

Bev's first customers were entertainers who had come to Maui to vacation. Friends in Los Angeles would give people her name and phone number and tell them "Call Bev, she'll cook for you." They called and she cooked.

After about five years, she decided to open Fresh Approach Catering and found an increasing demand for her cuisine. By 1987, Joe and Bev were looking for a place to house their burgeoning business. They found the old Haliimaile General Store, formerly a mercantile establishment for a plantation community in the Upcountry area of Maui.

They had conceived the place as a take-out deli and catering headquarters as well as a gourmet eat-in with about five or six tables. On the day they opened there were one hundred people waiting to get in. Almost instantly, Haliimaile General Store became a restaurant.

Bev is usually in the open kitchen and Joe trades stories with customers and helps with wine selection. You can count on great food in large quantities, and plenty of smiles.

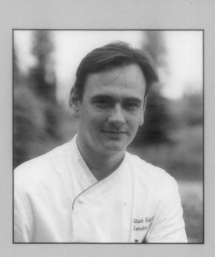

PATRICK CALLAREC

The Dining Room, The Ritz-Carlton Kapalua, Kapalua, Maui

French-born Patrick Callarec came to the culinary arts in the classic French way. At the age of thirteen he entered culinary school and began spending his summers in Nice. Callarec was not on the beach, but peeling potatoes in the restaurant kitchens of this Riviera town.

Inspired by the home cuisine of his father and grandmother in his native Perigueux, Callarec apprenticed in 1975 at the Martinez Hotel, then moved to the five-star Carlton Hotel, both in Cannes. In 1981 he went to Canada, where he was a saucier at Café de l'Auberge in Toronto's Inn on the Park, then moved on to Guy Calluaud's La Bonne Auberge.

Callarec went next to Dallas, Texas, where he served as executive chef for three years at the Grand Kempinski Hotel. He joined the Ritz-Carlton chain in Marina del Rey, California. When the 550-room Ritz-Carlton Kapalua opened on the island's west side, Callarec relocated to Maui to command the kitchens.

Moano and Kahuku Prawns with Molokai Sweet Potatoes

Patrick Callarec
The Dining Room
The Ritz-Carlton Kapalua
Kapalua, Maui

Serves 4

Large freshwater Kahuku prawns are farmed on the island of Oahu and are widely popular with Hawaiian chefs, who often cook them whole, leaving the heads and whiskers on. Moano is reef fish, a member of the goatfish family. Any white fish with a high fat content can be substituted. Callarec likes to leave the skin on to give the dish a distinctive iodine flavor.

1 tablespoon olive oil
4 Kahuku prawns or jumbo-sized
   shrimp, shelled and deveined
Four 2-ounce moano fillets, skin on
Salt and freshly ground pepper to taste
4 Molokai sweet potatoes

Wasabi Aïoli
2 egg yolks
1 garlic clove
Juice of ½ lemon
1 tablespoon wasabi powder
1 cup olive oil
Salt and freshly ground pepper

Lemongrass Bouillabaisse
8 ounces redfish fillet or boned
   white-fleshed fish fillet
3 tablespoons olive oil
½ small onion
1 leek, cut into 3-inch lengths,
   white part only
½ celery stalk
¼ teaspoon cracked peppercorns
1 tomato
1 teaspoon saffron threads
1 garlic clove
¼ fresh bunch parsley
¼ fennel bulb
1 fresh thyme sprig
1 bay leaf
1 star anise pod
½ stalk lemongrass, white part only
1 kaffir lime leaf
1 teaspoon minced fresh ginger
½ cup dry white wine
1 tablespoon Pernod
2 cups fish stock (page 200)
   or clam juice

½ cup heavy (whipping) cream
Salt to taste
3 tablespoons cornstarch mixed
  with ¼ cup water

In a large sauté pan or skillet over high heat, heat the oil and cook the prawns and fillets on both sides until the prawns are pink, the fillet meat flakes, and the skin is crisp, about 40 seconds on each side. Set aside.

With a sharp knife, carve a 2½-inch-by-2-inch-diameter cylinder out of the center of each sweet potato. Discard the sweet potato parings. Cook the sweet potato cylinders in boiling salted water for 15 minutes, or until tender. With a slotted spoon, remove from the water and drain. Scoop out the center of the potato cylinder with a melon baller. Set aside potato balls for the bouillabaisse.

To make the aïoli: Put all the ingredients except the oil, salt, and pepper in a blender or food processor and process until frothy. With the machine running, gradually add the oil. Add salt and pepper.

To make the bouillabaisse: Cut the fish into 1½-inch pieces. In a stockpot over high heat, heat the olive oil, and sauté the fish for 2 minutes, or until it browns lightly on each side. Add the onion, leek, celery, and peppercorns and cook for 4 minutes, or until the vegetables are tender. Add the tomato, saffron, garlic, herbs, spices, wine, and Pernod. Continue to cook until the mixture is reduced to about two-thirds. Add the fish stock or clam juice, and bring to a boil. Reduce heat to simmer and cook until liquid is reduced by one-third. Add the cream and simmer for 5 minutes, or until the cream is completely incorporated into the sauce. Add salt and whisk in the diluted cornstarch. Continue to cook until the cornstarch thickens the sauce.

To assemble: Add the sweet potatoes to the bouillabaisse and simmer to heat through. Place on the plates. Lean 1 fillet and 1 prawn against each sweet potato. Place a spoonful of aïoli in the center of the sweet potato. Drizzle the sauce on and around the fish and sweet potatoes.

Moano and Kahuku Prawns with Molokai Sweet Potatoes; Patrick Callarec, The Dining Room, The Ritz-Carlton Kapalua, Kapalua, Maui

Nori-seared Ahi with Citrus-Garlic Miso Sauce and Shiitake "Chopsticks"

Tod Kawachi
Roy's Kahana Bar & Grill
Kahana, Maui

Serves 4

This tasty appetizer is worth the effort: fans of seared ahi are surrounded by splashes of four sauces and criss-crossed with mushroom-filled "chopsticks". Ginger, mustard, spicy-hot shichimi, and other Asian flavors accent the tuna.

Spicy Sesame Aïoli

¼ cup mayonnaise (page 195)
½ teaspoon black sesame seeds
Pinch of shichimi
½ teaspoon minced fresh ginger
½ teaspoon minced garlic
2 tablespoons plain rice wine vinegar
Pinch of salt
½ teaspoon Asian sesame oil
½ teaspoon white sesame seeds

Scallion-infused Oil

1½ green onions, including some green tops
Pinch of grated fresh ginger
½ cup olive oil
Pinch of salt
½ teaspoon water

Soy-Mustard Sauce

¼ cup Colman's dry mustard
2 tablespoons hot water
2 tablespoons plain rice wine vinegar
¼ cup soy sauce

Citrus-Garlic Miso Sauce

½ tablespoon minced fresh ginger
½ tablespoon minced garlic
1 cup fish stock (page 200) or clam juice
¼ cup white miso paste
Juice of ½ orange
Juice of ½ lemon
Juice of ½ lime
½ tablespoon soy sauce

"Chopsticks"

½ tablespoon Asian sesame oil
2 tablespoons finely chopped green onions
1 tablespoon grated fresh ginger
⅓ ounce dried shiitake mushrooms, soaked in warm water to cover for 30 minutes
⅓ ounce fresh shiitakes, stemmed and finely chopped
1 tablespoon sake
1 tablespoon soy sauce
4 lumpia wrappers
1 egg white with 1 teaspoon water for egg wash
¼ cup canola oil for frying

12 ounces sashimi-grade ahi tuna
Salt to taste
1 tablespoon cracked pepper
½ cup furikake
2 tablespoons black sesame seeds
2 tablespoons white sesame seeds
2 tablespoons canola oil

Garnish

¼ cup finely chopped green onions

To make the aïoli: Combine all the ingredients except the sesame seeds in a blender and process until smooth. Fold in the seeds.

To make the infused oil: Place all ingredients in a blender or food processor and process until smooth. Strain through a fine-meshed sieve and set aside.

To make the soy-mustard sauce: In a small bowl, mix the Colman's mustard with the hot water to form a paste. Mix in the rice vinegar and the soy sauce, stirring until smooth. Strain through a fine-meshed sieve and set aside.

To make the miso sauce: In a small saucepan, combine the ginger, garlic, and fish stock or clam juice and bring to a boil over medium-high heat. Whisk in the white miso paste, then the citrus juices and soy sauce. Bring to a boil. Strain through a fine-meshed sieve. Set aside and keep warm.

To make the shiitake "chopsticks": In a small sauté pan or skillet over high heat, heat the sesame oil and sauté the green onions, ginger, and mushrooms until soft, about 3 minutes. Add the sake and soy sauce and stir to scrape up the browned bits from the bottom of the pan. Cook until the mixture is dry. Set aside and let cool. In a blender or food processor, puree the mixture until smooth.

Cut each lumpia wrapper in half diagonally and place a long thin line of mushroom mix along one edge of the wrapper. Carefully roll tightly to form a long thin chopstick shape and seal closed with a little egg wash. Repeat to fill and roll the remaining wrappers. Fry the wrappers until brown and crisp, about 1 to 2 minutes. Using a slotted spatula, transfer to paper towels to drain.

Season the ahi with salt and pepper, then roll in the furikake and sesame seeds. In a large sauté pan or skillet over high heat, heat the oil and sear the ahi for 30 seconds per side, or until the outside is seared and the center is still rare.

To serve: Cut the ahi into very thin slices and place on the center of each plate. Drizzle the miso sauce, aïoli, oil, and soy-mustard sauce around the fish. Cross 2 shiitake chopsticks on each plate. Garnish with green onions and serve at once.

Nori-seared Ahi with Citrus-Garlic Miso Sauce and Shiitake "Chopsticks"; Tod Kawachi, Roy's Kahana Bar & Grill, Kahana, Maui

Nori-wrapped Peppercorn-crusted Tuna with Mizuna, Enoki, and Wasabi

Kelly Degala
Gordon Biersch Brewery Restaurant
Honolulu, Oahu

Serves 4

The rolled nori gives the tuna in this dish the look of contemporary cone sushi. The sansho peppercorns may be replaced with Cajun-style spice rub. Mizuna, a Japanese salad green, may be replaced with a leafy green cabbage such as baby bok choy.

12 ounces ahi tuna fillet, cut into
  2-inch cubes
2 tablespoons ground Sansho or other
  fine-quality peppercorns
¼ cup peanut oil

Eggplant Chips
Olive oil cooking spray
1 Japanese eggplant, cut lengthwise
  into thin slices
Hawaiian or kosher salt and freshly
  ground black pepper to taste

Olive oil for brushing
2 tablespoons furikake
1 tablespoon black sesame seeds
1 tablespoons white sesame seeds
1 cup wasabi paste mixed with
  enough water to make a liquid
1 cup dark soy sauce
8 nori sheets, halved lengthwise
¼ cup mizuna or other leafy
  salad greens
2 cups daikon sprouts
2 cups enoki mushrooms
¼ cup tobiko

16 shiso leaves
⅛ cup pickled ginger for garnish

To prepare the ahi: Roll the tuna cubes in the peppercorns to coat. In a large sauté pan or skillet over high heat, heat the peanut oil for 1 minute, or until it ripples. It should not smoke. Sear the cubes about 30 seconds on each side, or until opaque on the outside and rare inside. Drain on paper towels and let cool.

To make the eggplant chips: Preheat the oven to 450°F. Spray a baking sheet with olive oil and lay the eggplant slices on it. Spray the eggplant with olive-oil cooking spray and season with salt and pepper. Bake for about 15 minutes, or until browned and crispy. Set aside.

To serve: Brush each plate with olive oil and sprinkle it with furikake and sesame seeds. Put the wasabi paste that has been diluted and the soy sauce into squeeze bottles. Drizzle the wasabi and soy sauce alternately in a criss-cross pattern on the bottom of each plate. Lay each sheet of nori flat on a work surface. Divide the greens, eggplant chips, daikon sprouts, mushrooms, and seared tuna among the nori sheets, and layer them in the center of each sheet. Roll each sheet of nori into a cone and place 2 cones on each plate. Spoon 1½ teaspoons tobiko inside the top of each cone.
Lay 2 shiso leaves at the base of each cone and garnish with pickled ginger.

Nori-wrapped Peppercorn-crusted Tuna with Mizuna, Enoki, and Wasabi; Kelly Degala, Gordon Biersch Brewery Restaurant, Honolulu, Oahu

*Peking-Style Squab with Foie Gras and Pineapple Tatin with Persimmon Sauce;
Bradley Montgomery, The Dining Room, The Ritz-Carlton Kapalua, Kapalua,
Maui*

Peking-Style Squab with Foie Gras and Pineapple Tatin with Persimmon Sauce

Bradley Montgomery
The Dining Room
The Ritz-Carlton Kapalua
Kapalua, Maui

Blend the flavors of foie gras, pineapple, and persimmon with squab
and you have a melding of China,
France, and the Pacific. The tatin is
a fruit tart baked with the fruit on
the bottom of the pan, then turned
fruit-side-up for presentation. Prepare
the tatin a day ahead.

Serves 4

Pineapple Tatin
6 tablespoons sugar
6 tablespoons unsalted butter
1 cup finely diced fresh pineapple
Pinch of salt
Four 2-inch-diameter puff
  pastry rounds

Peking Squab
2 quarts boiling water
¼ cup baking soda
4 squab
5 cups honey
4 cups water
Few drops of natural red food coloring
1 cup hoisin sauce
4 teaspoons minced fresh ginger
4 teaspoons minced garlic

Foie Gras
Four 1- to 1½-ounce slices
  foie gras, chilled and scored
  in a criss-cross pattern
Chinese five-spice powder to taste
Salt and freshly ground pepper to taste

Persimmon Sauce
4 fresh ripe Fuyu persimmons
1 tablespoon pickled ginger
Salt and freshly ground pepper to taste

To make the tatin: Preheat oven
to 350°F. In a large sauté pan or
skillet, cook sugar and butter over
medium heat until the sugar dissolves
and the mixture turns a light amber.
Add the pineapple and salt. Stir and
continue to cook until the caramel
is reduced and the pineapple is coated
with a thick layer of sauce. Transfer the
pineapple to 4 ramekins and lightly
press down on it with the back of a
spoon to remove any air bubbles. Top
the pineapple in each ramekin with a
round of puff pastry. Poke
holes in the pastry and, using a knife,
tuck it down around the pineapple
in the ramekin. Place the ramekins
in a baking pan and add warm water
to halfway up the sides of the ramekins. Bake for 15 to 20 minutes,
or until lightly browned. Remove from
oven and allow to rest overnight in the
refrigerator. To unmold, dip each
ramekin in hot water and turn out
onto a plate, using a knife to loosen
the edges.

To prepare the squabs: Preheat the oven
to 425°F. Place a wire rack on the top
rung of the oven and another on the
bottom. In a large saucepan over
medium-high heat, bring the water and
the baking soda to a boil. Tie the legs
of squab together with string and dip
it into the water twice. This will cause
the surface of the skin to tighten.
Repeat with other squabs.

In a small saucepan, mix 4 cups
of the honey, the water, and red food
coloring. Bring to a boil over medium-
high heat. Dip the squab quickly into
the boiling mixture 4 or 5 times,
or until it turns pink. In a small bowl,
combine the hoisin sauce, the
remaining 1 cup honey, ginger,
and garlic. Rub the inside of each
squab with the mixture. Thread
a chopstick or metal skewer through
the tied legs of each squab. Hang
the squabs from the top rack with
the chopstick placed across the rungs
securing them. Place the pan on
the bottom rack below the hanging
squab. Bake for 10 to 15 minutes,
or until lightly browned with crisp
shiny skin and firm flesh. Set aside.

To prepare the foie gras: Heat a large
dry sauté pan or skillet over high heat
until the pan is very hot. Dust the foie
gras with five-spice powder, salt, and

*Puna Goat Cheese and Vegetable
Terrine; Amy Ferguson-Ota, The
Dining Room, The Ritz-Carlton
Mauna Lani, Kohala Coast, Hawaii*

pepper. Turn off the heat. Sear the scored side first for 15 to 20 seconds until well browned. Turn the heat back on to medium-low and repeat on the other side. With a slotted spoon, remove the foie gras from the pan. Set aside.

To make the persimmon sauce: Poach the persimmons in boiling water until very soft. Remove the skin and puree the fruit in a blender or food processor with the pickled ginger until smooth. Season with salt and pepper.

To serve: Pour the persimmon sauce on each plate and unmold a tatin on top of the sauce. Place a squab beside the tatin and the seared foie gras, scored-side up, beside that.

Puna Goat Cheese and Vegetable Terrine

Amy Ferguson-Ota
The Dining Room
The Ritz-Carlton Mauna Lani
Kohala Coast, Hawaii

Like all good chefs, Ferguson-Ota looks for the finest local products — in this case, goat cheese made in the Puna district of the Big Island. The goat cheese between each layer helps bind this terrine.

Makes one 8-by-1/2-inch terrine

3 ounces fresh shiitake mushrooms, stemmed and sliced, or 1 ounce dried shiitakes, soaked in hot water for 30 minutes
6 large Japanese eggplants, sliced lengthwise into 1/4-inch slices
3 large zucchini, sliced lengthwise into 1/4-inch slices
1 medium yellow squash, sliced crosswise into 1/4-inch slices
1 Maui or other sweet white onion, finely diced
12 garlic cloves
Olive oil for brushing and sprinkling
Salt to taste
10 ounces crumbled Puna or other fresh white goat cheese
3 red bell peppers, roasted, peeled, and seeded (page 197)
1 tablespoon chopped basil leaves
1 cup white mushrooms, sliced
1 ripe tomato, peeled and seeded (page 203)
Balsamic vinegar for sprinkling
Freshly ground black pepper to taste
8 sprigs of fresh basil

BRADLEY MONTGOMERY
The Dining Room, The Ritz-Carlton Kapalua, Kapalua, Maui

When Bradley Montgomery presided over the kitchen of the Ritz-Carlton Kapalua's signature restaurant, The Grill, he brought to it an elegant California style that drew from his culinary background, a style that included an abundance of fresh produce presented in a straightforward manner.

After graduating from the California Culinary Academy in 1989, he worked for such top San Francisco restaurants as Jeremiah Towers' Stars, Acquerello, and Etrusca.

Montgomery was at the Ritz-Carlton, San Francisco, where he had been part of the opening team at The Terrace, when he was picked for the Maui position. Recently, he was made executive sous-chef for the entire hotel, and is in charge of the training and supervision of a staff of sixty, as well as the menu development for four food outlets.

To make the terrine: Preheat the oven to 350°F. If using dried shiitakes, drain them, reserving the soaking liquid for another use. Salt the eggplant slices and let sit for 30 minutes; rinse with cold water. Arrange the shiitakes, eggplants, zucchini, squash, onion, and garlic on an oiled baking sheet. Brush with olive oil and sprinkle with salt. Roast for 10 minutes. Set aside and cool. Squeeze half of the garlic cloves out of the skins and chop.

Line a 2-quart loaf pan, terrine, or triangular mold with plastic wrap, leaving 4 inches of plastic wrap hanging over each edge of the pan. Arrange the vegetables in the pan: Lay the eggplant and zucchini slices across the pan, alternating the vegetables and overlapping the slices to form a continuous layer. Sprinkle with

onion. Using your fingers or the back of a spoon, spread a thin layer of cheese on top of the onion. Top with a layer of peppers, and a layer of basil. Top with a thin layer of cheese. Sprinkle with mushrooms and the chopped garlic, and top with another layer of cheese. Place the squash slices over the cheese. Put the tomatoes over the squash, and top with basil. Press down gently with your fingers. Fold the plastic wrap over the top of the mold, and refrigerate for 3 hours.

To serve: Lift the mold out of the pan. Slice through the plastic with a serrated knife. Peel off the plastic and arrange a slice on each chilled plate. Sprinkle with olive oil, balsamic vinegar, and pepper. Garnish with a sprig of basil and the unpeeled roasted garlic cloves.

STEVE AMARAL
Kea Lani Hotel Suites & Villas, Wailea, Maui

Fresh ingredients are more important than anything else to Kea Lani executive chef Steve Amaral. In order to get them, he's established his own gardens on the grounds of the Maui hotel, and enlisted local farmers to grow the fresh fruits and vegetables he needs every day to serve his international clientele.

Amaral also pays a great deal of attention to local fish and meat products, serving naturally raised beef, cold-water lobsters from the Big Island of Hawaii, and a myriad of fresh island fish.

It was Amaral who first opened the luxury hotel in 1986 and put his personal stamp on everything that left the kitchen. Prior to moving to Hawaii, the Massachusetts native trained in France and at the Culinary Institute of America in New York. He is certified by the American Culinary Federation and belongs to Les Amis de' Escoffier, Chaîne des Rôtisseurs, and the Maui Chefs' Association.

Oahu Rock Shrimp with Sprout Slaw and Asian Cocktail Sauce

Steve Amaral
Kea Lani Hotel Suites & Villas
Wailea, Maui

Serves 4

Sprouts of all kinds are delicious in this slaw. Try mung and azuki bean sprouts or lentil sprouts, available in natural foods stores. They all work well. If you cannot find the purple Okinawan sweet potato, a regular sweet potato will do fine.

Asian Sprout Slaw
¼ cup sunflower sprouts
¼ cup daikon sprouts
¼ cup fresh pea sprouts
¼ cup fresh bean sprouts
2 tablespoons shredded cabbage
Pinch of mustard seeds
¼ cup peanut or olive oil
2 tablespoons pickled ginger, thinly sliced
1 teaspoon plain rice wine vinegar
Pinch of black sesame seeds
Pinch of toasted white sesame seeds (see page 196)

Asian Cocktail Sauce
½ cup sweet chili paste
5 curry leaves, crumbled
½ teaspoon dried marjoram
1 teaspoon toasted white sesame seeds (see page 196)
4 kaffir lime leaves, crumbled
¼ lemongrass stalk, cut into thin, diagonal slices
10 fresh cilantro leaves, chopped
½ cup ketchup

Crisp Sweet Potato Garnish
1 Okinawan purple sweet potato, peeled and shredded
¼ cup canola oil

8 ounces cooked jumbo shrimp

To make the slaw: Put the sprouts and cabbage in a small bowl. Soak the mustard seeds in boiling water for 5 minutes. Mix the oil, ginger, mustard seeds, and rice vinegar together. Pour over the sprout mixture and stir. Refrigerate for 1 hour, stirring once or twice. Sprinkle with the sesame seeds.

To make the cocktail sauce: In a small bowl, mix all the ingredients together. Cover and refrigerate until ready to use.

To make the crisp sweet potato: Peel the sweet potato and cut it into matchsticks. Put the matchsticks in a bowl of ice water to keep them from turning color. In a wok or deep-fryer, heat oil to 350°F, or until sizzling. Drain the sweet potato sticks and pat them dry on paper towels. Drop the sticks into the hot oil and cook about 5 minutes, or until crisp. Using a slotted spoon, transfer the sticks to paper towels to drain.

To serve: Place one-fourth of the sprout slaw in the middle of a 3-inch diameter ring mold in the center of a plate. Press the slaw down to compact it. Steam the shrimp over boiling water for 2 minutes, or until firm. Top the slaw with 2 pieces of cooked shrimp. Carefully remove the cookie cutter mold. Top with one-fourth of the shredded sweet potato. Spoon 2 tablespoons cocktail sauce on the side. Repeat with the remaining plates.

Oahu Rock Shrimp with Sprout Slaw and Asian Cocktail Sauce; Steve Amaral, Kea Lani Hotel Suites & Villas, Wailea, Maui

Seared Smoked Ahi with Lychee Salsa and Ogo-Wasabi Sauce

Gary Strehl
Hawaii Prince Hotel Waikiki
Honolulu, Oahu

Serves 4

Seared ahi has become a favorite in many island restaurants serving regional cuisine. Ogo is a kind of sea-weed found on island beaches. You can omit it entirely from the wasabi sauce and still have good results. The same goes for inamona, a traditional paste made from kukui nuts. The lychee salsa has a fresh, clean flavor and tastes wonderful with any light fish.

Macadamia Nut Pesto

1½ cups fresh cilantro leaves
¼ cup olive oil
¼ cup macadamia nuts
2 garlic cloves
¼ cup grated Parmesan cheese

1½ pounds ahi tuna, cut into
   2-by-2-inch strips
2 tablespoons olive oil

Ogo-Wasabi Sauce

½ tablespoon wasabi paste
¼ teaspoon dry mustard mixed with
   enough water to make a paste
1 teaspoon Dijon mustard
3 tablespoons soy sauce
4 tablespoons plain yogurt
2 teaspoons snipped fresh dill
1 teaspoon inamona paste (optional)
2 tablespoons minced ogo (seaweed),
   optional

Lychee Salsa

3 tablespoons finely chopped
   red radish
2 tablespoons finely chopped daikon
1 tablespoon minced fresh cilantro
3 tablespoons finely chopped lychee
1 teaspoon minced fresh opal basil
2 tablespoons finely chopped jícama
2 tablespoons finely chopped Maui or
   other sweet white onion
2 tablespoons finely chopped
   cucumber

Seared Smoked Ahi with Lychee Salsa and Ogo-Wasabi Sauce; Gary Strehl,
Hawaii Prince Hotel Waikiki, Honolulu, Oahu

½ teaspoon Asian sesame oil
2 tablespoons fresh lime juice
2 tablespoons plain rice wine vinegar
1 Hawaiian or Thai chili, minced, or
   hot pepper sauce to taste
2 tablespoons olive oil
Salt to taste

Garnish
4 ogo sprigs
4 fresh cilantro sprigs
Minced red and green seaweeds
   (optional)

To make the pesto: Combine all the ingredients in a blender or food processor, and grind to a coarse puree.

Prepare a smoker (page 198). Brush the strips of ahi with the pesto and place in a smoker for about 15 minutes, or until the fish is smoked but still raw. In a medium sauté pan or skillet over high heat, heat the oil and quickly sear the outside of the fish on all sides for 30 seconds. The fish will be raw in the center and cooked on the outside edges. Cool the fish, then with a sharp knife slice the ahi into ¼-inch-thick slices.

To make the wasabi sauce: In a small bowl, mix all the ingredients together. Set aside.

To make the lychee salsa: Combine the radish, daikon, cilantro, lychee, basil, jícama, onion, and cucumber in a medium bowl. In a small bowl, mix the remaining salsa ingredients to make a dressing. Combine the dressing with the vegetable mixture. Taste and adjust the seasoning. Cover and refrigerate.

To serve: Spoon one-fourth of the lychee salsa onto each plate. Lay 4 slices of seared ahi on one side of the salsa mound. Spoon 1 tablespoon of the pesto and 1 tablespoon of the ogo sauce next to each other on each plate. Garnish with a sprig of ogo and cilantro, and optional seaweed.

Gary Strehl
Hawaii Prince Hotel Waikiki, Honolulu, Oahu

Gary Strehl has a way of mixing his international culinary background with good ol' American recipes. As one of the leading proponents of new Hawaiian regional cuisine, Strehl combines solid culinary technique with the fresh local foods of Hawaii and Asia.

After graduation from the Culinary Institute of America, the Rutherford, New Jersey, native trained in Hong Kong, Bangkok, New York, and Hawaii with chefs of Chinese, Thai, French, and Swiss backgrounds. He combined what they taught him about seasonings and cooking techniques with the national trend toward more health-conscious food, and developed his own brand of regional cuisine.

Today Strehl eliminates the large quantities of butter, salt, and cream found in classic European dishes in favor of chilies, spicy salsas, and chutneys.

He still believes that formal European training is essential in learning the basics of professional cooking, but when hiring staff for his Hawaii Prince kitchen, he also looks for creative flair. Strehl has learned a great deal by paying attention to the home-cooking preferences of his island staff.

He first came to Hawaii as executive sous-chef for Rock Resorts at the Kapalua Bay Hotel, after training with the Regent International Hotel chain in Asia. In the mid-1980s, Strehl opened the Maui Prince as executive chef, and was selected to open the Hawaii Prince in Honolulu in 1990.

EDWIN GOTO
The Lodge at Koele, Lanai City, Lanai

Chefs who find themselves directing kitchens on Hawaii's neighbor islands have to work a little harder to get the freshest produce and meat. They can order what they want and have it flown in, or they can get local backyard farmers and hotel staff to help out. Edwin Goto has done the latter.

As executive chef at the elegant Lodge at Koele on the island of Lanai, which is owned by the Dole Food Company, Goto has developed a cuisine that is both sophisticated and reflective of what is available locally (fresh fish, venison, and garden vegetables).

Goto, a Japanese American born on the island of Oahu, was influenced by an uncle who served as executive chef aboard a Matson cruise ship in the 1950s. He, like most islanders with large families, was fascinated by the cooking at family gatherings.

He trained first at Kapiolani Community College and worked in the kitchens of the Ilikai and Island Colony hotels. In 1983, he joined chef Khamten Tanhchaleun at the Halekulani's La Mer restaurant.

San Francisco called, and in 1987 Goto headed for the West Coast where he worked at the Hotel Nikko's Les Célébrités, the Park Hyatt's Park Grill, and 1001 Nob Hill. He returned to Hawaii and the Lodge at Koele in 1992.

Goto's style is American and hearty. It's perfectly in keeping with the hotel's quiet elegance and warmth.

Seared Lanai Venison Carpaccio with Crisp Herb Salad

Edwin Goto
The Lodge at Koele
Lanai City, Lanai

Serves 4

The venison in this salad is readily available on the island of Lanai. If you are unable to get fresh venison, beef tenderloin may be substituted.

Spice-Rubbed Venison
2 tablespoons sweet paprika
1 tablespoon sugar
2 tablespoons salt
2 tablespoons chili powder
1 teaspoon cayenne pepper
1 teaspoon garlic powder
1 tablespoon ground pepper
8 ounces fresh venison loin

Mustard Sauce
2 tablespoons whole-grain mustard
½ cup crème fraîche or sour cream

Dressing
¼ cup olive oil
2 tablespoons plain rice wine vinegar
Salt and freshly ground pepper to taste
Pinch of sugar

Herb Salad
1 cup toasted croutons (page 192)
¼ cup fresh chervil leaves
¼ cup 1-inch pieces fresh chives
¼ cup fresh flat-leaf parsley sprigs
¼ cup frisée (curly endive)
¼ cup coarsely chopped radicchio

Garnish
¼ cup finely diced red onion
¼ cup grated Parmesan cheese

To prepare the venison: In a small bowl, combine the paprika, sugar, salt, chili powder, cayenne, garlic powder, and pepper and mix thoroughly. Roll the venison loin in the spice mixture, coating it thoroughly, and shake off the excess. Heat a dry heavy, medium skillet over medium-high heat until very hot. Add the venison and sear for 25 or 30 seconds on each side, or until it is evenly browned. Place the loin on a plate and refrigerate for 30 minutes.

To make the mustard sauce: In a small bowl, combine the ingredients and mix well. Cover and refrigerate.

Seared Lanai Venison Carpaccio with Crisp Herb Salad; Edwin Goto, The Lodge at Koele, Lanai City, Lanai

To make the dressing: In a small bowl, whisk the olive oil and vinegar together. Add the salt, pepper, and sugar. Set aside.

Crush the croutons into small pieces in a blender or food processor. Set aside.

To assemble: Remove the loin from the refrigerator and place it on a cutting board. Using a sharp knife, cut it against the grain into 1/16-inch-thick slices. Spread 1 tablespoon mustard sauce into an 1/8-inch-thick layer around the outer edge of each plate. Overlap the venison slices on top of the mustard sauce, completely covering the sauce. Toss the herb salad ingredients with the croutons and the dressing. Arrange the salad on the center of the plate. Sprinkle the red onions and Parmesan around the salad and on top of the venison.

Seared Pacific Shrimp with Soba Noodles, Crabmeat, and Asian Vegetables, and Ginger-Miso Dressing

Dominique Jamain
The Maile Restaurant
Kahala Hilton
Honolulu, Oahu

Serves 4

The origins of this dish are obviously Japanese. Soba, or buckwheat noodles; miso; togarashi, a spicy Japanese pepper; takuan, a pungent, pickled radish; and black sesame seeds, also called goma — all are available at an Asian grocery.

8 ounces soba noodles

12 tiger shrimp, peeled and deveined
1 tablespoon cornstarch
Salt and freshly ground pepper to taste
1 tablespoon canola oil

2 ounces fresh lump crabmeat
1/4 cup Ginger-Miso Dressing
   (recipe follows)

Asian Vegetables
1/2 cup julienned daikon radish
1/2 cup julienned carrots
1/2 cup julienned cucumber, unpeeled
1/2 cup julienned takuan radish
1/2 cup shiso leaves, cut into shreds

Garnish
12 red endive leaves
3 stalks green onions, including some green tops, cut on the diagonal
1 1/2 tablespoons black sesame seeds

In a large pot of boiling, salted water, cook the soba noodles for 6 to 8 minutes, or until tender. Rinse under cold water and set aside. In a medium bowl, toss the shrimp with the cornstarch. Let sit at room temperature for 30 minutes.

Sprinkle the shrimp with the salt and pepper. In a large sauté pan or skillet over medium-high heat, heat the oil and sauté the shrimp for 2 minutes, or until they turn pink. Set aside. Mix the crabmeat gently into the soba noodles with the dressing. Combine all the Asian vegetables with the noodle mixture.

To serve: Divide the soba noodle mixture among 4 salad plates. Place 3 shrimp on top of each serving. Decorate the outer edges of each plate with endive leaves, green onions, and sesame seeds.

Ginger-Miso Dressing
Makes 1 3/4 cups

1/2 cup white miso paste
1/4 cup soy sauce
1/4 cup plain rice wine vinegar
1/3 cup chicken stock (see page 199)
1/4 cup sugar
1 teaspoon minced ginger
Togarashi to taste

Combine all the ingredients in a small bowl and whisk to blend. Refrigerate for 30 minutes.

Seared Pacific Shrimp with Soba Noodles, Crabmeat, and Asian Vegetables, and Ginger-Miso Dressing; Dominique Jamain, The Maile Restaurant, Kahala Hilton, Honolulu, Oahu

Spicy Island Ahi Poke with Tobiko Caviar on Seared Furikake Rice Cakes

Mako Segawa-Gonzales
Roy's Poipu Bar & Grill
Poipu, Kauai

Serves 4

The Japanese flavors of wasabi, tobiko, daikon sprouts, rice, and furikake dominate this appetizer, a hot sauce poured over soothing rice cakes. Adjust the heat to your own taste by increasing or decreasing the wasabi and chili.

Spicy Ahi Poke
1 tablespoon Asian sesame oil
1 teaspoon togarashi
1 tablespoon Colman's mustard
1 tablespoon wasabi paste
2 tablespoons soy sauce
1 fresh Hawaiian or Thai chili
1 teaspoon salt
2 tablespoons spicy tobiko
2 tablespoons daikon sprouts
1 tablespoon minced onion
1 tablespoon minced green onion tops
6 ounces ahi tuna, cut into ¼-inch dice

Seared Furikake Rice Cake
2 cups steamed sticky rice (page 197)
½ cup plain rice wine vinegar
2 tablespoons water
2 tablespoons furikake
1 tablespoon Asian sesame oil

Garnish
2 tablespoons spicy tobiko
1 tablespoon white sesame seeds
Chili oil to taste (page 188)
¼ cup minced green onion tops

To make the ahi poke: In a medium bowl, mix all ingredients except the ahi into a paste. Add the ahi cubes, stir to coat, and let sit at room temperature for 15 minutes.

To make the rice cakes: Spread the rice onto a baking sheet. In a small bowl, combine the vinegar and water. Dip your fingers in the vinegar mixture and pat the rice into a 6-inch-by-8-inch firm, flat rectangle about ½-inch thick. Sprinkle the furikake on the rice and let the rice cool completely. Using a 2-inch biscuit cutter, cut out twelve rounds of rice. In a medium sauté pan or skillet over medium-high heat, heat the sesame oil. Sear the rice cakes furikake-side down for 2 minutes, or until they are lightly browned. Turn and repeat on the other side.

To assemble: Place 3 rice cakes in the center of each plate, overlapping them slightly. Spoon the poke mixture on top. Sprinkle tobiko and sesame seeds around the edge of each plate. Drizzle chili oil on top of the poke. Sprinkle the green onions over all.

Spicy Island Ahi Poke with Tobiko Caviar on Seared Furikake Rice Cakes; Mako Segawa-Gonzales, Roy's Poipu Bar & Grill, Poipu, Kauai

Steamed Seafood Laulau

Michael Longworth
Sam Choy's Diamond Head
  Restaurant
Honolulu, Oahu

Serves 4

One of the most traditional of Hawaiian dishes, laulau originally consisted of salted meat and fish wrapped in luau leaves (the green tops of the taro plant), then in ti leaves, and steamed in an imu, or underground oven. This updated version is lighter. Aluminum foil, banana leaves, or corn husks may replace the ti leaves.

Herb Sauce

1½ cups mayonnaise
1 tablespoon soy sauce
1 tablespoon snipped fresh dill

Laulau

2 carrots, peeled and cut into
  fine julienne
2 zucchini, cut into fine julienne
1 cup sliced stemmed fresh shiitake
  mushrooms or dried shiitakes
  soaked in warm water for
  30 minutes and squeezed dry
8 ti leaves
8 squid, cleaned (page 198)
8 large shrimp, peeled
  and deveined (page 198)
8 sea scallops
Salt and freshly ground pepper to taste

To make the herb sauce: Mix the mayonnaise, soy sauce, and dill together and set aside.

To make the laulau: Mix the carrots and zucchini together and divide into 4 equal portions. Divide the mushrooms into 4 portions. Remove the hard rib from the ti leaves to make them flexible, or bake on high in a microwave oven for 1 minute to soften. Lay one ti leaf across another at a right angle to form a cross. Or, spread out four 8-inch squares of aluminum foil. Place 1 portion of the carrot mixture in the center of the leaves and top with 2 pieces *each* of squid, shrimp, and scallops. Add salt and pepper. Spread 1 or 2 tablespoons of the herb sauce in a thin layer on top of the seafood, and top with 1 portion of the mushrooms. Gather up the ti leaves, or 4 pieces of aluminum foil, to make a purse and tie with string to make a bundle. Repeat to make 4 bundles. Put the bundles in a steamer or double boiler, cover, and steam over boiling water for 15 minutes.

To serve: If using leaves, place each bundle in the center of a plate at the table. If using aluminum foil, remove the steamed food and place in the center of each plate, and top with the cooking juices.

Steamed Seafood Laulau; Michael Longworth, Sam Choy's Diamond Head Restaurant, Honolulu, Oahu

Tempura of Keahole Baby Lobster; Corey Waite, Coast Grill, Hapuna Beach Prince Hotel, Mauna Kea Resort, Kamuela, Hawaii

Tempura of Keahole Baby Lobster

Corey Waite
Coast Grill
Hapuna Beach Prince Hotel,
Mauna Kea Resort
Kamuela, Hawaii

Serves 4

Maki sushi and tempura, both popular island dishes, are combined to make a crunchy, rich, yet tart appetizer. Japanese tobiko, caviar that has been flavored with pungent wasabi, is used to flavor the sauce. The baby keahole lobsters are soft-shelled, and are used whole.

Vinegared Rice

1 cup short-grain white rice
¼ cup plain rice wine vinegar
1½ teaspoons sugar
1½ teaspoons salt
1 cup plus 1 tablespoon water

Tempura Roll

¼ cup freshly cooked lobster meat
¼ cup mayonnaise (page 195)
Salt and ground white pepper to taste
1 tablespoon fresh lime juice
1 ounce spicy tobiko
2 nori sheets
16 shiso leaves
16 Keahole baby lobsters or
   large prawns

Wasabi Butter Sauce

1 teaspoon canola oil
½ shallot, minced
½ bay leaf
1 teaspoon wasabi paste
2 tablespoons soy sauce
2 tablespoons coconut milk
½ cup (1 stick) unsalted butter, cut
   into tablespoon-sized pieces
1 tablespoon wasabi tobiko

Tempura Batter

½ cup all-purpose flour
½ cup cornstarch
1 egg
1 cup ice water
1 teaspoon shichimi or cayenne
   pepper

½ cup peanut oil

To make the rice: Wash the rice gently until the water runs clear. Let it drain for 1 hour. Meanwhile, in a small saucepan, combine the vinegar, salt, and sugar and stir over low heat until the sugar and salt dissolve. Bring to a boil and let cool. In a medium saucepan over medium-high heat, bring the rice and the water to a boil. Cover and reduce the heat to low. Steam for 15 to 20 minutes, or until all the water has evaporated and the rice is soft. Transfer the rice to a wooden bowl and add the vinegar mixture. Mix well without smashing the rice. Set aside at room temperature.

To make the tempura roll: In a small bowl, combine the lobster meat, mayonnaise, salt, pepper, lime juice, and tobiko and mix well. Place one of the nori sheets, dull-side up, on a sushi mat or dish towel. Moisten your hands and spread half of the rice mixture evenly over the nori sheet. Place 8 of the shiso leaves in the center of the rice. Place half of the lobster mixture and half of the tobiko on the shiso. Kill the lobsters by inserting the point of a sharp knife into the back where the tail joins the body. If using prawns, completely shell them. Place 8 of the baby lobsters or prawns in the center of the roll and roll up tightly. Repeat to fill and roll the remaining nori sheet. Cut the rolls in half crosswise.

To make the sauce: In a small saucepan over medium-high heat, heat the oil and sauté the shallot and bay leaf until the shallot is translucent, about 3 minutes. Add the wasabi paste, soy sauce, and coconut milk. Bring to a simmer and slowly whisk in the butter. Strain through a fine-meshed sieve. Stir the tobiko in gently. Set aside and keep warm.

To make the batter: In a medium bowl, combine all the ingredients and mix well. If the batter is too thick, add more ice water.

In a wok over medium-high heat, heat the oil until a drop of batter into the oil sizzles. Dip the rolls in the batter and deep-fry until the batter is crisp and golden brown and the inside of the roll is still cool, about 1 to 2 minutes. Remove the rolls from the oil and drain well on paper towels. Slice each half into thirds.

To serve: Pool one-fourth of the sauce on each of 4 salad plates and place 3 slices of tempura on top.

Wok-charred Ahi

Peter Merriman
Merriman's Restaurant
Waimea, Hawaii

Serves 4

This variation on sashimi has become a staple of Hawaiian cuisine. Instead of being served raw, the ahi has been seared on the outside and remains rare on the inside. The dipping sauce is salty and hot.

Dipping Sauce
¼ cup soy sauce
1 tablespoon mirin or sweet sherry
1 tablespoon fresh lime juice
1 tablespoon wasabi powder
½ teaspoon water

½ cup clarified unsalted butter (page 186)
2 teaspoons grated fresh ginger

2 teaspoons minced shallots
2 teaspoons red pepper flakes
1 teaspoon dried marjoram
½ teaspoon cayenne pepper
1 teaspoon salt
Juice from ½ lemon
Two 4-inch squares 1¼-inch-thick ahi (4 ounces each)

To make the dipping sauce: In a small bowl, combine the soy sauce, mirin or sweet sherry, and lime juice. Mix the wasabi and water together to make a paste, and add it to the soy mixture.

In a shallow bowl, combine all the ingredients except the ahi and mix well. Heat a wok or large skillet over high heat until the pan is very hot. Coat the ahi in the butter mixture on all sides. Sear in the hot pan for 20 seconds on each side. Cut into ⅛-inch-thick slices and serve with the dipping sauce.

Wok-charred Ahi; Peter Merriman, Merriman's Restaurant, Waimea, Hawaii

Maui Onion Soup with Goat Cheese; Gerard Kaleohano, Mid-Pacific Country Club, Lanikai, Oahu

Soups and Salads

Salads and hot climates go hand in hand. Hawaii chefs have given the simple green salad new meaning by incorporating crisp wonton wrappers, fiddlehead ferns, and bean thread noodles. The dressings are innovative: the vinaigrettes use such ingredients as sesame oil, chili paste, papaya, and wasabi and can be used on salads and vegetable dishes of your own design.

Island soups are just as fresh and bright, making use of the abundance of island seafood and local vegetables, as in the Hawaiian version of bouillabaisse, and caramelized Maui onion soup.

Ahi and Taro Salad; Mark Ellman, Avalon Restaurant & Bar, Lahaina, Maui

Ahi and Taro Salad

Mark Ellman
Avalon Restaurant & Bar
Lahaina, Maui

Serves 4

Raw ahi, taro root, macadamia nuts, and a spike of chili pepper water are molded into a colorful salad topped with two colors of tobiko, or caviar. A puree of cilantro and macadamia nut oil adds a piquant flavor note.

8 ounces taro root, peeled and
　cut into ½-inch cubes

Cilantro Puree
4 cups packed fresh cilantro leaves
2 cups macadamia nut oil or walnut oil
Salt and freshly ground pepper to taste

12 ounces sashimi-grade ahi tuna,
　cut into ½-inch cubes
1 garlic clove, minced
½ Maui or other sweet white
　onion, minced
1 carrot, chopped
1 beet, peeled and cut into
　fine julienne
1 cup macadamia nuts, finely chopped
2 teaspoons minced fresh ginger
1 cup soy sauce
2 teaspoons Asian sesame oil
¼ cup finely chopped ogo (seaweed)
4 teaspoons chili pepper water
　(page 197)
¼ cup diced macadamia nuts, toasted
　(page 196)

4 teaspoons white sesame seeds,
　toasted (page 196)

½ cup black tobiko or salmon caviar
½ cup green tobiko

To cook the taro: Scrub the outside of the taro root with a brush. Put in a saucepan with enough boiling salted water to cover the taro. Cover and simmer for 1½ hours, or until tender. Remove the taro, drain, and let cool. With a sharp knife, remove the outer peel and cut into cubes.

To make the cilantro puree: In a blender or food processor, combine the cilantro and oil and puree. Stir in the salt and pepper. Set aside.

In a large bowl, combine all the remaining ingredients except the tobiko or salmon caviar. Toss and let sit for 15 minutes. Line a baking pan with parchment paper or aluminum foil. Place four 4-inch ring molds on the prepared baking pan. Divide the salad among the molds and gently pack down to firm. Refrigerate for at least 1 hour.

To serve: Lift the rings with a spatula and place on plates. Run the tip of a small sharp knife around the molds to loosen, and lift the molds. Pour one fourth of the puree around each salad mold. Top each salad with a teaspoon of black tobiko, and ½ teaspoon of green tobiko, or spoon the caviar on top.

Caramelized Maui Onion Soup

David Paul Johnson
David Paul's Lahaina Grill
Lahaina, Maui

Serves 4

Maui's sweet white onions are juicier than yellow onions, therefore they cook a little faster. This is a wonderful soup for a cold day. If you are in a hurry, you can substitute canned low-salt chicken broth for the chicken stock.

Caramelized Maui Onion Soup; David Paul Johnson, David Paul's Lahaina Grill, Lahaina, Maui

4 large Maui or other sweet white
onions, cut into thin slices
1 tablespoon sugar
1 teaspoon salt
¼ cup clarified unsalted butter or
olive oil (page 186)
¼ cup dry white wine
¼ cup dry sherry

2 quarts chicken stock (recipe follows)
¼ cup flour mixed with ¼ cup water
Salt and freshly ground pepper
¼ cup grated Parmesan cheese
1 cup toasted sourdough croutons
(page 192)

In a large bowl, combine the onions, sugar, and salt and stir to mix well. In a large, heavy saucepan over high heat, heat the butter or oil until almost smoking. Add the onions and stir until the onions begin to brown, about 3 minutes. Reduce heat to low and stir until the onions are soft and golden brown. Stir in the white wine and sherry. Set aside.

Return the caramelized onions to the stove and add the strained stock. Bring to a boil, reduce heat to medium, and cook to reduce to about 6 cups. Stir in the flour mixture and return to a boil. Simmer for 5 to 10 minutes. Season and serve with cheese and croutons.

David Paul's Chicken Stock
Makes 8 cups

2 tablespoons olive oil
5 pounds bony chicken parts, skin,
and trimmings
1 carrot, chopped
2 celery stalks, chopped
1 large onion, chopped
1 large leek, chopped, white part only
1 cup dry white wine
4 quarts cold water
1 cup port
Assorted fresh herbs tied in
a cheesecloth square

In a large stockpot over high heat, heat the oil and cook the chicken until it is well browned. Add the vegetables and continue to cook until they soften. Add the white wine, stirring to scrape up the small bits for 2 minutes. Add the cold water, port, and herb packet and bring to a boil. Reduce heat and simmer to reduce to 8 cups. Strain the stock ingredients through a medium-meshed sieve.

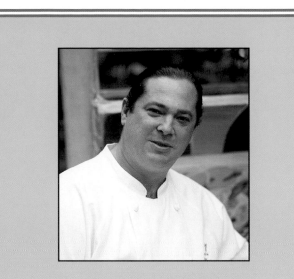

Mark Ellman
Avalon Restaurant & Bar, Lahaina, Maui

Mark Ellman has always loved two things: food and rock 'n' roll.

Perhaps his originality as a chef comes from the fact that his culinary skills are self-taught. Ellman began as a teenager flipping burgers at a place called Texas Tommy's on Topanga Canyon Boulevard in the San Fernando Valley. By the time he was eighteen he was working for French chef Tony LeBlanc at Yellowfinger's in Los Angeles. While there, he went from pantry boy to luncheon chef to head chef when they opened a new cafe.

In 1977, he and his wife Judy began their own catering company called Can't Rock and Roll, But Sure Can Cook, and geared it to the entertainment industry. They provided location and studio food for such rock and pop stars as Earth, Wind and Fire, Ronnie and Hubert Laws, the Moody Blues, Neil Diamond, Frankie Valli, and the Beach Boys. The diverse tastes of these artists pushed Ellman to try a wide range of cooking styles and ingredients.

Next, he opened a small restaurant serving peasant-style food from France and Italy called Cuisine Cuisine. Here he made his own pasta and sauces and marketed them to specialty markets throughout Southern California.

He also worked as chef at Kathy Gallagher's in Beverly Hills, and Cafe Ronchetti and Kilgore Trout's, both in Colorado.

In 1985, Mark and Judy moved to Maui, and in 1988 they opened the Avalon Restaurant & Bar in the old whaling port of Lahaina. Mark's sister Gerry has joined him as his assistant chef, and together they create innovative dishes that combine the cuisine of California with those of Indonesia, Vietnam, Thailand, China, and Japan.

KELLY DEGALA
Gordon Biersch Brewery Restaurant, Honolulu, Oahu

Kelly Degala had to leave to come home again. As a young man, he worked in Honolulu restaurants, but it wasn't until he found himself far from home in cold and rainy Seattle that his love of cooking and his commitment to a vocation solidified.

Degala became acquainted with the new, fresh cuisine of the Pacific Northwest at Cafe Sport, where he learned both the business and culinary ends of running a stylish cafe. His talents were honed further when he apprenticed with Caprial Pence in the kitchen of the four-star Fullers restaurant in the Seattle Sheraton Hotel.

Degala returned to Hawaii in 1994 to open Harlequin restaurant and Cafe Picasso in the Alana Waikiki Hotel. The venture was short-lived, but he had come back to his culinary roots. Here he began creating dishes that reflected his Filipino heritage, as well as other cultures of the Pacific Rim. He also discovered he had a real flair for presentation.

At the Gordon Biersch Brewery in the trendy new Aloha Marketplace on Honolulu's waterfront, Degala serves up healthful ingredients and exotic flavors that draw from American, Asian, and other influences, especially Mediterranean.

The restaurant has an open, friendly atmosphere that allows diners to watch the brewing process behind large windows, as well as ships passing in the harbor. Degala's cuisine makes the experience perfect.

Grilled Kauai Prawns and Bean Thread Noodles with a Strawberry Papaya Vinaigrette

Kelly Degala
Gordon Biersch Brewery Restaurant
Honolulu, Oahu

Serves 4

Large freshwater prawns are prepared here with the head, whiskers, and tail intact. The lumpia cups and fried bean thread noodles can be prepared ahead of time and kept in an airtight container for assembly. Solo and strawberry papayas are the most plentiful in Hawaii; however, you can use any variety for the vinaigrette.

Strawberry Papaya Vinaigrette
1 cup finely chopped strawberry, or solo, or regular papaya
1 tablespoon grated fresh ginger
2 tablespoons fresh orange juice
2 tablespoons mirin or sweet sherry
¼ cup Thai or other sweet chili paste
¼ cup macadamia nut or peanut oil
Hawaiian or kosher salt and freshly ground pepper to taste

Lumpia Cups
Peanut oil for frying
2 lumpia wrappers

One 8-ounce package rice stick noodles

16 large unshelled Kauai or other freshwater prawns or jumbo shrimp
Olive oil for coating
Hawaiian or kosher salt to taste

Salad Bouquets
4 green onions, green part only
4 large lettuce leaves
2 handfuls (2 ounces) mixed baby greens

Okinawan Sweet Potato Puree
2½ pounds Okinawan or regular sweet potatoes
¾ cup (1½ sticks) unsalted butter, cut into pieces
Salt and freshly ground pepper to taste

Garnish

4 fresh opal basil sprigs
1 red bell pepper, seeded, deribbed, and diced
1 yellow bell pepper, seeded, deribbed, and diced

To make the vinaigrette: Put the papaya, ginger, orange juice, mirin or sherry, and chili sauce in a blender and puree. With the machine running, gradually add the oil. Add salt and pepper. Set aside.

To make the lumpia cups: In a deep wok or deep fryer, heat 2 inches of the oil to 375°F, or until almost smoking. Cut each lumpia wrapper in half on the diagonal, making 2 triangles. Put 1 triangle in the hot oil and press to the bottom of the wok or fryer with a slotted wooden spoon. Hold it there for 15 seconds, or until a cup is formed. Continue to fry for 1 minute, or until browned. With a slotted spoon, transfer to paper towels to drain. Repeat to cook the remaining triangles. Reserve the oil.

To make the noodles: Cut a package of noodles into 4 portions. Drop ¼ of the noodles into the same hot oil used for the lumpia cups. They will triple in size immediately. With a slotted spoon, remove and drain on paper towels. Repeat with the remaining noodles. Set aside.

To prepare the prawns: Soak 16 bamboo skewers in water for at least 15 minutes. Light a fire in a charcoal grill or preheat a gas grill. Run the bamboo skewers lengthwise through the unshelled prawns or shrimp to hold the shellfish straight during cooking. Coat the prawns or shrimp with oil, then sprinkle with salt. Grill the prawns or shrimp over a medium-hot fire, turning frequently, until they turn pink, about 3 minutes. Set aside.

To make the bouquets: Blanch the green onions in boiling water for 30 seconds. Drain. Fill each large lettuce leaf with one fourth of the mixed greens. Place 1 grilled prawn or shrimp inside each bouquet of greens. Tie around each bouquet with a blanched green onion.

To make the sweet potato puree: Peel and cube the sweet potatoes. Place in a medium saucepan of salted water and bring to a boil. Cook until tender, about 25 minutes. Drain. Add the butter, salt, and pepper, and mash.

To serve: Place ¼ cup sweet potato puree on half of each plate. Place a lumpia cup on the other half of each plate, then place a bouquet across each lumpia cup. Ladle a generous portion of the vinaigrette over each prawn or shrimp. Garnish with a spray of fried bean thread noodles and a sprig of basil. Scatter the diced red and yellow peppers on top of the vinaigrette.

Grilled Kauai Prawns and Bean Thread Noodles with a Strawberry Papaya Vinaigrette; Kelly Degala, Gordon Biersch Brewery Restaurant, Honolulu, Oahu

Grilled Shrimp and Star Fruit Salad; Peter Merriman, Merriman's Restaurant, Waimea, Hawaii

Grilled Shrimp and Star Fruit Salad

Peter Merriman
Merriman's Restaurant
Waimea, Hawaii

Serves 4

Spicy and *exotic* are the best words to describe this colorful and attractive salad. If star fruit is difficult to find, mango makes a wonderful substitute.

¼ cup olive oil
2 tablespoons minced shallots
2 tablespoons minced fresh cilantro
Salt and freshly ground pepper to taste
16 to 20 large shrimp, peeled with
    head left on
1 tablespoon minced fresh ginger
½ cup fresh lime juice
⅛ teaspoon red pepper flakes
2 tablespoons chopped fresh mint
1 ripe star fruit, sliced thin
4 handfuls (4 ounces) watercress or
    arugula sprigs

In a nonaluminum baking dish, combine the oil, shallots, cilantro, salt, and pepper. Skewer 4 or 5 shrimp on each of 4 sets of parallel skewers, running the skewer through the head and tail of each shrimp and leaving space between shrimp. Marinate at room temperature for 1 hour, or cover and refrigerate for up to 8 hours. Let the shrimp sit at room temperature for 30 minutes before cooking.

Light a fire in a charcoal or gas grill, or preheat the broiler. Combine the ginger, lime juice, pepper flakes, mint, and star fruit in a small bowl; toss to mix. Grill or broil the shrimp for 1 minute on each side, or until pink. Set aside. Make a bed of watercress or arugula on each of 4 salad plates and place one fourth of the star fruit mixture on top of each. Take the shrimp off the skewers and place 4 or 5 on top of each salad.

Maui Onion Soup with Goat Cheese; Gerard Kaleohano, Mid-Pacific Country Club, Lanikai, Oahu

Maui Onion Soup with Goat Cheese

Gerard Kaleohano
Mid-Pacific Country Club
Lanikai, Oahu

Serves 4

The savory onion soup is covered by a single large toasted crouton topped with cheese and pineapple. Canned pineapple works as well as fresh in this sweet-tart topping. In Hawaii, taro bread is available in specialty foods stores. Any flavorful loaf of uncut bread such as potato bread will do.

4 tablespoons unsalted butter
4 Maui or other sweet white onions,
   cut into thin slices
1 cup Madeira
1½ quarts beef stock (page 200)
Salt and freshly ground pepper to taste

Taro Loaf Croutons

2 slices taro bread or potato bread
2 tablespoons unsalted butter
   at room temperature
2 tablespoons grated Parmesan cheese

Goat Cheese Topping

4 Swiss cheese slices cut
   to fit croutons
4 tablespoons fresh white goat cheese
4 tablespoons minced pineapple
4 tablespoons brown sugar
Ground cinnamon for sprinkling

To make the soup: In a deep pot, melt the butter over medium heat and sauté the onions until tender. Add the Madeira and cook for 4 to 5 minutes. Add the stock and cook for 20 to 30 minutes, or until somewhat reduced. Periodically remove the foam that comes to the top. Add salt and pepper.

To make the croutons: Preheat the oven to 325°F. Cut the bread in half diagonally, and cut into long thin slices. Beat the butter until smooth and blend the cheese into the butter. Spread the slices of bread with the butter mixture and place on a baking sheet. Bake about 20 minutes until golden. Increase the oven heat to 375°F.

To finish the soup: Ladle the soup into ovenproof soup dishes. Place a crouton on top of each serving. On top of each crouton place a slice of Swiss cheese and 1 tablespoon each of the goat cheese, pineapple, and brown sugar. Sprinkle with cinnamon. Bake the soup for 4 to 7 minutes, or until the cheese melts.

PETER MERRIMAN
Merriman's Restaurant, Waimea, Hawaii

With his big smile and his baseball cap, Peter Merriman still looks like a kid. But this kid was whipping up Eggs Benedict while still at Boy Scout camp. At sixteen, he introduced his football teammates at Elizabeth Forward School in Pennsylvania to salade niçoise.

Peter Merriman's boyish good looks belie the intensity with which he approaches cooking. On the Big Island of Hawaii, where he opened his first free-standing restaurant, he uses only the freshest lamb and beef from local ranches. His lokelani (rose) tomatoes are vine-ripened, and the juicy red strawberries come from nearby.

While still a teenager, Merriman learned to cook from Ferdinand Metz, an executive with the H. J. Heinz Company, who went on to head the prestigious Culinary Institute of America. After graduation from the University of Pennsylvania, Merriman enrolled in an apprentice program run by the American Culinary Federation, which gave him the opportunity to study at the Woodstock Inn in Vermont.

After working in resorts in the United States and Europe, he settled into the kitchen at the Four Seasons in Washington, D.C. From there he took a position at the newly opened Mauna Lani Bay Hotel & Bungalows on the Big Island.

At Mauna Lani, Merriman worked his way up from saucier to banquet chef, then to executive chef at the Gallery Restaurant. It was here, at the age of twenty-eight, that he gained his reputation as a proponent of the new Hawaiian regional cuisine.

He and his wife Vicki opened their own restaurant, Merriman's, in Opelo Plaza in 1988. In 1994, he became partners with TS Restaurants in the new Hula Grill & Bar at the Kaanapali Resort on Maui.

GERARD KALEOHANO
Mid-Pacific Country Club, Lanikai, Oahu

Gerard Kaleohano has received an honor not bestowed on many Hawaiian chefs: he prepared lunch for the President of the United States, Bill Clinton, while the Clintons were on vacation on Oahu. Then again, given the quality and creativity of Gerard Kaleohano's dishes, perhaps the President himself also felt honored.

Kaleohano, a native Hawaiian, serves as chef de cuisine at the Mid-Pacific Country Club on Oahu. Here he is responsible for catering banquets, weddings, wine tastings, business luncheons, and the day-in-and day-out table service.

He has had a close association with such leaders of the new Hawaii Regional Cuisine movement as Sam Choy, Beverly Gannon, Alan Wong, Gordon Hopkins, and Russell Siu.

Kaleohano is devoted to his family and community. On his days off you can find him surfing or improving his self-defense techniques. He has also worked with the Kailua Neighborhood Board, Big Brothers, Big Sisters, and the Aloha United Way.

Nalo Green Salad with Crispy Wontons and Tangerine Vinaigrette

Gerard Kaleohano
Mid-Pacific Country Club
Lanikai, Oahu

Serves 6

The Waimanalo district on the island of Oahu has in recent years become a big producer of fresh gourmet produce. Locals affectionately refer to the area as Nalo. The egg yolks in the vinaigrette can be deleted, if you like. This salad would be delicious with any of the duck entrees in this book.

Crispy Wontons
2 cups peanut oil
One 3-ounce package (24) wonton
  wrappers, cut into julienne

Tangerine Vinaigrette
6 to 8 egg yolks
¾ cup whole-grain Dijon mustard

2 tablespoons cider vinegar
2 cups tangerine juice or orange
  juice concentrate
¾ cup sugar
2 tablespoons salt
1 tablespoon ground pepper
¼ cup macadamia nut oil or walnut oil

1 head butter lettuce
1 head radicchio
1 head red leaf lettuce
6 cups stemmed Okinawan spinach
  or arugula
4 chives, snipped
2 tablespoons cider vinegar
1 tablespoon sugar
Salt and freshly ground pepper to taste
1 red bell pepper, seeded, deribbed,
  and diced (page 196)

Garnish
1 orange, cut into 6 to 8
  crosswise slices
1 teaspoon black sesame seeds
6 to 12 edible flowers

To make the wontons: In a wok over medium heat, heat the oil until a wonton strip sizzles and rises to the top when submerged. Add the wonton strips and cook until brown and crisp, about 30 seconds to 1 minute. Using a slotted spoon, transfer to paper towels to drain.

To make the vinaigrette: In a blender, beat the egg yolks until thickened. Add all the other ingredients except the oil and blend. With the machine running, gradually add the oil to make a smooth sauce.

Tear the lettuce and radicchio leaves into bite-sized pieces. In a large bowl, mix the lettuces and spinach, or arugula.

Submerge the chives in ice water until crisp, about 3 minutes. In a small bowl, combine the vinegar, sugar, salt, and pepper. Add the diced pepper and mix.

To serve: Toss the greens with some of the vinaigrette. Swirl vinaigrette on each plate. Mound about 1½ cups of crispy wontons in the center of each plate. Garnish the borders with the bell pepper mixture and orange slices. Arrange the greens on top of the pepper and orange slices. Drizzle more vinaigrette on top if desired. Sprinkle with sesame seeds and garnish with chives and 1 or 2 flowers.

Smoked Nairagi Sashimi with Fresh Ogo Salad

Roy Yamaguchi
Roy's Restaurant
Honolulu, Oahu

Serves 4

Begin curing and smoking the nairagi two days ahead. The fish and ogo give a fresh sea flavor to the salad, while the peppers add plenty of heat.

Marinade
1/2 cup brown sugar
1 cup white sugar
3 tablespoons salt
1 sprig fresh basil, minced
1/2 sweet white onion, minced
2 sprigs fresh dill, chopped

12 ounces sashimi-grade nairagi or
    other firm-fleshed fish

Wasabi Vinaigrette
4 tablespoons rice wine vinegar
4 tablespoons lemon juice
1/4 cup olive oil
1/2 cup sesame seed oil
1/2 cup soy sauce
1 teaspoon wasabi paste
4 tablespoons Lingham chili sauce
    or other chili sauce
1 Hawaiian or Thai chili, minced

Ogo Salad (below)
8 ounces mung bean sprouts
2 Japanese cucumbers, peeled, seeded,
    and cut into julienne
2 carrots, peeled and cut into julienne
4 ounces enoki mushrooms
8 chive stalks
1/8 teaspoon shichimi
2 tablespoons black sesame seeds

Ogo Salad
1-1/2 pounds fresh ogo
1 tomato, cut into julienne
1 sweet white onion, cut into julienne
4 green onions, tops only, minced
1/2 cup sesame seed oil
1/2 cup olive oil
1/2 cup soy sauce
2 Hawaiian or Thai chilies, crushed
3 tablespoons ground fresh ginger
4 fresh garlic cloves, finely minced
3 tablespoons lemon juice

To cure and smoke the fish: Combine all marinade ingredients in a nonaluminum bowl. Place the fish in a zipper sealed plastic bag and pour in the marinade. Press out all the air and seal the bag. Squeeze the bag to distribute the marinade evenly and refrigerate overnight. Prepare a smoker (page 198). When the smoker is ready, remove the fish from the marinade and blot with paper towels. Place the fish on a wire rack. Place the sheet pan in the smoker and place the rack on the ice. Cold smoke for 1 hour. Refrigerate.

To make the salad: Combine the ogo, tomato, onions, and green onions in a bowl. In a separate bowl, whisk together the sesame oil, olive oil, soy, chilies, ginger, garlic, and lemon juice. Toss the seaweed mixture with the dressing and refrigerate.

To serve: Whisk together the vinegar, lemon juice, oils, soy sauce, wasabi, chili sauce and chili. With a very sharp knife, slice the fish paper-thin. On each of four salad plates, place a small mound of ogo salad. Place a few sprouts, cucumbers, and carrots over the ogo. Top with slices of fish. Repeat two more times to create a tower of salad and drizzle the vinaigrette over the fish. Garnish with enoki and chives, and sprinkle with shichimi and sesame seeds.

Smoked Nairagi Sashimi with Fresh Ogo Salad; Roy Yamaguchi, Roy's Restaurant, Honolulu, Oahu

Nalo Green Salad with Crispy Wontons and Tangerine Vinaigrette; Gerard Kaleohano, Mid-Pacific Country Club, Lanikai, Oahu

Ono Poke with Crisp Wontons and Ogo Vinaigrette

Alex Stanislaw
The Plantation House Restaurant
Kapalua, Maui

Serves 4

This napoleonlike salad layers ono poke with wontons to create a tall salad with fresh sea flavor, plus a little crunch. Ahi tuna, or any firm-fleshed fish, can be substituted for ono. If the ogo is not available, use 1 tablespoon dried Japanese nori.

Poke

1 pound ono, cut into ¼-inch dice
½ small Maui or other sweet white
   onion, diced
3 tomatoes, seeded and diced
   (page 203)
1 teaspoon plain rice wine vinegar
1 teaspoon soy sauce
Pinch of Hawaiian or kosher salt
1 teaspoon shichimi

Ogo Vinaigrette

½ cup ogo
½ cup plain rice wine vinegar
1 tablespoon black sesame seeds
Juice of 3 limes
Salt and freshly ground pepper to taste
1 cup peanut oil
½ Maui or other sweet white
   onion, diced

2 cups peanut oil
8 square wonton wrappers, cut
   in half diagonally
Snipped fresh chives for garnish

Ono Poke with Crisp Wontons and Ogo Vinaigrette; Alex Stanislaw, The Plantation House Restaurant, Kapalua, Maui

To prepare the poke: In a medium bowl, combine all the ingredients. Cover and refrigerate for at least 2 hours or overnight.

To prepare the vinaigrette: Combine all the vinaigrette ingredients except the oil and onion in a blender. With the machine running, gradually add the oil. Stir in the onion.

To make the wonton: In a wok over medium heat, heat the oil until a wonton strip sizzles and rises to the top when submerged. Add the wonton strips and cook until brown and crisp, about 30 seconds. Using a slotted spoon, transfer to paper towels to drain.

To serve: Place 2 tablespoons of poke in the center of each plate and top with a wonton triangle. Place 2 more tablespoons of poke on the wonton, then another wonton on top. Mound a final 2 tablespoons of poke on the second wonton. Drizzle the stack and the plate with the dressing and garnish with chives.

ALEX STANISLAW
The Plantation House Restaurant, Kapalua, Maui

Alex Stanislaw's family centered life around the hearth. His grandmother always kept a stockpot simmering on the stove, and nothing was ever wasted. The noodles were homemade, leftovers showed up in the next day's salads, and the flavors were decidedly Eastern European, reflecting the family heritage.

But Stanislaw grew up wanting to be a filmmaker. In the mid-1970s he studied cinematography at Syracuse University and took a job in the kitchen of a swank country club. Even though much of what he cooked was the "meat and potatoes" food beloved by the country club set, he had access to a rich variety of seafood from East Coast waters.

"Any smart chef uses the best ingredients available, and that usually means working with the farmers and local community," he says.

Stanislaw found to his surprise that he loved to cook, and decided that he should enter formal training. He enrolled in the Culinary Institute of America's fifteen-month intensive program. After graduating with honors, he moved to Maui and a position at the Kapalua Bay Hotel, where he stayed for three years.

He was the chef at Erik's Seafood Grotto in Kihei, Maui, for seven years before becoming executive chef at the posh Plantation House. His unique cultural background and island experience have made the restaurant's fare exceptional.

PHILIPPE PADOVANI

The Manele Bay Hotel, Lanai City, Lanai

When Philippe Padovani was a young boy, his parents fed farmers and herders from their small snack shop in the Australian outback.

When he was fourteen, his family returned to France, where he had been born, and he entered the esteemed culinary school École Gaston Lenôtre in Plaisir, France. His career as a chef led him to restaurants in Antibes and Grenoble before he joined the award-winning Restaurant La Tour Rose in Lyons.

It was while he was in Lyons that he began consulting for the Halekulani Hotel's La Mer restaurant. Before long, he moved to Honolulu to become the hotel's corporate chef.

When Ritz-Carlton opened a new hotel at Mauna Lani on the Big Island, Padovani became executive chef, in charge of creating menus that reflected the atmosphere of the islands, while maintaining the high style the hotel chain is known for. Here he became part of the small cadre of chefs who began the culinary movement known as Hawaii Regional Cuisine.

Padovani is currently overseeing the cooking at the luxurious Manele Bay Hotel on the island of Lanai. He has also participated in many international food festivals, including the Hawaiian Food Festival in Bangkok, Thailand, the Hawaii Regional Cuisine Festival in Singapore, and Big Island Bounty at Mauna Lani.

Ahi and Onaga Poke with Green Papaya Salad and Lime Vinaigrette

Philippe Padovani
The Manele Bay Hotel
Lanai City, Lanai

Serves 4

Green papaya salad was introduced to Hawaii by immigrants from Southeast Asia. Its crunchy, fresh flavor has become a favorite in the last decade. This poke is an updated version of the traditional Hawaiian dish. If onaga is not available, any firm white-meat fish will do.

Poke
One 8-ounce block sashimi-grade ahi tuna
One 8-ounce block onaga
2 tablespoons wasabi paste
4 teaspoons red tobiko or salmon caviar
4 teaspoons pickled ginger
2 teaspoons white sesame seed, toasted (page 196)
4 teaspoons finely snipped fresh chives
4 teaspoons ogo (seaweed)
6 tablespoons olive oil
Salt and freshly ground white pepper to taste

Lime Vinaigrette
2 tablespoons fresh lime juice
Salt and freshly ground white pepper to taste
6 tablespoons olive oil

Green Papaya Salad
1½ pounds green papaya
4 teaspoons wasabi paste
4 teaspoons red tobiko or salmon caviar
4 teaspoons finely snipped fresh chives

To prepare the poke: Cut the ahi and onaga into ¼-inch dice. In a medium bowl, toss the fish with all the other poke ingredients and refrigerate for about 30 minutes.

To make the vinaigrette: Combine all the ingredients in a screw top jar and shake vigorously. Set aside.

To make the salad: Wash, peel, and pit the green papaya. Cut the papaya into shreds. Combine the papaya, wasabi, tobiko, and chives and mix with the lime vinaigrette to taste. Refrigerate for about 30 minutes, or until chilled.

To serve: In the middle of each of 4 chilled plates, place equal amounts of poke in a 4-inch circle. Place the papaya salad around the poke.

Red and White Sashimi Salad

Alan Wong
Alan Wong's Restaurant
Honolulu, Oahu

Serves 4

This fresh-tasting salad is sparked with the sharp bite of chilies and ginger. The recipe will serve 2 as an entree.

Wonton Garnish
2 cups peanut oil
8 square wonton wrappers, cut into julienne

3 ounces sashimi-grade ahi tuna
3 ounces sashimi-grade onaga
2 cups shredded won bok (napa cabbage)
½ large carrot, peeled and julienned

1 cup snow peas, julienned
½ cup shredded red cabbage
¼ Hawaii or Thai chili, minced
2 fresh kaffir lime leaves, thinly sliced
4 cilantro sprigs
1 small green onion, cut into julienne,
   including the green top
¼ cup macadamia nuts, toasted and
   coarsely chopped (page 196)
1 tablespoon chopped fresh
   cilantro leaves
Soy Vinaigrette (recipe follows)
2 teaspoons wasabi paste

To make the wonton garnish: In a wok over medium heat, heat the oil until a wonton strip sizzles and rises to the top when submerged. Add the wonton strips and cook until brown and crisp, about 1 minute. Using a slotted spoon, transfer to paper towels to drain.

With a very sharp chef's knife or Chinese cleaver, cut the ahi into 1-by-2-inch blocks, then slice into very thin, nearly transparent slices. Repeat with the onaga. In a large bowl, toss the won bok, carrot, snow peas, and cabbage together. Add the onaga, chili, lime leaves, cilantro, and green onion, and toss.

To serve: Divide the salad among 4 plates, then fan slices of ahi around the top. Garnish each serving with macadamia nuts and cilantro. Ladle vinaigrette on the plate around the greens and place ¼-inch dabs of wasabi evenly around the plate.

Soy Vinaigrette
Juice, pulp, and grated zest of 2 limes
1 cup water
1 cup soy sauce
1 cup canola oil
1 cup plain rice wine vinegar
1 cup sugar
1 cup mirin or sweet sherry
½ head of garlic
1 tablespoon grated fresh ginger
1½ teaspoons Asian sesame oil
2 Hawaiian or Thai chilies, seeded
   and chopped

Scoop the pulp out of the limes with a small sharp knife. In a small bowl, combine all the ingredients. Mix well, cover, and refrigerate for at least 2 hours. Strain through a fine-meshed sieve before using. May be kept in the refrigerator for up to 3 days.

Ahi and Onaga Poke with Green Papaya Salad and Lime Vinaigrette; Philippe Padovani, The Manele Bay Hotel, Lanai City, Lanai

Red and White Sashimi Salad; Alan Wong, Alan Wong's Restaurant, Honolulu, Oahu

Seared Spicy Ahi with Ogo-Wasabi Sauce and Fiddlehead Fern Salad; Daniel Delbrel, La Cascata, Princeville Hotel, Princeville, Kauai

Seared Spicy Ahi with Ogo-Wasabi Sauce and Fiddlehead Fern Salad

Daniel Delbrel
La Cascata
Princeville Hotel
Princeville, Kauai

Serves 4

Fiddlehead ferns, also known as pohole, have a delicate green flavor that complements the spicy tuna in this dish. Baby Blue Lake green beans may also be used.

Two 7-ounce ahi tuna blocks
2 tablespoons Cajun spice mix
3 tablespoons oil

Ogo-Wasabi Sauce
1 teaspoon Asian sesame oil
1 teaspoon minced onion
1 roasted garlic clove (page 198)
Leaves from 1 fresh thyme sprig
2 bay leaves
10 peppercorns
¼ cup distilled white vinegar
¼ cup dry white wine
2 tablespoons heavy (whipping) cream
½ cup (1 stick) cold unsalted butter, cut into tablespoon-sized pieces
2 teaspoons chopped ogo (seaweed)
1 teaspoon wasabi paste
Salt and freshly ground pepper to taste

Fiddlehead Fern Salad
2 ounces fiddlehead ferns (pohole), or haricots verts, or baby Blue Lake green beans
1 tablespoon slivered Maui or other sweet white onion
1 tomato, seeded and julienned (page 203)

Vinaigrette
2 tablespoons soy sauce
2 tablespoons plain rice wine vinegar
1 teaspoon Asian sesame oil
1 teaspoon fish sauce, preferably Tiparos

To prepare the ahi: Roll each fish block lightly in the Cajun spice. In a medium sauté pan or skillet over high heat, heat the oil and sear the ahi on all sides for about 20 seconds on each side. The fish will still be rare on the inside. Drain on paper towels and slice ¼ inch thick.

To prepare the ogo sauce: In a medium saucepan over high heat, heat the oil and sauté the onion for 5 seconds. Add the garlic, thyme, and bay leaves and sauté for 5 seconds. Add the peppercorns and saute for 10 seconds. Add the vinegar and sauté for 20 seconds. Cook to reduce until the pan is nearly dry. Add the white wine and cook for 4 to 5 minutes. Add the cream

and cook to reduce until thick. Reduce heat to low and whisk in the butter, 1 piece at a time. Do not boil. Remove from heat and strain the sauce by pushing it through a sieve with a wooden spoon. Return to low heat and whisk in the ogo and wasabi. Cook for another 30 seconds. Add salt and pepper. Set aside and keep warm over tepid water.

To make the salad: Trim the ends of the ferns or beans. Blanch the ferns for 1 second in boiling water, then plunge them into ice water. If using green beans, blanch for 30 seconds, or until crisp-tender, then plunge into ice water. Drain and dry the vegetables on paper towels. Combine with the onion and tomato.

To make the vinaigrette: Whisk the soy sauce and vinegar together, then whisk in the sesame oil and fish sauce.

To serve: Mix the vinaigrette and salad. Place some salad on one side of each plate. Spoon 2 to 3 tablespoons of the ogo sauce onto each plate and fan out one-fourth of the seared ahi on top of it and alongside the salad.

Spicy Thai Beef Salad with Lemongrass-Mint Vinaigrette and Toasted Macadamia Nuts

Roy Yamaguchi
Roy's Restaurant
Honolulu, Oahu

Serves 4

Ginger is the piquant note in the marinade, the vinaigrette, and the vegetables for this entree salad. The greens and stir-fry are topped with marinated, seared steak slices.

Marinade
½ cup hoisin sauce
2 tablespoons soy sauce
½ tablespoon minced fresh ginger
1 tablespoon red wine vinegar
2 tablespoons sugar

Four 4-ounce New York steaks, cut into 1-to-2-inch strips
3 tablespoons Asian sesame oil
Salt and freshly ground pepper to taste

Lemongrass-Mint Vinaigrette
¼ cup olive oil
1 teaspoon minced lemongrass

1 teaspoon minced shallots
1 teaspoon minced fresh ginger
2 cloves garlic, minced
1 tablespoon minced kaffir lime leaves
½ teaspoon sugar
½ tablespoon soy sauce
½ tablespoon fish sauce
2 tablespoons fresh lemon juice

Vegetable Stir-fry
2 tablespoons olive oil
½ cup fresh bean sprouts
¼ cup shredded radicchio
½ Maui or other sweet white onion,
   cut in ½-inch-thick rings
1 tablespoon minced fresh ginger
1 tablespoon minced garlic
20 fresh mint leaves
20 fresh basil leaves
½ cup watercress sprigs, chopped
½ cup shiitake mushrooms,
   stemmed and sliced
2 ounces Chinese bean thread noodles

Garnish
4 handfuls (4 ounces) mixed
   baby greens
2 tablespoons macadamia nuts, toasted
   and crushed (page 196)

To make the marinade: In a shallow dish, combine all the marinade ingredients. Add the steak strips and let sit at room temperature for 5 minutes. In a large sauté pan or skillet over high heat, heat the sesame oil and sauté the steak for 5 minutes on each side for medium rare. Sprinkle with salt and pepper. Using a slotted spoon, transfer the steak to a plate. Set aside.

To make the vinaigrette: In the same pan over high heat, heat the olive oil and sauté the lemongrass, shallot, ginger, garlic and lime leaves for about 10 seconds, or until lightly browned. Stir in the remaining ingredients. Set aside.

To make the stir-fry: In a large sauté pan or skillet over high heat, heat the olive oil and sauté all the remaining ingredients except the noodles for 1 minute. Add the noodles and cook for 1 minute. Set aside.

To serve: Divide the salad greens among 4 salad plates. Divide the stir-fry sprout mixture over the greens, then top with the beef. Drizzle vinaigrette around the salads and garnish with the macadamia nuts.

Spicy Thai Beef Salad with Lemongrass-Mint Vinaigrette and Toasted Macadamia Nuts; Roy Yamaguchi, Roy's Restaurant, Honolulu, Oahu

Togarashi Seared Beef Poke with Chilled Spicy Tomato Soup; Thomas B.H. Wong, The Surf Room, Royal Hawaiian Waikiki Sheraton, Honolulu, Oahu

Togarashi Seared Beef Poke with Chilled Spicy Tomato Soup

Thomas B. H. Wong
The Surf Room
Royal Hawaiian Waikiki Sheraton
Honolulu, Oahu

Serves 4

Poke is traditionally a mix of raw diced fish, onions, limu (seaweed), and Hawaiian salt; however, this variation using sautéed beef is very good. If prepared in advance, the flavors have an even better chance to meld into a spicy and delicious dish. Prepared togarashi spice mix, found at Asian markets, can be used if you prefer.

Togarashi Spice Mix
1½ teaspoons cayenne pepper
1½ teaspoons paprika
1 teaspoon red pepper flakes
1 teaspoon ground pepper
1 teaspoon white sesame seeds, toasted (page 196)
1 teaspoon black sesame seeds
1 teaspoon cumin seeds, toasted (page 196)
1 teaspoon mustard seeds, toasted (page 196)

1 pound beef sirloin, cut into ½-inch dice
2 tablespoons peanut oil
½ Maui or other sweet white onion, diced
1 garlic clove, minced

1 tomato, seeded and diced (page 203)
Minced fresh cilantro to taste
Chili pepper water to taste (page 197)
1 tablespoon soy sauce

1 teaspoon Hawaiian or kosher salt
1 teaspoon patis fish sauce
Chilled Spicy Tomato Soup (recipe follows)

2 green onions, cut into julienne including some green tops for garnish

To make the togarashi spice mix: Grind all the spice mix ingredients in a spice grinder.

Season the beef with the togarashi spice mix. In a sauté pan or skillet over high heat, heat the oil and sauté the beef until it is seared on the outside and rare on the inside, about 2 minutes. Remove the meat from the pan and refrigerate it for 1 hour. Add all the remaining ingredients except the soup to the seared beef and mix well. Taste and adjust the seasoning.

To serve: Ladle one fourth of the tomato soup into each dish. Place a portion of the beef poke in the center of the soup and garnish with the green onion.

Chilled Spicy Tomato Soup
½ cup olive oil
1 Maui or other sweet white onion, cut into ½-inch dice
2 garlic cloves, coarsely chopped
4 vine-ripened tomatoes, quartered
½ cup tarragon vinegar
1½ teaspoons chili pepper water (page 197)
3 tablespoons fish sauce, preferably Tiparos brand

In a saucepan over medium heat, heat ¼ cup of the oil and sauté the onion and garlic. Add the tomatoes and simmer 2 to 3 minutes, until all the ingredients are tender. Transfer to a blender and puree. With the machine running, gradually add the remaining oil, then the vinegar, chili water, and fish sauce. Cover and refrigerate for 2 to 3 hours before serving.

Venison Pipikaula with Kau Orange Vinaigrette

Thomas B. H. Wong
The Surf Room
Royal Hawaiian Waikiki Sheraton
Honolulu, Oahu

Makes 3 pounds

Pipikaula is Hawaiian-style beef jerky. Hunters on the islands of Hawaii, Lanai, Molokai, and Maui all have their favorite recipe for this spicy treat.

2 cups soy sauce

Venison Pipikaula with Kau Orange Vinaigrette; Thomas B.H. Wong, The Surf Room, Royal Hawaiian Waikiki Sheraton, Honolulu, Oahu

2 cups packed brown sugar
2 cups warm water
½ tablespoon red pepper flakes
½ cup dry sherry
1 tablespoon Asian sesame oil
Two 2-inch pieces fresh ginger, peeled
   and cut into thin slices
6 garlic cloves, minced
3 pounds venison loin
Two 3-inch mesquite wood chunks

12 red-tipped lettuce or
   radicchio leaves
Kea Orange Vinaigrette
   (recipe follows)
4 pieces lavosh

Combine all the ingredients except the venison, wood, and vinaigrette in a deep nonaluminum container. Add the venison, cover, and refrigerate for 24 hours.

Drain the venison, wrap it in cheesecloth, and tie the ends tightly. Lightly oil the cheesecloth. Prepare a smoker (page 198), using the mesquite. Place the venison in the smoker and smoke for 30 minutes. Preheat the oven to 450°F. Transfer the venison to a rack set in a roasting pan and bake for 25 minutes for medium. Let cool. Cut into thin 3-inch strips. Store in an airtight container and refrigerate for 4 to 6 weeks.

To serve: Arrange overlapping slices on each plate. Place 3 leaves of lettuce or radicchio to one side of the slices, and pour a tablespoon of vinaigrette over the leaves. Garnish with a piece of lavosh.

Kau Orange Vinaigrette
Makes 3 cups

2 Kau or Valencia oranges, peeled
   and chopped
½ Maui or other sweet white onion,
   coarsely chopped
1 garlic clove, chopped
Salt and freshly ground pepper to taste
2 cups olive oil
¾ cup plain rice wine vinegar
1 teaspoon chili pepper water
   (page 197)
Patis fish sauce to taste

Combine the oranges, onion, garlic, salt, and pepper in a blender or food processor and puree. With the machine running, gradually add the oil, then the vinegar. Stir in the chili water and fish sauce. Refrigerate. Dressing keeps for up to 1 week.

Thomas B. H. Wong
*The Surf Room, Royal Hawaiian Waikiki Sheraton,
Honolulu, Oahu*

Thomas Wong is one of those chefs who prepare high-quality food for great numbers of people year after year, yet are rarely known by name. Prior to joining the historic Royal Hawaiian in 1993, Wong had spent most of his culinary career on the mainland.

When he arrived, the menu still reflected the heyday of so-called continental cuisine. But in came Wong and out went the old menu. People on vacation want comfort food that also gives them a sense of the place they're visiting, says Wong.

Visitors to the Surf Room sit almost literally on the famous beach at Waikiki and dine on Wong's traditional venison pipikaula, tomato soup with togarashi beef poke, and ginger sake breast of duck. His intimate knowledge of island cooking goes back to his childhood when he accompanied his grandmother on shopping trips to Honolulu's Chinatown.

Wong, who is executive sous-chef, has over fifteen years of culinary experience. He received a culinary arts certificate from Kapiolani Community College before entering the Culinary Institute of America where he earned an Associate of Science degree in occupational studies. After school, he apprenticed at the Greenbrier Hotel in White Sulphur Springs, West Virginia. He also worked as chef at the Ice House Cafe in Herndon, Virginia, and as chef tournant at La Chaumière in Los Angeles.

He now serves on the Culinary Advisory Board at Kapiolani Community College and is a member of the American Culinary Federation, the National Ice Carving Association, and Chaînes des Rôtisseurs.

Crispy Thai-Style Chicken; Amy Ferguson-Ota, The Dining Room, The Ritz-Carlton Mauna Lani, Kohala Coast, Hawaii

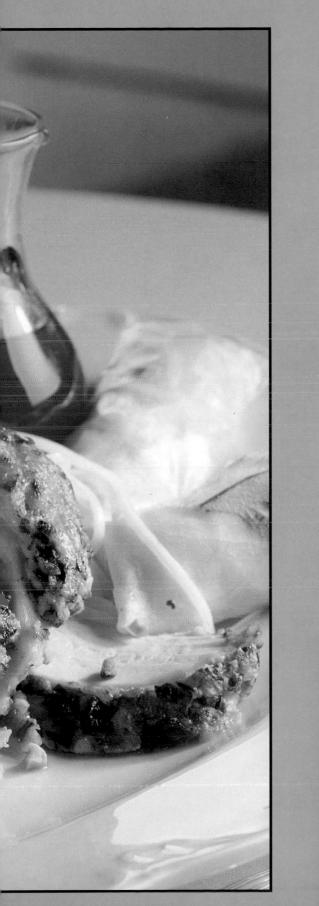

Poultry and Meats

Although fruits and vegetables are playing a larger role in most people's diet and are an important focus for chefs as well, meat and poultry remain favorites with most diners.

Here, you'll find these main-course basics with a Hawaiian lilt, like a rack of lamb with a crust of macadamia nuts or a marinade of *kecap manis,* a sweet soy sauce. New ways to prepare chicken include grilled, blackened, and Thai-style. And duck gets Asian treatment with sake, ginger, or shiitake mushrooms.

Beef Tenderloin and Poached Oysters with Essence of Pinot Noir and Chervil Sauce

George Mavrothalassitis
La Mer
Halekulani Hotel
Honolulu, Oahu

Serves 4

The silky texture and fresh taste of oysters pair with the perfect beef tenderloins. The rich wine sauce and piquant chervil sauce add the perfect contrasts to this surf-and-turf variation.

4 tablespoons olive oil
Four 6-ounce beef tenderloin fillets
2 bunches spinach, well washed and stemmed
4 large fresh oysters, shucked

Essence of Pinot Noir
2 tablespoons olive oil
1 Maui onion or other sweet white onion, finely sliced
1 bottle Pinot Noir wine
½ cup carrot, peeled and chopped
Salt and freshly ground pepper to taste

Chervil Sauce
2 tablespoons extra-virgin olive oil
1 onion, finely sliced

1 cup dry white wine
½ cup minced fresh chervil
Salt and freshly ground pepper to taste

To prepare the fillets: Preheat the oven to 350°F. In a large sauté pan or skillet over medium-high heat, heat 2 tablespoons of the olive oil and cook the fillets for 3 to 4 minutes on each side. Bake for 6 to 7 minutes for medium rare.

Place the spinach in the top of a steamer, and place the oysters on the spinach. Steam the spinach and oysters over boiling water in a medium covered pot for 3 to 4 minutes, until the oysters have firmed. With a spoon, set the oysters aside on a plate. Drain the spinach well. In a large saucepan over medium heat, heat the remaining 2 tablespoons of olive oil and sauté the spinach for 2 minutes. Set aside.

To make the essence: In a medium saucepan on low heat, heat the olive oil and sauté the onion for 10 minutes. Add one third of the wine and cook to reduce until almost dry. Add another third of the wine and cook to reduce again until almost dry. Add the last third of the wine and cook to reduce by half. Strain, reserving the onion.

In a steamer over boiling water, steam the carrots for 5 minutes, or until tender. Remove and put in a blender or food processor with a little water reserved from the steamer. Puree until smooth. Add the carrot puree to the sauce. Simmer the sauce for 10 minutes. Puree in a blender or food processor until very smooth. Add salt and pepper.

To make the chervil sauce: In a medium saucepan over low heat, heat the olive oil and sauté the onion for 3 minutes, or until translucent. Add the white wine and simmer for 25 minutes. In a food processor or blender, combine the onion mixture and chervil. Puree to a smooth sauce. Add salt and pepper.

To serve: Make a bed of spinach in the center of each plate. Top with a fillet. Top the fillet with one fourth of the reserved onion. Place 1 oyster on the onions. Surround with essence of Pinot Noir and cover the oyster with chervil sauce.

Beef Tenderloin and Poached Oysters with Essence of Pinot Noir and Chervil Sauce; George Mavrothalassitis, La Mer, Halekulani Hotel, Honolulu, Oahu

Blackened Jawaiian Spice Chicken Breasts with Banana-Rum Sauce and Chili Corn Cakes

Beverly Gannon
Haliimaile General Store
Haliimaile, Maui

Serves 8

Blackened Jawaiian chicken combines a Caribbean influence with Hawaiian ingredients in this dish. The term Jawaiian comes out of the island surf culture and denotes a blending of Jamaican reggae and Hawaiian influences in food, music, and lifestyle.

Jawaiian Spice Mix
2 tablespoons ground allspice
2 tablespoons ground cinnamon
2 teaspoons dried thyme
2 teaspoons dried rosemary
2 teaspoons dried chives
1 teaspoon salt
1 teaspoon sugar
2 teaspoons dried onion

8 boneless skinless chicken
   breast halves
6 tablespoons clarified butter
   (page 186)

Banana-Rum Sauce
2 tablespoons butter
½ cup chopped onion
½ cup chopped celery
2 garlic cloves, minced
4 bananas, cut into ½ inch pieces
2½ cups chicken stock (page 199)
½ cup sake
½ vanilla bean, halved lengthwise
Juice of 2 limes
3 star anise pods
½ cup rum

Chili Corn Cakes
1¼ cups milk
2 tablespoons butter, melted
3 eggs
¾ cup unbleached all-purpose flour
½ cup cornmeal
½ teaspoon baking powder
½ teaspoon baking soda
½ teaspoon salt
1 teaspoon sugar
1 cup fresh or frozen corn kernels
½ cup diced peeled green chilies
Peanut oil for frying

Fresh thyme sprigs for garnish

To make the spice mix and blacken the chicken: Combine all the spice ingredients and mix well. Preheat the oven to 350°F. Heat a large cast-iron skillet over high heat until smoking. Coat the chicken breasts with the spice mix. Add to the pan. Drizzle butter over the top of the breasts. Cook for 3 minutes, or until blackened on the bottom. Turn and drizzle more butter on the other side and blacken for another 3 minutes. Bake for about 10 minutes, or until done.

To make the banana-rum sauce: In a medium saucepan, melt the butter over medium heat and sauté the onions and celery for 2 minutes, or until the onion is translucent. Add the garlic and cook for 1 minute. Add the bananas and cook until they begin to caramelize. Add the stock, sake, vanilla bean, lime juice, and star anise, and simmer for 10 minutes. Remove the vanilla bean and star anise. Put the banana mixture into a blender or food processor and puree. Return to the saucepan and add the rum. Cook over medium heat for 2 minutes, or until thickened. Strain through a sieve.

To make the corn cakes: In a large bowl, beat the milk, butter, and eggs together. In a small bowl, stir the flour, cornmeal, baking powder, baking soda, salt, and sugar together. Add the dry ingredients to the wet ingredients. Stir just to combine. Gently blend in the corn and chilies.

In a large cast-iron skillet over medium heat, heat just enough oil to film the bottom of the pan. Add ¼ cup batter for each cake. Cook for 1 to 2 minutes on each side, or until golden brown. Repeat to cook the remaining batter. Remove to a plate and keep warm.

To serve: Ladle some sauce onto each plate and place a chicken breast on top. Cut the corn cakes in half and place one half on each side of the chicken. Garnish with thyme.

Blackened Jawaiian Spice Chicken Breasts with Banana-Rum Sauce and Chili Corn Cakes; Beverly Gannon, Haliimaile General Store, Haliimaile, Maui

Katsuo Sugiura (Chef Suki)
Ihilani Resort & Spa, Kapolei, Oahu

"Chef Suki," as he is affectionately called, has combined his passion for travel with his love of cooking. In the process, he's come up with a truly cross-cultural cuisine. Imagine, for instance, a green tea buckwheat pasta topped with wild mushrooms, garden vegetables, curried chicken, and tomato tarragon. It may be difficult to conjure up, but it's also delicious.

Or, imagine tea-smoked salmon and spices paired with an American caviar and dill mousseline. Wild, yes. The key, says Chef Suki, is not to overuse any one flavor, but instead to balance and blend them. "If I overuse the soy sauce the dish tends to be more Asian, but if I put in just the right amount, people say, 'What is this flavor?'"

Chef Suki was born in Japan forty-three years ago. Raised in Tokyo, he became interested in food at an early age. By the time he was in junior high school, he had also developed a keen interest in traveling outside the country.

In 1970, he received training in French cuisine in Yokohama. He then left for Europe and spent the next few years cooking in Finland, Norway, Germany, France, and Great Britain. In 1975, he was invited by the French Restaurant Association to study in New York City. He wanted to observe how French food was prepared outside of France, because his goal was to return to Japan and open a French restaurant.

Instead he was caught up in the cosmopolitan excitement of New York City. For the next few years he traveled across the United States to Chicago, Beverly Hills, Nashville, Miami, and Atlantic City (where he was the director of culinary arts for Donald Trump's Taj Mahal Casino Resort).

In 1993, Chef Suki moved to Honolulu to open the Ihilani Resort & Spa in the new resort community of Ko Olina. "The Pacific is new to me . . . I've tried to learn something from the people I worked with. I like to learn about my employees' culture and way of thinking," he says.

Five-Spice Smoked Rack of Lamb with Poha Berry and Ginger Butter

Katsuo Sugiura (Chef Suki)
Ihilani Resort & Spa
Kapolei, Oahu

Serves 4

The smoked lamb is treated to a fruity, yet spicy poha ginger sauce. Baby green beans provide the perfect touch of crunch and color for this dish.

Lamb Marinade
2 tablespoons peanut oil
8 unpeeled garlic cloves, crushed
1 cup chopped green onions, including some green tops
2 tablespoons sliced fresh ginger
3 cups dry sherry
2 cups water
10 star anise pods
1 cup hoisin sauce
2 teaspoons Chinese five-spice powder
4 tablespoons honey
2 tablespoons Asian sesame oil
½ cup soy sauce

Two 8-ounce boneless racks of lamb
2 cups (1 ounce) oolong tea leaves
4 cups (2 ounces) sawdust
Peanut oil for frying
1 cup (5 ounces) somen noodles
2 tablespoons olive oil

Poha Berry and Ginger Butter
1 cup poha berries, husked
½ cup sugar
3 tablespoons fruit-flavored vinegar
½ cup dry white wine
2 tablespoons sliced fresh ginger
1 cup veal or beef stock (page 200)
Salt and freshly ground pepper to taste
4 tablespoons cold unsalted butter, cut into tablespoon-sized pieces

2 pounds baby Blue Lake green beans
4 poha berries for garnish

To make the marinade: In a large saucepan, heat the peanut oil and sauté the garlic, green onion, and ginger for 3 minutes, or until the onion is translucent. Add the sherry, water, and star anise and cook for 3 minutes. Add the remaining ingredients and cook for 25 minutes. Let cool.

Pour the marinade into a shallow nonaluminum container. Add the lamb and turn to coat. Marinate for 15 to 30 minutes at room temperature.

Five-Spice Smoked Rack of Lamb with Poha Berry and Ginger Butter; Katsuo Sugiura (Chef Suki), Ihilani Resort & Spa, Kapolei, Oahu

To smoke the lamb: Remove the lamb from the marinade, and wipe the excess from the meat. Prepare a smoker according to manufacturer's instructions, using the tea and sawdust in place of wood chips (page 198). Smoke the lamb for 30 minutes.

In a wok or deep fryer, heat the oil to 350°F, or just rippling. With a slotted spoon, lower the somen noodles into the hot oil and fry until brown and crisp. The noodles will rise to the top of the oil. With a slotted spoon, remove the noodles. Drain on paper towels.

Preheat the oven to 350°F. Remove the lamb from the smoker and roll the lamb in the olive oil. Place the lamb in a roasting pan and bake for 25 to 30 minutes, until rare. Crush one half of the fried noodles with your hands and press onto the top of the lamb to make a crust. Reserve the remaining noodles. Cut the lamb into ½-inch-thick slices.

To make the poha butter: Puree the berries in a blender or food processor. In a heavy, medium, saucepan, cook the sugar over medium heat until light brown in color. Stir in the vinegar until the sugar dissolves. Add the berry puree, white wine, ginger, and stock. Cook to reduce the mixture by half. Add the salt and pepper. Add the butter and whisk for about 1 minute.

To serve: Spoon some sauce onto each plate. Divide the reserved noodles among the plates and place in the center of the sauce. Fan the lamb slices around the noodles. Place 3 bundles of green beans evenly on each plate, and garnish with a poha berry.

Crispy Thai-Style Chicken

Amy Ferguson-Ota
The Dining Room
The Ritz-Carlton Mauna Lani
Kohala Coast, Hawaii

Serves 4 to 6

Fish sauce is at the heart of Thai cuisine. Ferguson-Ota likes to serve this dish to her family at home with jasmine rice or rice noodles. The chicken marinates overnight, so start a day ahead.

Marinade

2 heaping tablespoons minced fresh lemongrass
6 large garlic cloves, minced
1 tablespoon grated fresh ginger
2 tablespoons fish sauce, preferably Tiparos
1 teaspoon Hawaiian or kosher salt
½ cup chopped green onions, including some green tops
2 tablespoons minced fresh cilantro

½ cup mochiko sweet rice flour or all-purpose flour
2 tablespoons cornstarch
2 egg whites

3 pounds boneless skinless chicken breasts or thighs
2 tablespoons peanut oil

Dressing

1 cup plain rice wine vinegar
½ cup water
½ cup sugar
¼ cup fish sauce, preferably Tiparos
2 Hawaiian or Thai chilies, or sambal olek to taste

Garnish

4 to 6 handfuls (4 to 6 ounces) mixed baby greens
4 tablespoons minced fresh cilantro
12 fresh cilantro leaves
4 tablespoons basil leaves, shredded

To make the marinade and chicken: In a large bowl, combine all the marinade ingredients and mix well. Add the chicken and stir to coat. Cover and marinate overnight. Remove from the marinade. In a large sauté pan or skillet over medium-high heat, heat the oil and sauté the chicken for 7 to 10 minutes on each side, or until the meat is opaque throughout and the juices run clear.

To make the dressing: Combine all the ingredients in a bowl and mix well.

To serve: Serve the chicken on a mound of baby greens. Garnish with herbs and drizzle with the dressing.

Crispy Thai-Style Chicken; Amy Ferguson-Ota, The Dining Room, The Ritz-Carlton Mauna Lani, Kohala Coast, Hawaii

Ginger Sake Breast of Duck and Duck Adobo; Thomas B.H. Wong, The Surf Room, Royal Hawaiian Waikiki Sheraton, Honolulu, Oahu

Ginger Sake Breast of Duck and Duck Adobo

Thomas B. H. Wong
The Surf Room
Royal Hawaiian Waikiki Sheraton
Honolulu, Oahu

Serves 6

Two preparations are combined to make this duck dish. The duck breasts are marinated in sake, soy sauce, and fresh ginger, and then roasted. The duck legs are braised with a thick brown sauce, a technique popular with Hawaii's Filipino population.

Marinade
2½ cups sake
1 cup soy sauce
1 tablespoon sugar
1 garlic clove, minced
2 tablespoons minced peeled
    fresh ginger
1 tablespoon Asian sesame oil
2 tablespoons olive oil
6 boneless duck breasts

Duck Adobo (recipe follows)

Stir -fried Vegetables
2 tablespoons peanut oil
½ cup each red, yellow, and green bell
    peppers, seeded, deribbed, and cut
    into julienne (see page 196)

½ cup chopped won bok
    (napa cabbage)
2 cups steamed short-grain rice
    (page 197)

To make the marinade and marinated duck: Combine all the marinade ingredients in a shallow nonaluminum container. Add the duck and turn it to coat. Marinate at room temperature for 2 hours, or cover and refrigerate for up to 6 hours. If refrigerated, remove from the refrigerator 30 minutes before cooking.

To cook the duck: Preheat the oven to 350°F. Remove the duck from the marinade. In a large sauté pan, or skillet over high heat, fry the duck breasts skin-side down for 4 minutes, or until brown and crisp. Turn and brown the other side of the breast. Put the breasts on a baking sheet and bake for 5 minutes, or until medium-rare.

To stir-fry the vegetables: In a wok or a medium sauté pan or skillet over medium-high heat, heat the oil and stir-fry the vegetables until crisp-tender, about 2 minutes.

Oil 4 cone-shaped or 2½-by-3-inch molds. When the rice has cooked, pack it into the molds while it is still warm. Set aside.

To serve: Unmold one cone of rice on each plate. Surround the rice with the vegetables. Slice the duck breasts

and fan the slices on the plates. Place one duck leg and some adobo sauce on each plate.

Duck Adobo
6 duck legs, thigh bone removed
2 tablespoons minced fresh ginger
1 garlic clove, minced
4 cups brown sauce (page 186)
1 cup raspberry vinegar
5 peppercorns, cracked
2 bay leaves
Salt and freshly ground pepper to taste

In a Dutch oven or a heatproof casserole over medium heat, brown the duck legs evenly on all sides. Add the ginger and garlic and sauté for 2 minutes, or until light brown. Add the remaining ingredients and bring to a boil. Reduce heat to a simmer. Cover and braise for 1½ to 2 hours, or until the legs are fork tender.

Grilled Chicken Napoleon with Shiitake and Spinach Ragout

James Gillespie
3660 on the Rise
Honolulu, Oahu

Serves 4

For a great country-style meal, this dish is hard to beat. It takes a little time to put together, and it's a bit on the spicy side, but it's well worth the effort.

Grilled Chicken Napoleon with Shiitake and Spinach Ragout; James Gillespie, 3660 on the Rise, Honolulu, Oahu

1 tablespoon Thai or Vietnamese chili
   paste
2 tablespoons vegetable oil
Juice and grated zest of 1 lemon
Salt and freshly ground pepper to taste
4 skinless boneless chicken
   breast halves

Shiitake and Spinach Ragout
½ cup heavy (whipping) cream
1 tablespoon soy sauce
1 tablespoon hoisin sauce
1 tablespoon Thai or Vietnamese
   chili paste
1 teaspoon vegetable oil
4 ounces shiitake mushrooms,
   stemmed and sliced
1 bunch fresh spinach, stemmed
½ teaspoon minced garlic

Roasted Pepper and Soy Jus
1 teaspoon vegetable oil
1 teaspoon minced garlic
1 tablespoon minced shallot
1 red bell pepper, roasted, peeled,
   and diced (page 196)
¼ cup soy sauce
¼ cup dry white wine
1 cup beef demi-glace (page 201)
¼ cup heavy (whipping) cream

Roasted Garlic Mashed Potatoes
4 unpeeled white or yellow
   potatoes, quartered
1 garlic bulb, roasted (page 198)
1 tablespoon vegetable oil
4 tablespoons butter
2 tablespoons heavy (whipping) cream
Salt and freshly ground pepper to taste

To prepare the chicken: Light a fire in a charcoal grill or preheat a gas grill. In a large bowl, mix the chili paste, oil, zest, juice, salt, and pepper. Add the chicken and toss to coat. Grill over a medium-hot fire for 7 to 10 minutes on each side, or until the meat is no longer opaque and the juices run clear.

To make the ragout: In a small saucepan, combine the cream, soy sauce, hoisin sauce, and chili paste. Cook over medium heat until reduced by half. In a large sauté pan or skillet over medium heat, heat the oil and sauté the mushrooms, spinach, and garlic for 2 minutes, or until crisp-tender. Add the cream mixture to the pan and stir. Set aside and keep warm.

To make the jus: In a medium saucepan over medium heat, heat the oil and sauté the garlic and shallot until translucent, about 3 minutes. Add the red pepper and sauté for 2 to 3 min-

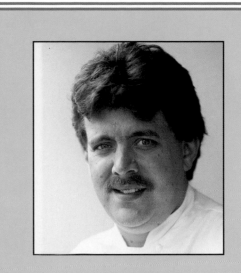

JAMES GILLESPIE
3660 on the Rise, Honolulu, Oahu

When *Honolulu Magazine* named 3660 on the Rise "Restaurant of the Year" in 1994, it was a credit to chef James Gillespie, who joined Gale Ogawa and Russell Siu in their Kaimuki neighborhood restaurant in 1992.

Gillespie had graduated from the Culinary Institute of America a decade earlier, then had opened and set the culinary standards for private clubs in Dallas, Los Angeles, and San Francisco.

The ninety-seat 3660 on the Rise serves traditional island dishes featuring foods from China, Japan, Thailand, and Korea, but gives them an updated twist. Their signature Ahi Katsu owes a debt to Japanese cuisine, the barbecued duck salad smacks of Chinese, and the grilled lamb with grilled vegetables and oheloberry sauce is, well, Hawaiian.

Located in a building that updates the traditional Hawaiian Territorial style of architecture, 3660 is located in Kaimuki, between two very fashionable neighborhoods: Kahala and Manoa. This proximity, along with Gillespie's consistently fine food, has made the restaurant tremendously popular with island residents.

utes. Add the soy sauce and wine to the pan and stir to scrape up the cooking juices from the bottom of the pan. Cook to reduce by half. Add the demi-glace, bring to a boil, and reduce heat to a simmer. Cook for 3 minutes to let the flavors develop. Add the cream and simmer for 1 minute. Set aside and keep warm.

To make the garlic mashed potatoes: Boil the potatoes in lightly salted water until tender. Drain and peel them. Place them back in the pan, and shake

over low heat for a few seconds to dry the potatoes. Squeeze the garlic puree from the bulb into the potatoes. Using a potato masher or a ricer, puree the potatoes and garlic. Beat in the butter, cream, salt, and pepper.

To assemble: Place a large spoonful of mashed potatoes in the center of each plate. Cut the chicken breast in half and place one half on the potato. Spoon the ragout onto the breast and place the second chicken half on top of the ragout. Top with the jus.

OnJin Kim
Hanatei Bistro, Honolulu, Oahu

OnJin Kim had cooked all over the world, in France, the United States, and Korea. But she was astounded by her reception in Japan. Here she was told falsely that women can't properly make sushi because their body temperature is higher than a man's, which adversely affects the molding of the rice.

But Kim sees hope for women in professional kitchens, even there. The owner of Hanatei Bistro, where she is executive chef, belongs to a new generation of Japanese men. From him she gets the support she needs to run her kitchen. "Things will be different," she says.

Kim's cuisine is exceedingly beautiful as well as good-tasting. Her menu is based on a blending of French and traditional Japanese cuisines, and the results are stunning.

As a student, she attended the American Conservatory of Music in Chicago and earned a master's degree in voice. During that time, she became acquainted with the many fine restaurants in the Chicago area.

Kim entered the Dumas Père School of French Cuisine in Illinois. After receiving her certificate in 1983 she attended Le Cordon Bleu, École de Cuisine et de Pâtisserie in Paris. From there she entered the Culinary Institute of America in New York.

Kim first gained attention in Hawaii culinary circles as the chef of the very upscale Bagwell's 2424 in the Hyatt Regency Waikiki. Food critic Nadine Kam of the *Honolulu Star-Bulletin* called her cuisine "simply soul-lifting."

Kim has been touted in the 1994 *Zagat Survey of Hawaii Restaurants and Hotels*. The 1994 *Frommer's Guide* placed a star next to Hanatei Bistro, marking it as a Frommer's Favorite, and she has been acclaimed in *Gourmet, Departures,* and André Gayot's *Tastes*.

Grilled Marinated Lamb Chops

OnJin Kim
Hanatei Bistro
Honolulu, Oahu

Serves 4

The straightforward flavor of grilled, marinated lamb chops is complemented by a rich spicy black bean sauce. Begin a day ahead to allow time for the lamb to marinate.

Black Bean Sauce
¾ cup mirin or sweet sherry
1 cup hoisin sauce
½ cup honey
¼ cup soy sauce
2 tablespoons curry powder

3 tablespoons Asian sesame oil
½ cup Chinese fermented black
  beans, rinsed, drained, and
  coarsely chopped
1 tablespoon chopped garlic
2 tablespoons momiji or other
  Asian chili paste
1 tablespoon grated orange zest

16 single lamb chops, trimmed of fat
2 fennel bulbs, cut and trimmed
Olive oil for coating
Steamed rice for serving (page 197)
4 fresh rosemary sprigs

To make the sauce: In a medium saucepan, combine all the sauce ingredients and cook over medium heat for 10 minutes. Let cool. Pour ½ cup of the sauce into a shallow nonaluminum container and add the lamb. Turn to coat. Cover and refrigerate overnight.

Remove the lamb from the refrigerator at least 30 minutes before cooking. Light a fire in a charcoal grill or preheat a gas grill or broiler. Barbecue the lamb over a medium-hot fire for 5 to 7 minutes on each side or until done. At the same time, brush the fennel slices with oil and grill them for 2 to 3 minutes on each side.

To serve: Ladle the black bean sauce on each plate and arrange 4 chops on top. Serve with the fennel and steamed rice. Garnish with a rosemary sprig.

Indonesian Grilled Lamb Chops with Ginger Cream

Mark Ellman
Avalon Restaurant & Bar
Lahaina, Maui

Serves 4

Kecap manis, a dark, sweet Indonesian soy sauce, gives these lamb chops a unique flavor. The ginger cream and basil puree balance the dish beautifully. The lamb marinates for 24 hours.

Marinade
2 cups kecap manis
2 cups minced peeled fresh ginger
¼ cup minced garlic
¼ cup Asian sesame oil
1 cup minced fresh mint
½ cup whole-grain mustard

2 pounds lamb loin chops, trimmed and sliced

Ginger Cream
4 cups heavy (whipping) cream
½ cup sliced peeled fresh ginger
Salt and freshly ground pepper to taste

Basil Puree
2 cups fresh basil leaves
2 cups olive oil
Salt and freshly ground pepper to taste
2 roasted garlic cloves (page 198)

Garnish
8 asparagus tips, blanched
4 tablespoons pickled ginger
White sesame seeds for sprinkling

To make the marinade: In a shallow nonaluminum container, combine all the marinade ingredients and mix. Add the lamb chops, turn to coat them, cover, and refrigerate for at least 24 hours.

Remove the lamb from the refrigerator 45 minutes before grilling. Light a fire in a charcoal grill or preheat a gas grill. Grill the lamb over a hot fire for 6 to 7 minutes on each side for medium-rare.

To make the ginger cream: In a small saucepan, combine the cream and ginger. Cook over medium-low heat until reduced by half, or until the mixture coats the back of a spoon. Add salt and pepper. Set aside and keep warm.

To make the basil puree: Puree all the ingredients in a blender or food processor, in batches if necessary.

To serve: Lace each plate with ginger cream and place one fourth of the lamb chops on top. Sprinkle with asparagus tips and pickled ginger, then drizzle with basil puree and scatter sesame seeds on top.

Indonesian Grilled Lamb Chops with Ginger Cream; Mark Ellman, Avalon Restaurant & Bar, Lahaina, Maui

Kalua Duck with Plum Wine Sauce and Lundberg Rice

David Paul Johnson
David Paul's Lahaina Grill
Lahaina, Maui

Serves 4

Moist pieces of duck are placed on top of a rich, nutty rice blend and then drizzled with rich plum wine sauce. The dish gets its name, Kalua Duck, from a traditional preparation for pork: Kalua pig is cooked slowly in an underground oven until it literally falls off the bones.

Kalua Duck

2 ducks, boned and cut into quarters, carcasses and trimmings reserved
2 tablespoons Hawaiian or kosher salt
1 tablespoon ground pepper
8 cups rendered duck fat or vegetable oil (page 198)
¼ cup liquid smoke (optional)
8 large garlic cloves
1 tablespoon peppercorns

Plum Wine Duck Sauce

2 reserved duck carcasses and trimmings, above, cut into 1-inch pieces
3 cups finely diced celery
3 cups finely diced carrots
3 cups finely diced onions
2 leeks, white part only, quartered
2 shallots, minced
2 cups Japanese plum wine
2 bay leaves
1 tablespoon peppercorns
4 quarts chicken stock (page 199) or water

Lundberg Rice

2 tablespoons unsalted butter
½ cup minced shallots
½ cup minced fresh parsley
¼ cup Japanese plum wine
2 cups Lundberg rice mix or other wild and brown rice mix
3 cups clarified chicken stock (page 199)

Steamed Vegetables

8 baby carrots, peeled
8 fresh baby corn
8 baby bok choy

To prepare the duck: Preheat the oven to 350°F. Season the ducks with the salt and pepper. Put the ducks in a Dutch oven. In a deep saucepan over medium-high heat, heat the fat or oil to 275°F, or until melted. Add the liquid smoke, if using. Pour over the duck to cover the duck completely. Add the garlic and peppercorns. Cover with a lid and bake for 2 to 3 hours, or until the meat starts to fall off the bones. Let cool to room temperature, then drain off the oil. Remove the meat from the bones. Return the duck and garlic to the pan.

To make the plum wine sauce: In a heavy, large pot, brown the duck bones and trimmings over high heat, rendering any fat. Pour off the fat and add the vegetables. Continue to brown, stirring, for 5 minutes. Add plum wine and stir to scrape up the browned bits from the bottom of the pan. Add the bay leaves, peppercorns, and stock or water. Bring to a boil and skim off the fat and foam. Cook over medium heat until reduced by half. Strain, skim the fat, and continue to cook to reduce to 1 or 2 cups of thick sauce. The total reduction time will be about 2 hours.

To make the rice: In a heavy, medium saucepan over medium heat, heat the butter and sauté the shallots and parsley until the shallots are translucent, about 3 minutes. Add the wine and stir. Add the rice and saute for 2 minutes. Add the stock, cover, and reduce heat to a simmer. Cook for 20 minutes, or until the liquid is absorbed. Fluff the rice with a fork and keep warm.

To steam the vegetables: Fill the bottom of a steamer with water and bring to a boil. Put the carrots, corn, and bok choy in the top of the steamer and cover. Steam until tender, about 12 minutes. Set aside and keep warm.

To serve: Reheat the duck in the oven on medium heat or in a skillet. Place a mound of rice in the center of each plate and some of the duck on the rice. Circle the sauce around the rice. Cross a baby carrot and a piece of baby corn on each side of the duck. Garnish with the roasted garlic and bok choy.

Kalua Duck with Plum Wine Sauce and Lundberg Rice; David Paul Johnson, David Paul's Lahaina Grill, Lahaina, Maui

Nanakuli Chicken Breasts with Shiitake Mushrooms and Steamed Baby Vegetables

Dominique Jamain
The Maile Restaurant
Kahala Hilton
Honolulu, Oahu

Serves 4

The marinade can also be used for a simple dish of grilled chicken. Nanakuli, a beachside community on the north-west corner of the island of Oahu, is the definition of "Hawaiian country." Begin a day ahead.

Marinade
½ cup chopped fresh basil
¼ cup Thai chili sauce
5 minced shallots
6 tablespoons minced fresh cilantro
¼ cup chopped fresh ginger
2 tablespoons chopped garlic
2 teaspoons chopped fresh lemongrass
1 cup soy sauce
1 cup unsweetened coconut milk
¼ cup vegetable oil
2 tablespoons sugar

4 large skinless boneless
  chicken breasts
2 tablespoons oil

Steamed Baby Vegetables
4 baby bok choy
8 fresh baby corn
2 tablespoons olive oil
12 Japanese eggplants, cut into
  ¼-inch diagonal slices
6 ounces shiitake mushrooms,
  stemmed and sliced
2 cups cooked jasmine rice (page 197)

Herb Sauce
4 cups chicken stock (page 199)
2 shallots, minced
¼ cup Marinade, above
1 tablespoon heavy (whipping) cream
1 teaspoon unsalted butter
Salt and freshly ground pepper to taste
4 fresh basil leaves, cut into fine shreds

Garnish
Black sesame seeds
4 fresh basil sprigs

To make the marinade: Put the basil, chili sauce, shallots, cilantro, ginger, garlic, and lemongrass in a blender or food processor and puree. Add the remaining ingredients and blend until smooth. Pour into a shallow nonalu-

Nanakuli Chicken Breasts with Shiitake Mushrooms and Steamed Baby Vegetables; Dominique Jamain, The Maile Restaurant, Kahala Hilton, Honolulu, Oahu

minum container and add the chicken breasts. Turn to coat. Cover and refrigerate for 24 hours.

To prepare the chicken: Preheat the oven to 350°F. Remove from the refrigerator 30 minutes before cooking. Remove from the marinade and reserve ¼ cup of the marinade. In a large sauté pan or skillet over medium-high heat, heat the oil and sauté the chicken breasts for 3 minutes on each side, or until lightly browned. Bake for 8 to 10 minutes, or until opaque throughout. Remove the chicken from the oven and place on a wire rack. Let rest for 10 minutes.

To prepare the vegetables: Fill the bottom of a steamer with water and bring to a boil. Put the bok choy and corn in the top of the steamer. Cover and steam for 12 minutes, or until tender. Set aside. In a medium sauté pan or skillet over medium-high heat, heat the oil and sauté the eggplant for 3 to 4 minutes, or until lightly browned. Remove from the pan and

set aside. In the same pan, sauté the mushrooms for 2 to 3 minutes, or until tender. Set aside. Oil 4 2½-inch-by-3-inch molds. When the rice has cooked, pack it into the molds while it is still warm. Set aside.

To make the sauce: In a medium, heavy saucepan, combine the chicken stock and shallots. Cook over medium heat to reduce to ½ cup. Pour into a blender or food processor, add the reserved marinade, and puree. Strain through a sieve. Return to the saucepan and place over low heat. Stir in the cream and butter. Add the salt and pepper. Set aside and keep warm. Just before serving, stir in the basil.

To serve: Arrange the vegetables and unmold the rice on one side of each plate. Place the shiitake mushrooms to one side. Cut the breast meat in thin slices and arrange a fan shape, overlapping some of the mushrooms. Garnish the rice with the sesame seeds and place a basil sprig in the center of each dish.

DANIEL DELBREL

La Cascata, Princeville Hotel, Princeville, Kauai

Daniel Delbrel arrived on the Garden Island of Kauai in 1992 — just in time to experience the devastating Hurricane Iniki. Because of it, the Princeville Hotel was closed for a year, and Delbrel was given the opportunity to completely redesign the menus.

"We wanted our food to establish an identity for the hotel, but we didn't want to just serve 'hotel food,'" says Delbrel, who says he loves rich food as well as the next guy, but has cut down on butter and cream in his cooking. Instead, he uses olive oil and lots of spices like garlic and ginger. He creates appealing dishes that are also good for you.

At Princeville's more casual restaurant, Cafe Hanalei, Delbrel serves Pacific Rim cuisine, blending the flavors of Hawaii and the Pacific with his traditional French cooking style. In the signature restaurant, La Cascata, the emphasis is on the Mediterranean food of Provence and the Italian Riviera.

Delbrel is a "hands on" executive chef. Even though he has the responsibility for a large staff, you will find him personally supervising much of the preparation and presentation.

Born in France, Delbrel came up through the classical ranks of French cuisine. After culinary school, he apprenticed in Cannes and Paris in several restaurants ranked in the Michelin Guide. After coming to America, he worked as a saucier in the Ritz-Carlton in Boston before moving to the Ritz-Carlton in Chicago as executive sous-chef. From there he went to the Four Seasons Hotel in Newport Beach, California, for a year. He moved to Hawaii in 1988 to take over Le Soleil restaurant in the Mauna Lani Bay Hotel and Bungalows on the Kohala Coast.

Delbrel has appeared in *Chocolatier, San Francisco Focus,* and *Bon Appétit,* among others.

Roasted Rack of Lamb with Macadamia Honey, Minted Papaya and Star Fruit Salsa, and Cabernet Sauce

Daniel Delbrel
La Cascata
Princeville Hotel
Princeville, Kauai

Serves 4

Lamb gets a new treatment, first with a macadamia honey marinade, then a rich Cabernet sauce. The surprise is the topping of minted papaya and star fruit salsa.

Spiced Sherry
15 white peppercorns
1 whole nutmeg
2 cloves
½ cup dry sherry
½ cup sugar
2 teaspoons grated lime zest
One ½-inch piece fresh ginger

Macadamia Honey Marinade
¼ cup macadamia nut honey or other flavorful honey
¼ cup white vinegar

Lamb Marinade
2 tablespoons minced garlic
1 tablespoon minced fresh thyme
2 tablespoons Macadamia Honey Marinade, above
2 tablespoons olive oil

4 racks of lamb (4 ribs per person)

Cabernet Sauce
2 tablespoons olive oil
8 ounces lamb bones and scraps
2 carrots, peeled and finely chopped
1 onion, coarsely chopped
2 garlic cloves
1 celery stalk, coarsely chopped
2 tablespoons tomato paste
½ cup Cabernet wine
1 pinch minced fresh thyme
1 pinch minced fresh rosemary
2 bay leaves
10 peppercorns

2 tablespoons olive oil

Minted Papaya and Star Fruit Salsa
½ cup diced papaya
½ cup diced star fruit

½ cup minced fresh mint
2 tablespoons Spiced Sherry, above

Seasonal Vegetables
1 summer squash, coarsely cubed
1 zucchini, coarsely cubed
1 cup green beans, cut into
   3-inch pieces
1 tomato, chopped
3 tablespoons butter
Salt and freshly ground pepper to taste

4 rosemary sprigs for garnish

To make the sherry: In a small sauté pan or skillet over high heat, toast the peppercorns, nutmeg, and cloves for about 1 minute, or until their fragrance is released. Remove from heat to cool for a few seconds. Return to heat and add the sherry and sugar. Add the lime zest and ginger and cook for 10 seconds. Let cool. Cover and let sit overnight.

To make the macadamia honey: In a small saucepan, combine the honey and vinegar. Bring to a boil over medium-high heat. Let cool. Cover and refrigerate until ready to use.

To make the marinade: In a shallow nonaluminum container, combine all the marinade ingredients. Add the lamb and coat it on all sides. Cover and refrigerate for at least 6 hours.

To make the Cabernet sauce: In a heavy pot over medium-high heat, heat the olive oil. Add the lamb pieces and brown. Reduce heat to medium, add the carrots, onion, garlic, and celery, and cook for 10 minutes. Add the remaining ingredients. Simmer for 45 minutes, or until reduced by half. Strain and reduce again to make a sauce. Set aside and keep warm.

To make the salsa: In a small bowl, combine all the salsa ingredients and gently mix. Refrigerate for 30 minutes.

To prepare the vegetables: Blanch the squash, zucchini, and beans separately in salted boiling water for 30 seconds. Drain and place in ice water. Drain again and toss with the remaining ingredients.

To prepare the lamb: Preheat the oven to 350°F. Season the lamb with salt and pepper. In a large ovenproof sauté pan or skillet over high heat, heat the oil and sear the lamb on all sides for 3 to 4 minutes, or until browned. Roast for 20 minutes for medium rare. Set aside and let rest.

To serve: Ladle ¼ cup Cabernet sauce onto each plate. Slice the lamb and arrange in a mound like a tepee with the bones upward in the center of the plate. Place ½ cup salsa and ¾ cup of the vegetables beside the lamb. Garnish with a sprig of rosemary.

Roasted Rack of Lamb with Macadamia Honey, Minted Papaya and Star Fruit Salsa, and Cabernet Sauce; Daniel Delbrel, La Cascata, Princeville Hotel, Princeville, Kauai

Roast Rack of Lamb with Sun-dried Tomato and Apple-smoked Bacon

Edwin Goto
The Lodge at Koele
Lanai City, Lanai

Serves 4

Rich and *hearty* are the best words to describe this dish. The lamb chops are placed on a creamy polenta filled with fragrant herbs and sauced with a delicious wine sauce. Start a day ahead to make the sauce.

Red Wine Jus

5 pounds veal bones
2 carrots, peeled and
   coarsely chopped
1 celery stalk, coarsely chopped
2 onions, coarsely chopped
1 whole garlic bulb, halved crosswise
4 cups dry red wine
5 quarts water
1 teaspoon peppercorns
1 fresh thyme sprig
1 fresh rosemary sprig
1 bay leaf
Hawaiian or kosher salt and freshly
   ground pepper to taste

Herbed Soft Polenta

½ cup (1 stick) unsalted butter
1 teaspoon minced garlic
1 teaspoon minced shallot
¼ teaspoon dried rosemary
½ teaspoon ground sage
1 teaspoon dried thyme
3 cups chicken stock (page 199)
1 teaspoon salt
1 cup heavy (whipping) cream
1 cup polenta
¼ teaspoon ground pepper
1 tablespoon grated Parmesan cheese
1 teaspoon minced fresh parsley
1 teaspoon minced fresh basil

Two 8-rib racks of lamb, frenched
Hawaiian or kosher salt and freshly
   ground pepper to taste
8 ounces thinly sliced
   apple-smoked bacon
20 sun-dried tomatoes, soaked in water
   and drained
¼ cup fresh basil leaves
¼ cup pine nuts, toasted (page 196)
3 tablespoons olive oil

4 fresh thyme sprigs for garnish

The day before serving, make the jus:
Preheat the oven to 400°F. Put the veal bones, carrots, celery, onions, and garlic in a large roasting pan and roast, turning twice, until lightly browned, about 40 minutes. Put the bones, vegetables, wine, and water in a large stockpot. Bring to a boil over medium-high heat, skimming to remove the foam that rises to the top. Add the peppercorns, thyme, rosemary, and bay leaf. Reduce heat and simmer for 4 hours. Let cool. Pour the stock through a sieve, cover, and refrigerate overnight. The next day, remove and discard the fat. Place the stock in a large saucepan over medium-high heat and cook until reduced to 1 cup. Season with salt and pepper.

To make the polenta: In a heavy, large saucepan, melt the butter over medium heat. Add the garlic, shallot, rosemary, sage, and thyme, and cook until the garlic and shallots are translucent, about 3 minutes. Add the stock, salt, and heavy cream. Increase heat to high and bring to a boil. Gradually stir the polenta into the boiling liquid and stir constantly until the mixture thickens, about 5 minutes. Reduce heat to low and cook the polenta for 35 to 45 minutes, stirring occasionally. Add the remaining ingredients. Stir to blend. Set aside and keep warm.

To prepare the lamb: Preheat the oven to 450°F. Cut the loin from the rack of bones. Trim all the excess fat and remove the silver skin. Butterfly the lamb by slicing it lengthwise three fourths of the way through. Open and lay out flat. Using the flat side of a mallet or a heavy pan, pound to an even thickness. Season with salt and pepper.

Lay the thinly sliced bacon on parchment or waxed paper, slightly overlapping each slice. Layer the lamb with the sun-dried tomatoes, basil, and pine nuts. Starting with the end of the lamb closest to you, begin rolling up tightly into a tube. Place the rolled lamb at one end of the bacon and wrap until the lamb is encased in bacon.

In a large ovenproof sauté pan or skillet over medium-high heat, heat the olive oil. Brown the lamb evenly on all sides. Pour off the fat and add the lamb bones. Bake for about 10 minutes, turning the lamb twice, to evenly brown on all sides.

Remove the lamb from the oven and place on a cutting board. Let rest for 5 minutes before slicing. Using a sharp knife, slice the loin in half crosswise. Cut 1 inch off the end of each half. Cut 2 halves into ¼-inch-thick diagonal slices. Slice the remaining pieces diagonally. Cut through the rack bones.

To serve: Mound the center of each plate with 1 cup of polenta. Stand the long slices of lamb around the mound. Ladle the red wine jus around the polenta and garnish with the bones and a sprig of thyme.

Roast Rack of Lamb with Sun-dried Tomato and Apple-smoked Bacon; Edwin Goto, The Lodge at Koele, Lanai City, Lanai

Salmon and Shrimp Gyoza with Sweet Chili Vinaigrette and Sweet Chili Beurre Blanc; Jean-Marie Josselin, A Pacific Café, Kapaa, Kauai

Fish and Shellfish

Thanks to the chefs of the new Hawaiian cuisine and the efforts of the State of Hawaii, a wide variety of reef and deepwater fish such as opah, kajiki, marlin, shark, and kumu are now as popular in island cooking as the more familiar onaga, opakapaka, and ahi tuna. Many of Hawaii's chefs draw from Asian techniques such as steaming and searing with hot oil, and smoking. Both recipes and techniques are adaptable to stateside fish, and substitutes are given.

Ahi Wellington Kailua on Hearts of Palm with Citrus-Herb Butter; Gerard Kaleohano, Mid-Pacific Country Club, Lanikai, Oahu

Ahi Wellington Kailua on Hearts of Palm with Citrus-Herb Butter

Gerard Kaleohano
Mid-Pacific Country Club
Lanikai, Oahu

Serves 4

This lighter version of beef Wellington uses ahi tuna and a pâté made with mushrooms instead of liver. The Asian ingredients give the dish a completely new taste.

Marinated Vegetables
¼ cup mirin or sweet sherry
1 cup bonito flakes
¼ cup soy sauce
4 cups hot water

1 carrot, peeled and cut into julienne
1 zucchini, cut into julienne

Mushroom Paste
12 bacon slices, minced
4 shallots, minced
10 ounces mushrooms, sliced
1 cup brandy

1 teaspoon Cajun spice mix
¼ cup macadamia nut or olive oil
3 pounds ahi tuna block
2 tablespoons olive oil
12 ounces puff pastry
12 to 15 shiso or inner romaine lettuce
   leaves
1 egg white, lightly beaten

1 pound (2 cups) hearts of palm, cut
   into crosswise slices
½ cup Citrus-Herb Butter (page 186)

Wasabi-Soy Sauce
1 tablespoon wasabi powder
1 cup soy sauce
¼ cup jackfruit extract or papaya
   puree
¼ cup chili pepper water (page 197)

Garnish
24 chives
12 fresh spinach leaves
4 fresh flowers

To make the marinated vegetables: In a large saucepan, combine the mirin or sherry, bonito flakes, soy sauce, and water. Bring to a slow boil and add the carrot and zucchini. Blanch for 30 seconds, drain, and plunge the vegetables into cold water. Drain and set aside.

To make the mushroom paste: In a medium sauté pan or skillet cook the bacon and shallots over medium-high heat until the fat is rendered. Add the mushrooms and brandy and cook until tender. While still hot, put the mixture in a blender or food processor and puree. Spread on parchment or waxed paper and let cool for 15 minutes.

To blacken the fish: Combine the spice mix and oil. Coat the ahi blocks with the spice paste. In a large sauté pan or skillet over high heat, heat the oil and sear the fish for 15 to 20 seconds on each side. The center of the fish will be raw.

To assemble: Preheat the oven to 350°F. Lay the puff pastry dough flat. Spread the center third of the pastry with a ¼-inch-thick layer of the mushroom paste. Lay half the shiso or romaine leaves on top. Layer with half the blanched vegetables. Place the seared ahi on the vegetables. Top with the rest of the vegetables. Cover with the remaining leaves. Wrap the dough around to encase the entire filling. Place the wellington on an oiled baking sheet, seam-side down. Brush the surface with the egg white. Bake for 8 to 12 minutes, or until golden brown.

To serve: Divide the hearts of palm among 4 plates. In a small sauté pan or skillet, melt the citrus-herb butter over low heat and pour over the hearts of palm. Slice the wellington into 2-inch pieces and place on top of the hearts

of palm. Whisk the sauce ingredients together and spoon some onto each plate. Tuck 6 chives into the edge of the crust, standing the chives vertically, and garnish with spinach leaves and flowers.

Ahi Katsu with Wasabi-Ginger Butter Sauce

Russell Siu
3660 on the Rise
Honolulu, Oahu

Serves 4

This is a fresh approach to a traditional Japanese dish. Panko, coarse Japanese bread crumbs, provide a crunchy crust for rare ahi, while wasabi and ginger combine with butter and cream to make a piquant dipping sauce.

8 sheets nori
2 bunches fresh spinach, stemmed
16 ounces fresh ahi tuna
Salt and freshly ground pepper to taste
4 eggs
½ cup water

Ahi Katsu with Wasabi-Ginger Butter Sauce; Russell Siu, 3660 on the Rise, Honolulu, Oahu

1 cup flour, plus ¼ cup flour
   for dusting
4 cups panko or other coarse
   bread crumbs

Wasabi-Ginger Butter Sauce
2 chopped shallots
3 tablespoons fresh ginger,
   peeled and chopped
2 tablespoons wasabi paste
½ cup rice vinegar
½ cup dry white wine
½ cup soy sauce
½ cup heavy (whipping) cream
1 cup (2 sticks) unsalted butter, cut
   into tablespoon-sized pieces

4 cups vegetable oil
Salt and freshly ground pepper to taste

Garnish
Sticky Rice (page 197)
1 tablespoon white sesame seeds
1 tablespoon black sesame seeds
Cucumber Salad (recipe follows)

To make the ahi: Spread the nori sheets, rough side up, on a work surface. Place a row of spinach leaves along one edge. Cut the ahi into pieces 1 inch thick by 1½ inches wide and as long as a nori wrapper. Place the ahi on the spinach leaves and season with salt and pepper. Top with another row of spinach leaves. Starting with the filled side, roll the nori up like a jelly roll. Moisten the edge of the nori with water and seal, leaving the ends open. Set aside.

In a large bowl, beat the eggs, water, and 1 cup of the flour together until blended. Place the remaining ½ cup flour in one plate and the panko in another. Dust the ahi rolls with the flour, dip them into the batter, and roll them in the panko until completely coated. Set aside.

To make the sauce: In a medium saucepan bring the shallots, ginger, wasabi, vinegar, wine, and soy sauce to a boil over medium-high heat and cook, stirring constantly, until reduced to about ½ cup. Add the cream and cook again until reduced to ½ cup. Reduce heat to low and whisk in the butter 1 piece at a time. Remove the pan from heat as necessary to keep the sauce just warm enough to melt each piece of butter. Keep warm over tepid water.

To serve: In a deep pan or fryer, heat the oil to 350°F, or until rippling, over

RUSSELL SIU
3660 on the Rise, Honolulu, Oahu

Russell Siu began cooking while he was still attending St. Louis High School in Honolulu. It was on-the-job training in family-run restaurants and fast-food outlets.

At the University of Hawaii he studied business administration, but later attended the food service division of Kapiolani Community College.

After school, he worked as sous-chef at the Westin Wailea Beach Hotel and Waiakea Village on the Big Island. For more than twelve years he served as executive chef at the prestigious Plaza Club in downtown Honolulu.

Siu's association with the Club Corporation of America, and his background in business as well as food service, enabled him to run the food and beverage operations in twenty-four private clubs in the organization's western region and Canada.

In 1981, he was invited to create Hawaiian food for Maxim Caterers in Hong Kong and at the World Trade Center Club in New York City. *Cook's Magazine* nominated him for a culinary award in 1983 as one of its Who's Who Among Chefs.

Siu is certified as an executive chef with the American Culinary Federation and is a member of the Chaîne des Rôtisseurs.

medium-high heat. Using tongs, place the rolls into the oil and cook 2 to 3 minutes, until the outside is golden brown. Drain on paper towels. With a sharp knife, cut the rolls crosswise into ½-inch slices. Place two tablespoon-sized mounds of sticky rice on each serving plate. Sprinkle the rice with white and black sesame seeds. Mound ½ cup of cucumber salad in the center of the plate. Pour one quarter of the sauce on one side of each plate, and fan the ahi roll slices over the sauce.

Cucumber Salad
Serves 4
½ cup sugar

¼ cup plus 2 tablespoons
   soy sauce
Juice of 2 lemons
¼ cup plus 2 tablespoons sesame oil
1½ cups salad oil
¼ cup sesame seeds, toasted
   (page 196)

1 large cucumber, peeled, seeded, and
   cut into matchsticks

Place the sugar, soy sauce, lemon juice, oils, and seeds in a large bowl. Whisk until blended and creamy. Add the cucumber strips and toss until coated. Chill in the refrigerator up to 1 hour.

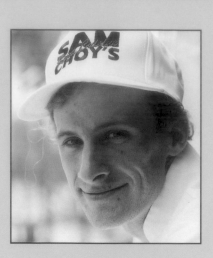

MICHAEL LONGWORTH
Sam Choy's Diamond Head Restaurant, Honolulu, Oahu

When Hawaii's Soul Food King, Sam Choy, opened a branch of his popular Kona restaurant just outside Waikiki, he named a thirty-one-year-old native of Boston, Massachusetts, as its executive chef.

Michael Longworth loves preparing "local-style" foods. His favorite is a version of Choy's Seafood Laulau, a fragrant combination of fresh island fish, local vegetables, scallops, and lobster tied up in a ti leaf and steamed to perfection.

He's not the sort of chef who enjoys being trapped in a hot kitchen without contact with diners. At Sam Choy's, the open Chef's Bar allows guests to watch their food being prepared, and lets Longworth hear and see their reactions, something he craves.

Before coming to Sam Choy's, Longworth worked as sous-chef at Honolulu's Black Orchid, World Cafe, and Nick's Fishmarket.

When he's not cooking, you can find him mountain biking in the hills around the island of Oahu, hiking, and swimming.

New Wave Marinated Ahi Salad

Michael Longworth
Sam Choy's Diamond Head
*   Restaurant*
Honolulu, Oahu

Serves 4

The trick to this hot and cold salad is to have everything ready before you begin to sear the fish. Assemble everything at once, adding the greens and noodles at the last minute.

Marinade
½ cup soy sauce
¼ cup vegetable oil
2 tablespoons mirin or sweet sherry
¼ teaspoon Asian sesame oil
¼ tablespoon minced fresh cilantro
2 tablespoons thinly sliced
   green onions
1 tablespoon minced garlic
1 tablespoon minced ginger
¼ teaspoon ground white pepper
1½ teaspoons Chinese five-spice mix
1 tablespoon black sesame seeds
1 Hawaiian or Thai chili pepper,
   seeded and minced, or 1 pinch
   red pepper flakes

6 ounces soba noodles

Twelve 2-ounce ahi tuna fillets,
   about ½-inch thick
¼ cup olive oil

¼ cup peanut oil
4 flour tortillas
4 handfuls (4 ounces) mixed
   baby greens

Garnish
Carrot, beet, and radish curls (page 203)
4 fresh cilantro sprigs
3 cucumber slices
3 tomato wedges
2 tablespoons black sesame seeds
½ cup macadamia nuts, chopped

Creamy Oriental Dressing
   (recipe follows)

Combine all the marinade ingredients in a shallow bowl and blend well. Bring a large pot of water to a rolling boil and boil the noodles until just tender to the bite, 5 to 6 minutes. Drain and rinse well in cold water; drain again. Toss the noodles with ½ cup of marinade. Cover and refrigerate for 20 to 30 minutes.

Marinate the ahi in the remaining marinade for 5 minutes. Drain and pat dry with paper towels. In a large sauté pan or skillet over high heat, heat the olive oil and sauté the ahi for 1 minute on each side. The fish will be raw on the inside.

In a deep sauté pan or skillet, heat the oil until it ripples. Using tongs, drop a tortilla in the hot oil and cook for 30 seconds, or until bubbles form in the top of the totilla. Turn and cook for 20 seconds, remove, and drain on paper towels. Repeat with remaining tortillas. Set aside and keep warm.

To serve: Place a fried flour tortilla on each salad plate, then arrange a handful of salad greens on top. Place some cold noodles on top of the greens, then arrange 3 fish fillets on top of that. Garnish with the vegetable curls, cilantro, cucumber, tomatoes, sesame seeds, and macadamia nuts. Pour ¼ cup dressing over the top of each salad.

Creamy Oriental Dressing
Makes 2½ cups

2 cups fresh orange juice
2 tablespoons sesame seeds,
   toasted (page 196)
3 tablespoons sugar
1 tablespoon salt
½ cup peanut or canola oil
3 tablespoons vinegar
2 tablespoons soy sauce

In a medium bowl, combine all ingredients and whisk together until creamy. Store, covered, in the refrigerator for up to 3 days.

Bouillabaisse de OnJin

OnJin Kim
Hanatei Bistro
Honolulu, Oahu

Serves 6

This bouillabaisse is true to the Mediterranean classic: local fish and shellfish cooked in a saffron-laced stock. The specific ingredients add the Hawaiian touch.

Fish Marinade

1 cup dry white wine
¼ teaspoon saffron threads
½ teaspoon fresh lemon juice
Salt to taste

1 pound salmon fillet, cut into twelve
    1½-inch-square pieces
1 pound opakapaka or other mild
    white-fleshed fish fillet, cut into
    twelve 1½-inch-square pieces
12 large shrimp, shelled and deveined
    (page 198)
18 sea scallops
3 lobster tails, cut in half lengthwise
6 crab claws, crushed

Marinara Sauce

2 tablespoons olive oil
½ onion, finely chopped
1 teaspoon minced fresh basil
½ teaspoon minced fresh thyme
½ teaspoon minced fresh oregano
½ teaspoon minced garlic
1 bay leaf
One 14½-ounce can diced tomatoes
    in juice
Salt and freshly ground pepper to taste
1 tablespoon tomato paste

Soup Stock

2 tablespoons olive oil
1 large leek, white part only, chopped
1 lemongrass stalk, white part only,
    diced
½ teaspoon saffron threads
1½ cup dry white wine
2 tablespoons fresh lemon juice
4 cups fish stock or clam juice
    (page 200)
1½ cups Marinara Sauce, above
½ teaspoon minced garlic
1 tablespoon minced fresh basil
1 tablespoon minced fresh parsley
1 tablespoon minced fresh cilantro
1 tablespoon Pernod

6 clams, scrubbed

Garnish

6 fresh chives
18 garlic bread croutons (page 192)

New Wave Marinated Ahi Salad;
Michael Longworth, Sam Choy's
Diamond Head Restaurant,
Honolulu, Oahu

To make the fish marinade: In a large nonaluminum saucepan, bring the wine, saffron, and lemon juice to a boil and cook until reduced by half. Add salt. Let cool. Add the fish and shellfish, except the clams, to the marinade. Cover and refrigerate for at least 1 hour, or up to 8 hours.

To make the marinara sauce: In a medium saucepan over medium heat, heat the oil until fragrant. Add the onion, basil, thyme, and oregano and sauté until the onion is tender, about 5 minutes. Add the garlic, bay leaf, tomatoes and juice, salt, and pepper, and simmer for 30 minutes, or until almost all the juice is evaporated. Add the tomato paste. Remove and discard the bay leaf. Set sauce aside.

To make the stock: In a large saucepan over medium-high heat, heat the oil until fragrant. Add the leek, lemongrass, and saffron, and sauté until the leek is evenly yellow from the saffron. Add the wine and lemon juice and bring to a boil. Cook until the liquid is reduced by half. Add the fish stock or clam juice, marinara sauce, and garlic and bring to a boil again. Add the basil and parsley. Reduce heat to a simmer and cook for 30 minutes. Add the cilantro and Pernod and remove from heat.

Bring the soup stock to a boil. Drain the marinade from the fish and shellfish. Add the lobster, salmon, opakapaka, and shrimp to the stock and cook for 2 minutes. Add the scallops, crab, and clams, and cook just until the clams open. Discard any clams that do not open.

To serve: Tie a knot in the center of each chive. Divide the bouillabaisse equally among 6 bowls. Garnish each with a chive and croutons.

Bouillabaisse de OnJin; OnJin Kim, Hanatei Bistro, Honolulu, Oahu

Portuguese Steamed Clams; Beverly Gannon, Haliimaile General Store, Haliimaile, Maui

Portuguese Steamed Clams

Beverly Gannon
Haliimaile General Store
Haliimaile, Maui

Serves 6

Inspired by the heritage of the Upcountry region of Maui, this dish combines clams and sausage with Pacific Rim seasonings of fresh ginger, chili paste, sake, and cilantro.

2 tablespoons olive oil
1 tablespoon minced garlic
½ cup minced fresh ginger
2 onions, finely chopped
3 red bell peppers, seeded, deribbed, and finely chopped (page 196)
8 ounces mild Portuguese sausage (linguiça), cut into ¼-inch chunks
1½ cups sake
6 cups reduced fish stock (page 200) or clam juice
1½ tablespoons Chinese chili paste
2 tomatoes, peeled, seeded, and coarsely diced (page 203)
5 dozen clams, scrubbed
½ cup fresh cilantro sprigs, chopped

In a large pot over medium heat, heat the oil and sauté the garlic, onions, and red peppers for 2 minutes, or until translucent. Add the sausage and sauté for 5 minutes, or until the sausage is slightly browned. Add the sake and stir to scrape up the browned bits from the bottom of the pan. Add

the fish stock or clam broth and cook until reduced by half. Add the chili paste, tomatoes, and clams. Cover and cook until the clams open, approximately 6 to 8 minutes. Discard any clams that do not open. Ladle the clams and broth into bowls and garnish with cilantro.

Salmon and Shrimp Gyoza with Sweet Chili Vinaigrette and Sweet Chili Beurre Blanc

Jean-Marie Josselin
A Pacific Café
Kapaa, Kauai

Serves 4

Gyoza are Japanese fried dumplings, enjoyed alone or with noodles at lunch, dinner, or as a snack. This contemporary version has a filling of salmon and shrimp, and is served with a rich lime-ginger sauce.

Lime-Ginger Sauce Base
1 cup dry white wine
2½ teaspoons minced fresh ginger
1 cup heavy (whipping) cream
1 cup (2 sticks) cold unsalted butter, cut into tablespoon-sized pieces
Juice of 1 lime
Salt and freshly ground pepper to taste

Thai Chili Vinaigrette
¾ cup olive oil
2 tablespoons mirin or sweet sherry
½ cup rice wine vinegar
1 tablespoon minced fresh cilantro
Salt and freshly ground pepper to taste

Filling
8 medium shrimp
8 to 10 ounces salmon fillet, skinned
1 egg
½ cup Thai chili paste
Salt and freshly ground pepper to taste
½ red bell pepper, seeded, deribbed, and diced (page 196)
1 fresh cilantro sprig, chopped

Gyoza
1 tablespoon cornstarch, plus cornstarch for dusting
2 tablespoons water
16 large dim sum or wonton wrappers
Filling, above
1 cup peanut oil for frying

1 tablespoon minced fresh cilantro
1 tablespoon Thai chili paste
4 fresh basil sprigs, stemmed and chopped
½ cup extra-virgin olive oil

1 cup shredded Chinese cabbage
2 red bell peppers, seeded, deribbed, and cut into julienne (page 196)
1 fresh cilantro sprig, stemmed and chopped

½ cup oyster sauce
½ cup Thai chili paste
1 tablespoon minced fresh cilantro
8 fresh flowers

To make the sauce base: In a medium, heavy saucepan, combine the wine and ginger and bring to a boil. Reduce heat to medium and cook to reduce to about ½ cup. Add the cream and cook to reduce to 1 cup. Reduce heat to low and whisk in the butter 1 piece at a

Salmon and Shrimp Gyoza with Sweet Chili Vinaigrette and Sweet Chili Beurre Blanc; Jean-Marie Josselin, A Pacific Café, Kapaa, Kauai

time. Remove the pan from heat as necessary to keep the sauce base just warm enough to melt each piece of butter. Add the lime juice, salt, and pepper. Keep warm over tepid water for up to 1 hour.

To make the vinaigrette: In blender or food processor, combine all ingredients and puree. Place in a squeeze bottle and refrigerate.

To make the filling: Reserve 3 shrimp. In a blender or food processor, combine the salmon, the remaining shrimp, the egg, chili paste, and seasoning. Puree until smooth. Cut the reserved 3 shrimp into small pieces and stir into the mixture with the red bell pepper and cilantro.

To make the gyoza: Mix the cornstarch with the water and moisten the edges of the wonton wrappers. Place 1 tablespoon of the filling in the center of a wrapper. With your fingers bring one point across the filling at an angle to the opposite corner, making 2 offset triangles. Grasp both outer points and pull around behind the filling, overlapping slightly. Press the ends together and dust the gyoza with cornstarch. Repeat with remaining wrappers. Bring a large pot of salted water to a boil and drop in the gyoza. Cook for 2 minutes, then remove with a slotted spoon and drain on paper towels.

In a large sauté pan or skillet over medium-high heat, heat the oil to 350°F, or until it ripples. Add the gyoza and cook for 1 minute, until the edges are crisp.

To finish the sauce: Put the sauce base, cilantro, and chili paste in a blender or food processor and puree.

In a blender or food processor, combine the basil and oil and puree until smooth. Put in a squeeze bottle.

To serve: Pool one fourth of the sauce on a serving plate. Toss the Chinese cabbage, peppers, and cilantro with the Thai chili vinaigrette and mound one-fourth in the center of the sauce. Place 4 gyoza in a radial pattern on the greens. Put the oyster sauce and the Thai chili paste in separate squeeze bottles. Drizzle oyster sauce, basil puree, and Thai chili paste over the entire dish. Garnish with a sprinkle of cilantro and 2 fresh flowers. Repeat with remaining dishes.

JEAN-MARIE JOSSELIN
A Pacific Café, Kapaa, Kauai

Josselin is one of the fathers of the new Hawaii Regional Cuisine. Born in France and schooled at the Culinary School of Paris, Josselin was a successful chef with the Rosewood Hotel chain when he arrived in the islands. After opening the much-praised Crescent Court Hotel in Dallas, he was sent to create a new cuisine for the Hotel Hana Maui. It was here that a profound change in his culinary style took place.

Introduced to Hawaiian fish, produce, and local foods, he concocted a sophisticated menu incorporating these new flavors. It was one of the first times island food had been presented as fine cuisine.

Josselin returned to the mainland to become executive chef of the Los Angeles Registry Hotel in 1986, but came back to Hawaii two years later to direct the kitchens of the lush bungalow-style Coco Palms Hotel on the island of Kauai. Here he commanded a crew of forty-five cooks and three kitchens. In 1990, he opened A Pacific Café in the nearby town of Kapaa. It was an instant success. In 1994, he opened another restaurant, A Pacific Café Maui, in Kihei.

A Pacific Café has received its share of accolades from the food media, including being named Best Restaurant on Kauai by *Honolulu Magazine,* and as one of the "best restaurants in the country" by *Bon Appétit.* Food critic Mimi Sheraton ranked A Pacific Café in her list of "fifty choice restaurants in the country" in *Condé Nast Traveler,* and noted food writer David Rosengarten sang its praises in *Departures.*

Josselin's cookbook, *A Taste of Hawaii: New Cooking from the Crossroads* (Stewart, Tabori & Chang), was the first written on the new island cuisine. He is also included in Janice Wald Henderson's *The New Cuisine of Hawaii* (Random House).

The chef has recently begun operating his own organic farm on Kauai, which produces as many as fifty different varieties of fruits and vegetables for his two restaurants. His wife Sophie, an artist, creates brilliantly colored ceramic tableware on which to display his culinary art.

GORDON HOPKINS
Roy's Restaurant, Honolulu, Oahu

It's Gordon Hopkins' "willingness to dream, then wake up and work like hell" that has made him so important to the Euro-Asian style of Roy Yamaguchi's flagship Hawaii Kai restaurant.

Hopkins' high energy and creativity have set the tone for the kitchen, attracting such guest chefs as Madeleine Kamman and James Beard Award winners Mark Miller of the Coyote Cafe and Bradley Ogden of the Lark Creek Inn. Hopkins has also served as guest chef at such high temples of California cuisine as Spago, Chinois on Main, and Citrus in Los Angeles.

Before joining Yamaguchi, Hopkins honed his craft in classic French kitchens across the mainland, from Chicago to New York and New Orleans. He is responsible for the nightly chef's specials that define Roy's distinctive style. You are likely to find dim sum, wood oven–baked pizza, and salads made with locally raised produce, along with an array of French-style sauces with Asian seasonings, topping a selection of six to eight kinds of fresh island fish.

Roy's kitchen helped to initiate the blending of island cuisine with classical techniques and presentation, and Gordon Hopkins has played a key role in the development of the new Hawaii Regional Cuisine.

Grilled Kajiki and Okinawan Sweet Potatoes with Peppercorn-Wasabi Vinaigrette

Gordon Hopkins
Roy's Restaurant
Honolulu, Oahu

Serves 4

Purple sweet potatoes make a colorful base for a tower of grilled fish and greens spiked with a spicy wasabi-based vinaigrette sauce. Nalo fern greens are suggested; the curled fern fiddleheads are very tender.

Mashed Purple Sweet Potatoes
2 pounds Okinawan or regular
    sweet potatoes
2 cups hot milk
2 tablespoons unsalted butter
Salt and freshly ground pepper to taste

Peppercorn-Wasabi Vinaigrette
1 cup Asian sesame oil
½ cup plain rice vinegar
1 tablespoon fresh lemon juice
1 teaspoon minced fresh ginger
1 tablespoon ginger juice
¼ teaspoon wasabi powder
1 teaspoon minced fresh garlic
1 tablespoon minced cilantro
2 green onions, green part only,
    finely chopped
⅛ teaspoon ground black peppercorns

Ponzu Sauce
1½ cup mirin or sweet sherry
½ cup soy sauce
Juice of 3 lemons
½ teaspoon red pepper flakes
1 tablespoon minced nori

Four 3-ounce pieces kajiki or
    swordfish
2 tablespoons minced nori

Garnish
1 tablespoon paprika
2 tablespoons furikake

1 cup Nalo ferns or baby salad greens
½ cup Peppercorn-Wasabi Vinaigrette
    (above)
¼ cup kaiware sprouts

4 tablespoons pickled ginger
8 chives, green part only
1 red bell pepper, seeded, deribbed, and julienned
1 tablespoon black sesame seeds, toasted (page 196)
1 tablespoon white sesame seeds, toasted (page 196)

To make the mashed sweet potatoes: Peel the sweet potatoes and cut into 1-inch dice. Cook the sweet potatoes in salted boiling water until tender, about 6 minutes. Drain. Combine the milk and butter and stir until the butter melts. Mash the potatoes with a masher or beater. Beat in the milk mixture. Add salt and pepper. Set aside and keep warm.

To make the vinaigrette: In a blender or food processor, puree all ingredients for 30 seconds, or until creamy.

To make the ponzu sauce: In a small saucepan, heat the mirin or sherry over medium-high heat for 4 minutes. Add the soy sauce, lemon juice, pepper flakes, and the nori. Cook for 1 minute.

To prepare the fish: Light a fire in a charcoal grill or preheat a gas grill. Five minutes before grilling, slice the fish into ⅛ inch slices. Coat the fish on all sides with 6 tablespoons ponzu sauce. Sprinkle with the nori. Cook the fillets over a medium-hot fire for 30 seconds per side, or until lightly seared on the outside.

To serve: Lightly dust the rim of the plates with paprika and furikake. Place some mashed sweet potatoes in the center of a plate. Place a few greens loosely on top of the potatoes. Place the grilled fish on top of the greens. Baste the fish with some of the remaining ponzu sauce. Add a layer of sprouts, ginger, 2 chives, and 2 strips of bell pepper. Drizzle the wasabi vinaigrette over and around the salad tower. Sprinkle with sesame seeds. Repeat with remaining plates.

Grilled Kajiki and Okinawan Sweet Potatoes with Peppercorn-Wasabi Vinaigrette; Gordon Hopkins; Roy's Restaurant, Honolulu, Oahu

Togarashi-seared Kumu with Pohole Fern Salad and Sesame Dressing

Amy Ferguson-Ota
The Dining Room
The Ritz-Carlton Mauna Lani
Kohala Coast, Hawaii

Serves 4

Kumu is a local favorite for its delicate flavor. The head is saved to make a rich fish stock. For this warm salad, the pan-seared fillets are stacked on a bed of blanched fern shoots accented with a sauce that blends ginger, soy, and chili flavors.

Eight 8-ounce kumu or red snapper
  fillets, skin left on one side
Hawaiian or kosher salt to taste

Togarashi to taste
Juice of 2 lemons
1 to 2 tablespoons peanut oil

Sesame Dressing
½ teaspoon minced garlic
1½ tablespoons minced pickled ginger
2½ tablespoons soy sauce
1 tablespoon soy sauce
2 tablespoons plain rice wine vinegar
1 teaspoon chili paste
1 teaspoon Asian sesame oil
1 teaspoon snipped fresh chives
1 teaspoon sugar

Fern Salad
1 pound fiddlehead ferns (pohole),
  blanched, or haricots verts or
  baby Blue Lake green beans
4 handfuls (4 ounces) mixed
  baby greens

1 small Maui or other sweet white
  onion, cut into ¼-inch strips
2 tomatoes, seeded, peeled, and cut
  into ¼-inch strips (page 203)

Garnish
1 tablespoon paprika
4 teaspoons togarashi
4 teaspoons snipped fresh chives

To prepare the fish: Score the fillets about ½ inch deep so they will not curl when fried. Use pliers to pull any visible bones from the fillets. Season with the salt, togarashi, and lemon juice. In a large sauté pan or skillet over high heat, heat the peanut oil and sear the fish for 1 minute on each side, or until opaque throughout. Set aside and keep warm.

Togarashi-seared Kumu with Pohole Fern Salad and Sesame Dressing; Amy Ferguson-Ota, The Dining Room, The Ritz-Carlton Mauna Lani, Kohala Coast, Hawaii

To make the salad: Whisk all the dressing ingredients together. Combine all the salad ingredients and toss with the dressing.

To serve: Lightly dust the rim of the plate with paprika. Pile salad in the middle of each plate. Top with the tomato strips. Lean 2 fillets against the greens on each plate, skin-side in. Drizzle dressing around the edges of the plate and sprinkle with togarashi and chives.

AMY FERGUSON-OTA

*The Dining Room, The Ritz-Carlton Mauna Lani,
Kohala Coast, Hawaii*

Women have always provided their families with meals, but it's rare when a woman serves as executive chef in a luxury hotel. Texan Amy Ferguson has been a trendsetter in this area twice. She was the first woman executive chef in the Rosewood Hotel chain when she took over responsibility for the Hotel Hana Maui's kitchens and she was also the first such chef for the Ritz-Carlton Hotels when she joined the staff at their hotel on the Big Island of Hawaii.

Papaya, chilies, avocados, and mangoes were already very familiar to Ferguson-Ota back home in Texas, where she worked for Che, Chez Lilliane, and Charley's 517 restaurants in Houston. She also opened the trendsetting Baby Routh for chef Stephen Pyles in Dallas. Now in Hawaii, she has reached even deeper into the native culture for exotic ingredients to use in her delightfully specialized cuisine. She uses the finest pohole (fiddlehead) ferns from the rain forests for her salads, and incorporates such island ingredients as ulu (breadfruit) for vichyssoise, guava for salad dressings, and ahi (tuna) for ahi cakes with a lime-cilantro mayonnaise.

Ferguson-Ota's basic training was classically French. She studied French at Laval University in Quebec City, Canada, before going to Paris to attend the American College, the Sorbonne, and Le Cordon Bleu.

Each year she serves as host of a culinary event called Big Island Bounty, where Hawaiian people and products are showcased. Working with local food product suppliers, she says, has given her the greatest satisfaction.

She was further honored by being selected to appear on Julia Child's PBS television series, *"Cooking with Master Chefs."*

GERARD REVERSADE

Gerard's at the Plantation Inn, Lahaina, Maui

Gerard Reversade is French, and the food he serves up in his charming Lahaina restaurant is French also. Unlike many chefs who wander from their homeland, Gascony-born Reversade has not gone far from the mother cuisine. It's true that he uses less cream and butter, and that he uses as many locally produced foods as he can, but his culinary heart is still in France. He serves local shiitake and oyster mushrooms in a classic puff pastry, his grilled scallop and prawn salad is served with a tomato confit, and his rack of lamb is accompanied with a potato galette.

Reversade first came to Maui in 1975 to open an extravagant restaurant called Rene's, which served hippopotamus and lion steaks. In 1977, the restaurant was destroyed by fire, and he moved to Honolulu to run the kitchen at the Café de Paris in Discovery Bay, a luxury condominium complex in Waikiki.

But Reversade was still enchanted with the small resort town of Lahaina, and in 1982 he returned to open his own restaurant, a small room that could barely hold thirty people. The floors were brick, ferns hung everywhere, and original art was on the walls.

Down the street from the restaurant, an inn was being built to replicate the gingerbread prettiness of a nineteenth-century inn. When it was completed, Reversade moved into the ground floor of the Plantation Inn.

The chef believes that French cuisine suffers from an image problem in the United States and particularly in Hawaii, where life is casual. Pretentious restaurants, he says, misrepresent what real French food is all about. Reversade's own cuisine is like that of his home in Gascony: simple, hearty, and earthy.

Roasted Opakapaka with Orange-Ginger Butter Sauce

Gerard Reversade
Gerard's at the Plantation Inn
Lahaina, Maui

Serves 4

When French technique meets fresh island fish, you get a refreshing dish like this roasted opakapaka. Cradled in puree and orange sections, the fish is moist and bright with island flavor.

1 whole opakapaka or other mild
    white-fleshed fish, about 2½ pounds
Salt and freshly ground pepper to taste
2 tablespoons extra-virgin olive oil
1 small bunch fresh savory
1 Hawaiian or Thai chili, seeded and
    chopped, or 1 pinch of red pepper
    flakes
½ orange, cut in ¼-inch slices

Potato-Carrot Puree

2 large potatoes, peeled and coarsely chopped
1 carrot, peeled and coarsely chopped
4 tablespoons unsalted butter
Salt, ground nutmeg, and white pepper to taste

Orange-Ginger Sauce

¼ cup water
½ cup (1 stick) unsalted butter, cut into pieces
2 teaspoons minced fresh ginger
1 Hawaiian or Thai chili, seeded and minced, or 1 pinch of red pepper flakes
Juice from 1 orange

1 orange, sectioned and seeded
2 green onions, green tops only, chopped

To prepare the fish: Preheat the oven to 450°F. Place the whole fish on a work surface. With a sharp knife, score the fish in a criss-cross pattern on each side. Sprinkle the fish cavity with salt and pepper. Fill the cavity with the savory and chili, and top the fish with orange slices. In a large ovenproof sauté pan or skillet over high heat, heat the olive oil and add the fish. Cook for 30 seconds on each side, then place the fish in the oven and bake for 25 to 30 minutes, or until the meat flakes but is still moist.

To make the puree: In a medium saucepan of salted, boiling water, cook the carrots and potatoes until tender, about 25 minutes. Drain and put the vegetables in a blender or food processor with the butter and seasonings. Puree. Set aside and keep warm.

To make the sauce: Add the water to a small saucepan and bring to a boil. Gradually add the butter, then the ginger, chili, and orange juice.

To serve: Arrange the fish on a platter. Place the puree in a large pastry bag fitted with a large star tip and pipe curving swirls of puree on each side of the fish. Pour the butter sauce over the top and arrange the orange sections around the outside. Sprinkle the top of the fish with the green onions.

Roasted Opakapaka with Orange-Ginger Butter Sauce; Gerard Reversade, Gerard's at the Plantation Inn, Lahaina, Maui

Jasmine Tea-steamed Fillet of Opakapaka with Coriander Butter Sauce

Russell Siu
3660 on the Rise
Honolulu, Oahu

Serves 4

Ginger brightens the crust on these fish fillets, coated with a silken cream reduction sauce. The simple but intensely flavored dish is garnished with a pick-up-sticks design of julienned carrot and green onion.

Four 5-ounce opakapaka fillets
Salt and freshly ground pepper to taste
1 cup fresh bread crumbs
1 tablespoon grated fresh ginger
2 large fresh cilantro sprigs, stemmed and minced (stems reserved)
3 cups water
2 jasmine tea bags

Coriander-Butter Sauce

1½ tablespoons coriander seeds
2 tablespoons dry white wine
2 tablespoons plain rice wine vinegar
Reserved cilantro stems, above
¼ cup heavy (whipping) cream
1 cup (2 sticks) unsalted butter, cut into tablespoon-sized pieces
Salt and freshly ground pepper to taste

Garnish

2 cups julienned green onions
1 carrot, peeled and cut into julienne
1 teaspoon finely diced fresh ginger

Sprinkle the fish with salt and pepper. In a small bowl, combine the bread crumbs, ginger, and chopped cilantro. Sprinkle this mixture over the fish. Put the fish in the top part of a steamer. In a small saucepan, bring the water to a boil. Set aside, add the tea, and steep for 3 minutes. Pour the tea into the bottom of the steamer, discarding the tea bags. Bring to a simmer, add the steamer section, cover, and steam for about 12 minutes, or until the fish flakes easily. Remove the fish from the pan and keep warm.

To make the sauce: In a heavy, medium saucepan, combine the coriander seeds, white wine, vinegar, and cilantro stems. Cook over medium-high heat until reduced by half. Reduce heat to medium, add the heavy cream, and cook to reduce by half again. Reduce heat to low and whisk in the butter 1 tablespoon at a time. Strain through a fine-meshed sieve and season with salt and pepper.

To serve: Place ¼ cup of sauce on each plate and place 1 fillet in the center. Garnish the top of the fish with green onions and carrot, and sprinkle the ginger over the plate.

Opakapaka CanoeHouse

Alan Wong
Alan Wong's Restaurant
Honolulu, Oahu

Serves 4

This is a signature dish of the CanoeHouse at the Mauna Lani Bay Hotel, where Alan Wong worked before opening his own restaurant. The opakapaka fillets are placed on a seared Chinese noodle pillow and bathed in a sauce of ginger, lemongrass, vegetables, clams, and shrimp. The dish resembles an Asian bouillabaisse.

Noodle Cakes

16 ounces dry Chinese egg noodles
Peanut oil for frying

Four 6-ounce opakapaka or other white-fleshed fish fillets
Salt and freshly ground pepper to taste
Olive oil for searing

CanoeHouse Sauce

2 tablespoons peanut oil
12 littleneck or other small clams, scrubbed
1 cup diced onion
¼ cup minced fresh ginger
1½ tablespoons minced garlic
1 lemongrass stalk, white part only, cut diagonally into 2-inch pieces
½ cup Chinese fermented black beans, rinsed
½ cup dry sherry
¼ cup Thai chili paste
½ cup chicken stock (page 199)
12 sugar snap peas, halved diagonally
1 cup fresh or frozen corn kernels
1 tomato, peeled and diced (page 203)
¼ cup garlic butter (page 187)

Garnish

4 fresh cilantro sprigs
4 green onions, julienned and placed in ½ cup ice water

To make the noodle cake: Preheat the oven to 350°F. Bring a large pot of water to a boil over high heat and add

Opakapaka CanoeHouse; Alan Wong, Alan Wong's Restaurant, Honolulu, Oahu

the noodles. Return to a boil and cook for 2 to 3 minutes, until tender. Drain. Heat a 5-inch nonstick skillet or sauté pan over high heat. While the noodles are still hot, place one fourth of the noodles in the hot skillet, forming them into a pillow shape with a spatula or slotted spoon. Sear for 30 seconds, or until brown; loosen and flip the noodle cake. Sear on the second side. Remove with a slotted spoon and place in an ovenproof pan. Repeat with remaining noodles, making a total of 4 cakes. Place the noodles in the oven and bake for 15 minutes.

To make the fillets: Preheat the oven to 350°F. Season the fillets with salt and pepper. Heat a large ovenproof sauté pan or skillet over medium-high heat. Add 2 tablespoons oil and heat until rippling, then add 1 fillet and sear on each side for 30 seconds. Remove the fillet with a spatula and place on an ovenproof dish. Repeat with the remaining fillets, adding oil as needed. The fish will be seared on the outside, and very rare inside. Bake for 15 minutes.

Meanwhile, to make the sauce: Heat a large skillet over medium-high heat, and add the oil. When the oil is hot, add the clams, onion, ginger, garlic, lemongrass, and black beans. Sauté for 1 minute, or until the vegetables are slightly translucent and beginning to brown. Pour the wine into the pan and stir to loosen the brown bits from the bottom. Add the chili paste, stock, peas, corn, tomato, and butter. Stir, cover, and cook until the clams open, 2 to 3 minutes. Remove any clams that have not opened and discard.

To serve: Remove the noodles and fish from the oven. Place a noodle cake in the center of each of 4 serving plates. Lean 1 fillet against each cake. Spoon clams and sauce over and around the fillets and cakes, dividing the clams equally among the plates. Garnish each plate with a cilantro sprig and a green onion curl.

Jasmine Tea-steamed Fillet of Opakapaka with Coriander Butter Sauce; Russell Siu, 3660 on the Rise, Honolulu, Oahu

Rich Forest; Alex Stanislaw, The Plantation House Restaurant, Kapalua, Maui

Rich Forest

Alex Stanislaw
The Plantation House Restaurant
Kapalua, Maui

Serves 4

A tall mold of fish, garlic mashed potatoes, spinach, and mushrooms shows off its layers. Any firm white fish can be used for the fillets. The chef names his dishes after the personality of each: He calls this Rich Forest because of its green and brown colors and earthy mushroom flavor.

Meunier Sauce
½ teaspoon olive oil
1 Maui or other sweet white onion, diced
2 cups dry red wine
½ cup (1 stick) unsalted butter
2 cups veal or beef stock (page 200)
1 tablespoon arrowroot diluted in 1 tablespoon water
Salt and freshly ground pepper to taste

Beurre Blanc
3 shallots, minced
1 teaspoon cracked pepper
1 cup dry white wine
½ cup heavy (whipping) cream
1 cup (2 sticks) unsalted butter, cut into tablespoon-sized pieces

Garlic Mashed Potatoes
6 white or yellow potatoes, peeled and chopped
½ cup (1 stick) unsalted butter
8 garlic cloves, diced
2 cups heavy (whipping) cream
Salt and freshly ground pepper to taste

3 day-old croissants, broken up
2 ounces dried mushrooms
Eight 4-ounce firm white fish fillets such as sole or halibut
6 tablespoons olive oil
6 garlic cloves, minced
1 pound fresh spinach, stemmed
Salt and freshly ground pepper to taste

Garnish
1 cup snipped fresh chives
½ cup minced fresh parsley

To make the meunier sauce: In a medium saucepan over medium-low heat, heat the olive oil and sauté the onion for 20 to 25 minutes, or until browned and caramelized. Add the red wine and cook over medium-high heat until evaporated. Add the butter, reduce heat to low, and cook until the butter browns. Add the veal or beef stock and simmer to reduce by one-fourth. Whisk in the diluted arrowroot and simmer until it begins to thicken. Add salt and pepper. Set aside and keep warm.

To make the beurre blanc: In a medium saucepan, combine the shallots, pepper, and wine and bring to a boil. Add the cream and cook to reduce by half. Remove from heat and whisk in the butter one tablespoon at a time. Return the pan to the stove as necessary to keep the mixture just warm enough to melt the butter. Strain through a fine-meshed sieve. Keep warm over tepid water.

To make the potatoes: Cook the potatoes in salted boiling water for 20 minutes, or until tender. Drain in a colander and let dry for 10 minutes. In the same saucepan, combine the butter, garlic, and cream and bring to a boil. Lower heat to a simmer and cook for 15 to 20 minutes. Put the potatoes in a medium bowl and beat, gradually adding the cream mixture. Season with salt and pepper.

In a blender or food processor, combine the stale croissants and dried mushrooms and grind to fine crumbs. Using a 3-inch ring mold, cut the fish fillets into circles. Sprinkle the fish with salt and dust with the crumbs.

Preheat the oven to 350°F. In a large ovenproof sauté pan or skillet over medium-high heat, heat 2 tablespoons of the oil and sauté the fish for 30 seconds on one side. Turn the fish and sauté for 30 seconds. Bake for 6 minutes, or until medium-rare. Set aside and keep warm.

In a large sauté pan or skillet over medium heat, heat the remaining 4 tablespoons oil and sauté the garlic for 3 minutes, or until translucent. Add the spinach and sauté until wilted. Add salt and pepper. Set aside and keep warm.

To serve: Place a 3-inch-diameter ring mold on each plate. Layer in one fourth of the spinach mixture, then a fish fillet, one fourth of the potatoes, and a second fish fillet. Remove the ring. Ladle 2 tablespoons beurre blanc on the top and 2 tablespoons of the meunier on top of that. Garnish with chives and parsley.

Sautéed Shrimp and Penne with Rice Cream Sauce

Alan Wong
Alan Wong's Restaurant
Honolulu, Oahu

Serves 4

Penne pasta are topped with a creamy rice-based sauce studded with beautiful seared shrimp. The ingenious Alfredo-style sauce is made without cream, and the only butter is used as an enrichment for the shrimp. You may cut the quantity of the butter if you wish.

Rice Cream Sauce

1 cup long-grain white rice
5½ cups fish stock (page 200) or clam juice
2½ cups water
1 tablespoon olive oil
1 tablespoon minced garlic
1 tablespoon minced shallot
¾ cup tomato water (see below)
1 cup dry white wine
4 cups chicken stock (page 199)
1½ tablespoons salt
24 large shrimp, peeled and deveined, tails left on
Salt and freshly ground pepper to taste
Flour for dredging
½ cup olive oil
2 teaspoons minced garlic
½ cup dry white wine
¾ cup tomato water (below)
2 teaspoons capers, drained
½ cup finely diced tomatoes
½ cup garlic-herb butter (page 187)
20 ounces penne pasta
4 tablespoons minced fresh Italian parsley

Garnish

8 tablespoons grated Parmesan cheese
4 fresh basil sprigs
2 tomatoes, peeled, seeded, and chopped (page 203)

Wash the rice. In a large saucepan, combine the rice, fish stock or clam juice, and water. Bring to a boil, then reduce heat to low and cook for 30 to 45 minutes, or until the liquid is absorbed and the rice is soft. Puree the rice in a blender or food processor until smooth.

In a large saucepan over medium-high heat, heat the oil and sauté the garlic and shallots for 2 minutes, until lightly browned and slightly translucent. Add the tomato water and white wine. Boil the mixture for 2 minutes, then add the chicken stock. When the stock boils, reduce heat to low and stir in the pureed rice. Add the salt and set aside.

Sprinkle the shrimp with salt and pepper and dredge lightly in flour. In a large sauté pan or skillet over medium-high heat, heat the olive oil until it ripples. Add the shrimp and sauté for 30 seconds on each side, or until golden. Add the garlic, wine, and tomato water, and stir to scrape up the browned bits from the bottom of the pan. Add the capers, tomatoes, garlic butter, parsley, and rice cream sauce. Cook and stir until the liquid has evaporated, 5 to 7 minutes. Season with salt and pepper.

Cook the pasta in a large pot of salted boiling water until al dente. Drain and toss with the shrimp sauce.

To serve: Divide among 4 shallow bowls. Garnish each with 2 tablespoons of cheese and a basil sprig. Place a tablespoon of chopped tomato over center of each.

Tomato Water

8 vine-ripened tomatoes
Pinch of salt

With a sharp small knife, cut the unpeeled tomatoes into chunks. Sprinkle with a pinch of salt and toss. Place the tomato chunks in a fine-meshed sieve over a bowl, or wrap in cheesecloth and place in a colander over a bowl. Refrigerate overnight and let drip. A clear tomato liquid will collect in the bowl. The tomato water may be used for suble flavoring; keep in a covered jar in the refrigerator up to 5 days.

Sautéed Shrimp and Penne with Rice Cream Sauce; Alan Wong, Alan Wong's Restaurant, Honolulu, Oahu

TOD KAWACHI
Roy's Kahana Bar & Grill, Kahana, Maui

Tod Kawachi was raised on Japanese and Chinese cuisines in his hometown of Seattle, Washington. His love of food led him to enroll in the culinary program at South Seattle Community College, where he graduated with honors in 1984.

Kawachi moved to Maui in 1985 to take a position at the Hyatt Regency Maui. It was here that he got his first taste of what would come to be called Hawaii Regional Cuisine.

Wanting to study more about food and wine, he returned to the mainland and the Napa Valley where he worked at the Meadowood Resort and Domaine Chandon restaurant, followed by stints in Los Angeles at Checkers Hotel, the Peninsula Beverly Hills, and the prestigious Hotel Bel-Air.

He was selected to attend a specialized program for professional chefs taught by Madeleine Kamman at Beringer Vineyards in May 1992. Later that year he returned to Hawaii and joined forces with chef Roy Yamaguchi. Kawachi assisted Yamaguchi in a food fair named for the famed island chef at the Nagoya Hilton in Japan in 1993.

As executive chef at Roy's Kahana Bar & Grill on Maui, Kawachi continues to promote the flavors of the Pacific Rim in his fine, fresh dishes.

Macadamia Nut-crusted Shutome and Vegetable Lumpia with Black Bean and Orange-Shrimp Butter Sauces

Tod Kawachi
Roy's Kahana Bar & Grill
Kahana, Maui

Serves 4

Crisp macadamia-crusted shutome fillets are served with beautiful vegetable lumpia and shiitake mushrooms. The companion sauces, a traditional black bean sauce and orange-shrimp butter, enhance the fresh sea flavors of the dish.

Black Bean Sauce
¼ cup Chinese fermented black beans
1 tablespoon peanut oil
1 tablespoon Asian sesame oil
½ tablespoon minced fresh ginger
½ tablespoon minced garlic
1 tablespoon chopped green onions
1½ tablespoons minced fresh cilantro
1 cup fish stock (page 200) or
    clam broth
Chili paste to taste

Vegetable Filling
½ cup dry rice noodles
2 tablespoons peanut oil
2 tablespoons Asian sesame oil
1 tablespoon minced garlic
1 tablespoon minced ginger
1 cup shredded won bok
    (napa cabbage)
½ cup shredded mustard greens
½ cup julienned celery
½ cup julienned carrots
½ cup mung bean sprouts
2 tablespoons oyster sauce
1 tablespoon white sesame seeds
Salt and freshly ground pepper to taste

4 lumpia wrappers

1 egg, beaten
2 cups peanut oil

Stir-fried Mushrooms
2 tablespoons peanut oil
1 tablespoon minced garlic
1 tablespoon minced fresh ginger
2 tablespoons oyster sauce
10 ounces shiitake mushrooms,
    stemmed and julienned
Salt and freshly ground pepper to taste

Orange-Shrimp Butter
Juice of 2 oranges
1 tablespoon plain rice vinegar
1 tablespoon minced fresh ginger

2 tablespoons shrimp paste
1 tablespoon minced shallots
1 tablespoon sake
1 cup dry white wine
2 tablespoons heavy (whipping) cream
1 cup (2 sticks) cold unsalted butter, cut into tablespoon-sized pieces

Twelve 3-ounce fresh shutome or swordfish fillets
Salt and freshly ground pepper
1 cup (5 ounces) macadamia nuts, finely ground
2 tablespoons peanut oil
2 tablespoons Asian sesame oil

Garnish
¼ cup scallion-infused oil (page 198)
¼ cup green onions, green part only, cut into 1-inch pieces
2 tablespoons white sesame seeds, toasted (page 196)
4 fresh cilantro sprigs

To make the black bean sauce: The day before serving, soak the black beans in water to cover overnight. Wash and drain the beans. In a medium saucepan over medium heat, heat the peanut and sesame oils. Add the ginger, garlic, green onions, and cilantro and sauté for 3 minutes. Add the black beans. Add the stock or broth and bring to a simmer for 5 minutes. Add the chili paste. Put the mixture in a blender or food processor and puree. Set aside and keep warm.

To make the vegetable lumpias: Bring a large pot of water to a boil and boil the noodles until tender, about 6 minutes. Drain in a colander. In a wok or large sauté pan or skillet over medium-high heat, heat the peanut and sesame oils until almost smoking. Add the garlic and ginger and stir-fry for 15 seconds, or until fragrant. Add the won bok, mustard greens, celery, carrots, and bean sprouts and stir-fry for 1 minute. Add 2 tablespoons of the oyster sauce, sesame seeds, and noodles. Pour into a colander to cool and drain. Season with salt and pepper

Lay 4 lumpia wrappers out on a work surface. Place one fourth of the cooled vegetables on the bottom half of each wrapper. Brush the top half of each wrapper lightly with the beaten egg. Fold up the bottom of each wrapper over the filling, then fold in the sides and roll up. In a wok or deep fryer over medium-high heat, heat the oil to 350°F, or until it ripples. Add the lumpia and cook for 2 minutes, or until

crisp and brown. Using tongs, transfer to paper towels to drain.

To make the mushrooms: In a medium sauté pan or skillet over medium-high heat, heat the oil and stir-fry the garlic, ginger, oyster sauce, and mushrooms for 1 minute. Add salt and pepper. Set aside and keep warm.

To make the orange-shrimp butter: In a medium saucepan, combine the orange juice, rice vinegar, and ginger, and simmer to reduce by half. Add the shrimp paste. In a medium, heavy saucepan over medium heat, sauté the shallots for 1 minute, until softened. Add the sake and wine and bring to a boil. Reduce heat to medium and cook to reduce to about ½ cup. Add the cream and cook to reduce to ½ cup. Reduce heat to low and whisk in the butter 1 piece at a time. Remove the pan from heat as necessary to keep the sauce base just warm enough to melt each piece of butter. Whisk the beurre blanc into the orange juice mix-ture. Strain through a fine-meshed sieve. Season to taste. Keep warm over tepid water for up to 1 hour.

Season the fillets with salt and pepper. Dredge one side of each in the macadamia nuts. In a large sauté pan or skillet over high heat, heat the oils until they ripple. Add the fillets, crusted-side down, and cook for 2 minutes, until golden. Turn and cook on the second side for 2 minutes, or until opaque throughout.

To serve: Slice each lumpia roll in half diagonally. Trim the ends flat and stand each half on end on the top portion of the plate. Place a small mound of the shiitake mushrooms on the plate, then overlap 3 shutome fillets on top and drizzle the sauces in equal amounts around the outside of the fish. Garnish with 5 drops of the oil, the green onions, and sesame seeds. Stand 1 cilantro sprig between the fillets and the lumpias. Repeat with remaining plates.

Macadamia Nut–crusted Shutome and Vegetable Lumpia with Black Bean and Orange-Shrimp Butter Sauces; Tod Kawachi, Roy's Kahana Bar & Grill, Kahana, Maui

Swordfish with a Crabmeat-Sesame Crust and Stir-fried Vegetables with Mirin-Cilantro Vinaigrette

Dominique Jamain
The Maile Restaurant
Kahala Hilton
Honolulu, Oahu

Serves 4

Medallions of broiled swordfish are protected from the heat of the broiler by a tasty crabmeat-sesame crust. While the crust is crunchy, the fish remains moist. The medallions rest on a bed of stir-fried vegetables dressed with mirin-cilantro vinaigrette.

Mirin-Cilantro Vinaigrette

1 cup soy sauce
¾ cup peanut oil
¾ cup plain rice vinegar
½ cup mirin or sweet sherry
¼ cup fresh lime juice
½ cup sugar
2 tablespoons grated fresh ginger
1½ teaspoons Asian sesame oil
1 tablespoon minced garlic
2 tablespoons chili pepper water
   (page 197)
1 teaspoon minced fresh red chili
½ cup chopped fresh cilantro

Eight 2½-ounce boneless, skinless
   swordfish medallions
¼ cup peanut oil
Salt and freshly ground pepper to taste

Crabmeat-Sesame Crust

⅔ cup fresh lump crabmeat
¼ cup panko (Japanese bread crumbs)
¼ teaspoon garlic powder
Salt and freshly ground pepper to taste
Pinch of black sesame seeds
1 teaspoon white sesame seeds,
   toasted (page 196)
1 teaspoon minced fresh parsley
1½ tablespoons mayonnaise
1 teaspoon garlic-herb butter at room
   temperature (page 187)

Stir-fried Vegetables

½ cup yellow bell peppers, seeded,
   deribbed, and halved (page 196)
1 ounce snow peas, halved lengthwise
1 ounce fresh bean sprouts
1 ounce baby corn, halved lengthwise

Swordfish with a Crabmeat-Sesame Crust and Stir-fried Vegetables with Mirin-Cilantro Vinaigrette; Dominique Jamain, The Maile Restaurant, Kahala Hilton, Honolulu, Oahu

½ cup red bell peppers, seeded,
   deribbed, and julienned (page 196)
1 ounce shiitake mushrooms,
   stemmed and cut into strips
¼ cup julienned celery
¼ cup julienned zucchini
¼ cup julienned choi sum (Chinese
   broccoli), or broccoli florets
¼ cup julienned peeled broccoli stems
1 cup shredded Chinese cabbage
½ cup chopped Maui or other
   sweet white onions
Salt and freshly ground pepper to taste
¼ cup peanut oil

Garnish
4 fresh cilantro sprigs
1 sheet nori, cut into fine strips

To make the vinaigrette base: One day
ahead, combine all the ingredients
except the cilantro in a medium bowl
and mix well. Cover and refrigerate
overnight to infuse flavors.

Coat the fish with oil and season
with salt and pepper. In a large sauté
pan or skillet over high heat, sear the
fish for 1 minute on each side.

To make the crust: Preheat the broiler.
Combine all the ingredients and blend
with your fingers. Coat each medallion
of fish evenly with a portion of the
crabmeat mixture. Place under the
broiler and cook for 3 minutes, or until
it forms a golden crust. Set aside and
keep warm.

To make the stir-fried vegetables: Season
the vegetables with salt and pepper. In
a wok or large sauté pan or skillet over
medium-high heat, heat the oil until it
ripples. Stir-fry the vegetables for 45
seconds, or until they soften and
brown slightly. Set aside and keep
warm.

To finish the vinaigrette: In a medium
saucepan over low heat, warm the
vinaigrette. Stir in the cilantro.

To serve: Place some of the stir-fried
vegetables in the center of each plate.
Place 2 medallions on top of the vegetables and pour ¼ cup warm vinaigrette around the vegetables. Garnish
with cilantro sprigs and nori.

Dominique Jamain
The Maile Restaurant, Kahala Hilton, Honolulu, Oahu

When Dominique Jamain first arrived in Honolulu, he was
introduced to produce and seasonings he'd never seen before.
They baffled and excited him all at once. Before long he was combining balsamic vinegar with mango for a coulis and putting
a bit of curry in his wild rice. Soon he had completely embraced
the flavors of Asia and Polynesia.

Jamain graduated from the College d'Enseignement Technique
in France in 1973 and began working in restaurants in the Loire
Valley. In 1976, he relocated to Montreal, where he joined the
Hilton Hotel chain as sous-chef at the Queen Elizabeth Hotel and
taught at La Salle College.

He was awarded silver medals from the Salon Culinaire
du Quebec in 1982, 1985, and 1987. In 1988, he won the grand
prize at the Bureau Laitier du Canada, a contest open to professional chefs throughout the country. In Hawaii, he was recognized
by the Hawaii Papaya Administration for his Papaya Trifle with
Galliano in their annual contest.

Jamain has participated in the annual Kapalua Wine
Symposium on the island of Maui, and was honored by the James
Beard Foundation in 1992 as one of the Great Hotel Chefs of
America. He has also appeared as guest chef aboard Cunard's
luxury liner *Queen Elizabeth II.*

Papillotte of Kumu with Basil, Seaweed, and Shiitake Mushrooms

George Mavrothalassitis
La Mer
Halekulani Hotel
Honolulu, Oahu

Serves 4

Kumu is a small member of the goatfish family, and like its cousins moano and weke, it's often fried whole. Steaming in parchment paper allows the fish to make its own sauce, enhanced by a surprising combination of ingredients.

4 tablespoons extra-virgin olive oil
8 ounces shiitake mushrooms, stemmed and sliced
1 cup thinly sliced Maui or other sweet white onions
1½ pounds kumu or red snapper fillets, skin on
1 cup ogo (seaweed)
4 fresh basil sprigs, stemmed and minced
¼ cup dry white wine
¼ cup olive oil
¼ cup fish stock (page 200), or clam juice mixed with ¼ cup water
Salt and freshly ground pepper to taste
1 egg yolk, beaten

In a medium sauté pan over medium-high heat, heat 2 tablespoons of the oil and sauté the mushrooms for 2 minutes, or until lightly browned on the edges. Remove the mushrooms from the pan and set aside. Heat the remaining oil in the pan and sauté the onions for 2 minutes, or until translucent. Set aside.

Preheat the oven to 450°F. Cut the fish into eight 1-inch-thick pieces. Cut 4 circles of parchment paper 14 inches in diameter. Fold the paper in half to make a center crease. Open the paper toward you and arrange the ingredients in the center: On 1 paper circle, layer one fourth of the onions, 2 fillets, and one fourth each of the mushrooms, ogo, basil, white wine, olive oil, and diluted fish stock. Salt and pepper to taste. Repeat with remaining 3 circles. Brush the inner edge of the paper with the beaten egg and fold the paper in half over the ingredients. Beginning at the crease, fold the cut edges upward and back over themselves in 2-inch sections, sealing as you work and forming a twisted edge. Paper clip the final twist to hold tightly. It will look like a large tart.

Place the papillottes in a large dry ovenproof skillet over medium-high heat just until they begin to puff. Place the skillet in the oven and bake for 8 minutes. The parchment will puff slightly. With scissors, cut an opening in the parchment paper to allow the steam to escape. Serve the packages at the table.

Wok Lobster with Lehua Honey and Black Bean Sauce

Patrick Callarec
The Dining Room
The Ritz-Carlton Kapalua
Kapalua, Maui

Serves 4

Although it looks elegant, this is a simple and quick dish to prepare. It is served family-style on a platter. The thick and fragrant lehua honey featured in the dish is made from the nectar of a plant that grows on the side of Maui's volcano.

Lehua Honey and Black Bean Sauce

1 teaspoon cornstarch
½ cup water
1 cup Chinese fermented black beans, rinsed and chopped
1 teaspoon sesame oil
1 teaspoon coconut oil
1 teaspoon minced garlic
1 teaspoon minced fresh ginger
½ teaspoon minced lemongrass
1 teaspoon minced green onion (white portion only)
1 teaspoon minced fresh cilantro
1 teaspoon grated orange zest
1 teaspoon chili paste
1 teaspoon soy sauce
1 teaspoon oyster sauce
1 teaspoon lehua honey or other fragrant honey
1½ cups chicken or fish stock (page 199 or 200) or clam juice

Papillotte of Kumu with Basil, Seaweed, and Shiitake Mushrooms; George Mavrothalassitis, La Mer, Halekulani Hotel, Honolulu, Oahu

Wok Lobster with Lehua Honey and Black Bean Sauce; Patrick Callarec, The Dining Room, The Ritz-Carlton Kapalua, Kapalua, Maui

Two 2-pound Maine lobsters or
   4 rock lobster tails
1 teaspoon sesame oil
1 teaspoon peanut oil

Noodles
One 12-ounce package fresh Chinese
   egg noodles
2 tablespoons sesame oil
2 tablespoons peanut oil

Garnish
1 teaspoon julienned green onions
4 fresh cilantro stems
6 orange zest strips

To make the sauce: In a small bowl, dissolve the cornstarch in the cold water and set aside. Coarsely chop half of the black beans. In a large wok over medium heat, heat the oil to rippling and stir-fry the chopped and whole beans, garlic, ginger, lemongrass, green onion, and cilantro until the vegetables are wilted. Add the zest and chili paste, and stir-fry for 1 minute. Stir in the soy sauce, oyster sauce, honey, and stock or clam juice. Bring to a boil and pour

in the cornstarch mixture, stirring until thickened. Simmer for 15 minutes. Remove from heat.

Bring a large pot of water to a boil. Kill the lobsters by making an incision in the back of the shell where the chest and tail meet. Immediately add the lobsters to the boiling water for 2 minutes. Using tongs, remove the lobsters and drain on paper towels. Place on a cutting board and cut the tail from the body where they join. Cut the tail into ¾-inch slices, keeping the meat inside the shell. Cut the claws away close to the body and cut the knuckles away at the claws, keeping the claws intact. Remove the legs. Pull the meat from the knuckles and crack the claws, removing the lower part of the shell to expose the meat. If using lobster tails, cut into medallions, keeping the meat inside the shell.

In a clean wok over high heat, heat sesame and peanut oils until rippling. Add the lobster and stir-fry for 1 minute. Add to the wok with the black

bean sauce, cover, return to medium heat, and cook for 2 minutes. Remove from heat.

To make the noodles: Bring a large pot of water to a boil and add the noodles. Cook for 7 minutes, then drain well and pat dry with a paper towel. In a large wok over high heat, combine 1 tablespoon sesame oil and 1 tablespoon peanut oil and heat to rippling. Put the noodles in the oil, shaping them into a cake with the back of a spoon. When the cake has turned a golden color on one side, about 2 minutes, turn it with a large spoon or spatula and reshape into a cake. Pour 1 tablespoon sesame oil and 1 tablespoon peanut oil around the edges of the cake and cook until golden brown on the second side, about 2 minutes.

To serve: Place the noodle cake in the center of a large platter. Split the body of the lobster in half lengthwise. Arrange all the lobster pieces or tails over and around the noodles. Pour the black bean sauce over and around the lobster. Garnish with green onions, cilantro sprigs, and orange zest.

Sam Choy

Sam Choy's Restaurants of Hawaii, Kailua Kona, Hawaii

Sam Choy's culinary roots lie deep in the home-cooking styles of Hawaii's ethnic families. The son of a Chinese father who loved to cook, and a Hawaiian-German mother, Choy puts as much importance on dining as a social event as on preparing fine food for its own sake.

Born in Laie, on the north shore of the island of Oahu, Choy grew up preparing luau feasts for visitors. When he wasn't helping his father cook at the family restaurant, Sam's Place, he was entertaining with a happy hula. He remembers wishing he could spend the rest of his life doing just that — and in a sense he has.

After high school, Choy attended culinary school at Honolulu's Kapiolani Community College, then worked at the Hyatt Kuilima Hotel near his home and later at the Kona Hilton Hotel on the Big Island. Today he owns two restaurants in Kailua Kona, and one near Waikiki in Honolulu. He's appeared on ABC's *Good Morning America,* "dished" with the likes of New Orleans' Paul Prudhomme, prepared a state dinner for Hawaii Governor John Waihee in Cologne, Germany, and been the subject of two cookbooks, *Sam Choy's Cuisine Hawaii* (Pleasant Hawaii, Inc.) and *Cooking from the Heart with Sam Choy* (Mutual Publishing).

Still, Sam Choy remains at heart a local boy who "did good." He's at his best reinterpreting island classics such as poke (raw fish with soy sauce, seaweed, onions, and chilies), lomi lomi salmon, and kalua pig. But ask for something upscale and you're likely to get a delicious plate of Ginger Crab on Deep-fried Opakapaka.

Sam Choy is one of the giants of Hawaiian cuisine.

Crusted Mahimahi with Crab Bisque

Sam Choy
Sam Choy's Restaurants of Hawaii
Kailua Kona, Hawaii

Serves 4

The Japanese bread crumbs called panko make this dish very "island" in flavor, and the coconut, spinach, and crabmeat in the bisque make it taste like a luau. The bisque is made of pureed taro leaves enriched with cream and coconut milk, forming a rich green halo around the fish.

Mashed Purple Sweet Potatoes

1 pound Okinawan or regular
  sweet potatoes
1 cup hot milk
1 tablespoon unsalted butter
Salt and freshly ground pepper to taste

Crab Bisque

4 tablespoons unsalted butter
2 onions, diced
2 tablespoons flour
2 cups heavy (whipping) cream
1 cup coconut milk
2 cups green taro leaves or frozen
  spinach, chopped
1½ cups fresh lump crabmeat
Salt and freshly ground pepper to taste

Crusted Mahimahi

1 cup panko (Japanese bread crumbs)
1 cup macadamia nuts, finely chopped
½ cup minced fresh parsley
Four 8-ounce mahimahi fillets
Salt and freshly ground pepper to taste
½ cup all-purpose flour
2 eggs, lightly beaten
¼ cup vegetable oil for frying

Sautéed Vegetables

2 tablespoons peanut oil
1 cup finely chopped onions
1 cup fresh bean sprouts
½ cup diagonally cut celery
5 ounces shiitake mushrooms,
  stemmed and sliced
3 ounces white mushrooms, sliced
1 red bell pepper, seeded, deribbed,
  and cut in julienne

Garnish

2 fresh cilantro sprigs
1 tablespoon black sesame seeds

To make the potatoes: Peel the sweet potatoes and cut into 1-inch dice. Cook the sweet potatoes in salted boiling water until tender, about 6 minutes. Drain. Combine the milk and butter and stir until the butter melts. Mash the potatoes with a masher or beater. Beat in the milk mixture. Add salt and pepper. Set aside and keep warm.

To make crab bisque: In a large saucepan, melt the butter and sauté the onions until translucent, about 3 minutes. Stir in the flour and blend well. Add the heavy cream and simmer for 5 minutes, stirring frequently. Stir in the coconut milk, taro or spinach, and crabmeat. Add salt and pepper. Reduce the heat to low and cook until the mixture thickens slightly.

To make the crusted mahimahi: In a shallow bowl, combine the panko, macadamia nuts, and parsley. Season the mahimahi with salt and pepper and dust with flour. Dip each fillet in the eggs, then the macadamia nut crust mixture, to coat on both sides. In a large sauté pan or skillet over medium-high heat, heat the oil and cook the mahimahi for 2 minutes on each side, or until golden brown.

To make the vegetables: In a medium sauté pan or skillet over medium-high heat, heat the oil and sauté the onions until translucent, 3 minutes. Add the remaining ingredients, reduce heat to medium, and sauté until tender, 3 to 5 minutes. Set aside and keep warm.

To serve: Put the mashed potatoes in the center of the serving platter. Place the crusted mahimahi fillets on top of the potatoes. Spoon the vegetables on one side of the plate. Pour the bisque completely around the fillets and vegetables. Garnish with cilantro sprigs and sesame seeds.

Crusted Mahimahi with Crab Bisque; Sam Choy, Sam Choy's Restaurants of Hawaii, Kailua Kona, Hawaii

Seared Mahimahi with Garlic-Sesame Crust and Lime-Ginger Sauce; Jean-Marie Josselin, A Pacific Café, Kapaa, Kauai

Seared Mahimahi with Garlic-Sesame Crust and Lime-Ginger Sauce

Jean-Marie Josselin
A Pacific Café
Kapaa, Kauai

Serves 4

The garlic-sesame crust seals the fish fillets as they cook, and they emerge succulent and flavorful. The golden brown fillets are beautifully presented on a bed of bok choy with a dramatic lime-ginger sauce dotted with dark oyster sauce, and colorful nori-lined taro lumpia.

Lime-Ginger Sauce
¾ cup dry white wine
2½ teaspoons minced fresh ginger
½ cup heavy (whipping) cream
1 cup (2 sticks) cold unsalted butter, cut into tablespoon-sized pieces
Juice of 1 lime
Salt and freshly ground pepper

Four 7-ounce mahimahi fillets
Salt and freshly ground pepper to taste
1½ cups (8 ounces) white sesame seeds
5 teaspoons minced garlic
½ cup (1 stick) unsalted butter at room temperature
3 tablespoons olive oil

1 tablespoon extra-virgin olive oil
2 cups baby bok choy, blanched

4 Taro Lumpia (recipe follows)

Garnish
½ cup peanut oil
4 shallots, white part only, cut into fine julienne
¼ cup oyster sauce
1 cup radish sprouts
½ cup red ginger
4 edible flowers

To make the sauce: In a heavy, medium saucepan, combine the wine and ginger. Bring to a boil, reduce heat to medium, and cook until reduced to ¼ cup. Add the cream and continue cooking until reduced to ½ cup. Reduce heat to low and whisk in the butter 1 piece at a time. Remove the pan from heat as necessary to keep the sauce just warm enough to melt each piece of butter. Whisk in the lime juice, salt, and pepper. Prepare up to 1 hour in advance and keep warm over tepid water.

Sprinkle the fillets with salt and pepper and set aside. In a medium bowl, combine the sesame seeds, garlic, butter, and salt and pepper to taste. Spread one side of the fillets evenly with this mixture.

In a large sauté pan or skillet over medium-high heat, heat the oil and cook the fillets on each side for 4 minutes, or until the crust is golden and crisp. With tongs or a spatula, lift the fish out of the pan and place on paper towels to drain.

In a large sauté pan or skillet, heat the olive oil over medium-high heat, and sauté the bok choy for 2 min-

utes, or until heated through. Place one fourth of the bok choy on each serving plate. Place a fillet on the bok choy on each plate.

In a heavy, small sauté pan or skillet over high heat, heat the peanut oil until rippling. Drop the shallots into the oil and fry for 30 seconds, or until light brown and crisp. Remove with a slotted spoon and drain on paper towels.

To assemble: Pour the lime-ginger sauce around the fish. Place the oyster sauce in a squeeze bottle and place dime-sized dots in the sauce around the fish. Sprinkle black sesame seeds lightly on the sauce. Cut the lumpia in half on the diagonal and stand 2 halves, points up, on each plate. Garnish the fish with the fried shallots, sprouts, ginger, and edible flowers.

Taro Lumpia
Makes 4

4 egg roll wrappers
2 nori sheets

1 tablespoon plus 2 cups peanut oil
1 garlic clove, minced
2 taro roots, cut into julienne
1 carrot, peeled and cut into julienne
1 egg yolk, beaten
2 cups peanut oil

Lay the egg roll wrappers flat. Cut the nori sheets in half and place a sheet on each wrapper.

In a small sauté pan or skillet over medium-high heat, heat the 1 tablespoon peanut oil and sauté the garlic 30 seconds, or until translucent. Add the taro and carrot and sauté for 2 minutes, or until tender. Divide the vegetables among the wrappers and place on the wrappers diagonally. Fold one point of a wrapper across the filling and tuck the end under the filling. Fold both sides of the wrapper together over the center. Brush the final point with egg and fold the point down over the package, pressing to seal. Repeat with remaining wrappers.

In a heavy, medium saucepan or deep fryer, heat the peanut oil over high heat to 350°F, or until rippling. With tongs, lift the lumpia and plunge into the oil. Fry, turning to brown all sides, until crisp, about 4 minutes. Lift the lumpia with the tongs and drain on paper towels.

Sautéed Mahimahi on Stir-fried Watercress with Ginger Beurre Blanc and Noodle Cakes

Peter Merriman
Merriman's Restaurant
Waimea, Hawaii

Serves 6

A mixture of French, Japanese, and Thai styles results in a dish that is creamy smooth with the sharp bite of peppers. Soba noodle cakes and curried stir-fried vegetables serve as a base for delicate mahimahi fillets and a ginger beurre blanc. Adjust the heat with the peppers, ginger, and chili sauce.

Curry Sauce

2 tablespoons grated galangal or
    fresh ginger
3 lemongrass stalks, white part only
4 kaffir lime leaves, chopped
1 shallot
4 garlic cloves
2 tablespoons Thai chili paste

Ginger Beurre Blanc

1½ cups dry white wine
2 tablespoons minced shallots
3 fresh parsley sprigs
3 white mushrooms, chopped
¼ cup pickled ginger, cut into julienne
2 tablespoons heavy (whipping) cream
1 cup (2 sticks) unsalted butter,
    cut into tablespoon-sized pieces
Salt and freshly ground pepper to taste

Noodle Cakes

2 pounds soba noodles
½ cup extra-virgin olive oil for frying

Six 6-ounce mahimahi fillets
Salt and freshly ground pepper to taste
1 cup cornstarch
¼ cup extra-virgin olive oil

Spicy Stir-fried Vegetables

1 tablespoon Curry Sauce, above
1 red bell pepper, seeded, deribbed,
    and cut into julienne
¼ cup white mushrooms, quartered
½ Maui or other sweet white onion,
    cut into julienne
¼ bunch watercress, stemmed
½ cup fresh bean sprouts
¼ cup Thai fish sauce

Garnish

2 tablespoons unsalted peanuts,
    chopped
¼ cup fresh cilantro leaves, chopped

To make the curry sauce: Grind all ingredients in a blender or a food processor until smooth. This can take 8 minutes or longer. Reserve or freeze until ready to use.

To make the beurre blanc: In a medium saucepan, combine the wine, shallots, parsley, mushrooms, and half of the pickled ginger. Cook over medium heat until almost evaporated. Add the cream and cook to reduce by half. Reduce heat to low and whisk in the butter 1 piece at a time. Remove the pan from the heat as necessary to keep the sauce just warm enough to melt each piece of butter. Remove from the heat and strain through a fine-meshed sieve. Add the remaining ginger, salt, and pepper. Keep warm over tepid water.

To prepare the noodle cakes: Bring a large pot of water to boil over high heat. Add the noodles and let boil until just soft to the bite, about 6 minutes. Drain in a colander. Divide the noodles into 6 equal portions. In a large sauté pan or skillet over medium-high heat, heat the oil until rippling. Add noodles, one portion at a time, pressing into a rectangle with the back of a spoon as they cook until they hold their shape. Cook on both sides until crisp and golden brown, about 3 minutes per side. Remove with a slotted spoon and drain on paper towels; set aside and keep warm. Repeat with remaining noodle portions.

Sprinkle the fillets with salt and pepper and coat them with cornstarch. In a large sauté pan or skillet over medium-high heat, heat the oil and cook the fillets for 3 minutes on each side, or until they flake easily and are golden brown.

To make the stir-fried vegetables: Heat a wok over high heat, add the curry sauce, and stir-fry for 30 seconds. Add the bell pepper, mushrooms, onion, and watercress. Stir-fry for 1 minute. Add the bean sprouts and fish sauce. Set aside and keep warm.

To serve: Place the noodle cakes at one end of a serving platter. Spoon the vegetables down the center of the platter, moving the red pepper strips to the top center of the vegetables. Spoon the beurre blanc over the vegetables, letting the sauce pool on the platter. Place 3 fillets on each side of the vegetables, touching in the center. Sprinkle with the peanuts and cilantro.

Sautéed Mahimahi on Stir-fried Watercress with Ginger Beurre Blanc and Noodle Cakes; Peter Merriman, Merriman's Restaurant, Waimea, Hawaii

Lemongrass-grilled Mako Shark with Sticky Rice and Roasted Banana–Mint Sauce

Jacqueline Lau
Roy's Nicolina
Kahana, Maui

Serves 4

Sticky rice forms a bed for grilled shark fillets. The roasted banana sauce is an unusual choice, but adds to the Pacific Rim flavors in the dish.

Marinade
6 lemongrass stalks, white part only, finely chopped
2 teaspoons minced fresh ginger
1 teaspoon minced garlic
Juice of 2 limes
Juice of 2 lemons
Juice of 1 orange
½ cup Asian sesame oil

Four 3-ounce fillets mako shark

Roasted Banana–Mint Sauce Base
4 bananas
2 tablespoons sesame oil
6 star anise pods
4 tablespoons grated fresh ginger
2 lemongrass stalks, white part only, chopped
5 cups sake
2 cups mirin or sweet sherry
½ cup minced fresh cilantro
2 tablespoons plain rice wine vinegar

Sticky Rice
1 cup Thai sticky rice
6 cups water

2 tablespoons peanuts, toasted and chopped (page 196)
4 tablespoons shredded fresh mint
4 oak leaf lettuce leaves
1 cup red ogo or other seaweed
4 green onions, green part only, cut into julienne

Soak the rice in the water overnight

To make the marinade: In a medium bowl, combine all the marinade ingredients. Add the fillets, cover, and refrigerate for at least 6 hours and up to 12 hours.

To make the sauce base: Preheat the oven to 400°F. Peel the bananas and coat them with sesame oil. Roast in the oven for 15 to 20 minutes. Dice the roasted bananas into ¼-inch pieces. In a large pot, combine the remaining sauce ingredients and cook over medium heat to reduce by half. Strain the mixture. Add the bananas to the strained sauce. Set aside and keep warm for at least 30 minutes; this allows the banana flavor to be infused.

To make the sticky rice: Soak the rice and rinse it well. Place the rice in a medium saucepan and add water to cover 1 inch above the rice. Bring the water to a boil over high heat, swirl the rice, and cover. Lower the heat to medium-low, and cook for about 20 to

Lemongrass-grilled Mako Shark with Sticky Rice and Roasted Banana–Mint Sauce; Jacqueline Lau, Roy's Nicolina, Kahana, Maui

30 minutes, or until the water is absorbed. When the rice is ready it will be stuck together and translucent. Set the covered pan aside and keep warm.

Meanwhile, remove the fillets from the refrigerator at least 30 minutes before cooking. Light a fire in a charcoal or wood-burning grill. Just before serving, drain the fillets and cook over a medium-hot fire for 2 minutes per side, or until opaque throughout.

To serve: Place some sticky rice in the center of each plate and sprinkle with the toasted peanuts. Place a shark fillet on top of the rice. Stir the mint into the sauce and pour the roasted banana sauce around. Garnish with lettuce leaves, ogo, and green onions.

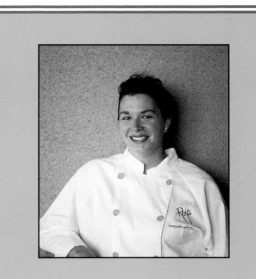

JACQUELINE LAU
Roy's Nicolina, Kahana, Maui

Jacqueline Lau's style of cuisine could be called "Southwest meets Pacific Rim." Lau, a Latina from California, arrived in Hawaii on vacation right after graduation from culinary school in California.

It was 1988, and Roy Yamaguchi had just opened his Hawaii Kai restaurant, causing all sorts of excitement around Honolulu. Lau signed on as pastry chef, and rode the wave of Euro-Asian cuisine being created at the trendsetting restaurant.

She was good enough to be noticed by Yamaguchi, who picked her to open his first international restaurant, Roy's Tokyo, in the fall of 1992. After two months as chef, she returned to Honolulu. Six months later, Yamaguchi sent her off again, this time to open his new restaurant on Guam. Back again in the flagship Hawaii Kai restaurant, she became a master of Roy's culinary style.

In 1993, Roy named her executive chef of his new establishment Nicolina, named after his young daughter. To this new venture, Lau, who is married to island-born Cleighton Lau, brought her culinary influences, creating menus that are resourceful and strikingly original.

Pan-seared Onaga Fillet with Pumpkin and Curry Sauce; Steve Amaral, Kea Lani Hotel Suites & Villas, Wailea, Maui

Pan-seared Onaga Fillet with Pumpkin and Curry Sauce

Steve Amaral
Kea Lani Hotel Suites & Villas
Wailea, Maui

Serves 4

Local vegetables stir-fried with green curry sauce add spicy heat to the creamy smoothness of seared, baked onaga. This is a good company dish: The curry paste and vegetable preparation can be done ahead of time, the onaga is ready after just a few minutes of preparation, and the vegetables are stir-fried at the last minute. Adjust the heat with the number of chilies used.

Green Curry Paste
2 shallots
2 garlic cloves
½ cup peanut oil
10 small green Thai chilies
10 coriander seeds, ground
10 cumin seeds, ground
10 black peppercorns
2 lemongrass stalks, white part only, chopped
1 inch galangal or fresh ginger, peeled and sliced
4 green onions, green part only, chopped
2 bunches fresh cilantro
10 kaffir lime leaves
10 fresh lemon basil leaves
3 kaffir lime zest strips

Four 6-ounce onaga or red snapper fillets, each 1¼ inches thick
¾ cup peanut oil
Salt and freshly ground pepper to taste

Vegetables
½ kabocha pumpkin or butternut squash, or 1 acorn squash
2 Yukon Gold potatoes
1 Japanese or Italian eggplant
2 tablespoons peanut oil
Salt and freshly ground pepper to taste

1 leek, cut into fine julienne
1 carrot, peeled and cut into fine julienne
2 green onions, green part only, cut into julienne

Curry Sauce
2 tablespoons peanut oil
2 lemongrass stalks, white part only, cut into 4-inch lengths
2 green Thai chilies, minced
1 inch galangal or fresh ginger, peeled and julienned
4 kaffir lime leaves
1 cup bamboo shoots, julienned
6 fresh basil sprigs
12 fresh cilantro sprigs
⅓ cup coconut milk
⅓ cup chicken stock (page 199)
Green Curry Paste, above
Vegetables, above
Salt and freshly ground pepper to taste
Fish sauce to taste, preferably Tiparos
Date palm or raw sugar to taste

Garnish
1 cup peanut oil
Blanched leeks, carrots, and green onions, above

To make the curry paste: Put all ingredients in a blender or food processor and blend until smooth. Set aside.

To prepare the fish: Cut each fillet crosswise into four 1½-inch-thick slices. In an ovenproof nonstick or seasoned cast-iron skillet over high heat, heat the oil until almost smoking. Sear the fish for 1 minute on each side, until crisp. Season with salt and pepper. Set aside and keep warm.

To prepare the vegetables: Cut the pumpkin or squash, potato, and eggplant into 1-inch cubes and coat with the oil. Season with salt and pepper, put in a roasting pan, and bake for 15 to 20 minutes, or until three-fourths cooked. Let cool to room temperature. (The vegetables will continue to cook as they cool.) Drain again and set aside.

Blanch the leek, carrot, and green onions in boiling water for 30 seconds. Drain and plunge into ice water. Set aside.

To make the curry: In a wok over high heat, heat the oil and stir-fry the lemongrass, chili, ginger, lime leaves, and bamboo shoots for 1 minute. Add the basil and cilantro, and stir-fry for 1 minute. Reduce heat to medium and add the coconut milk, stock, curry paste, and vegetables. Add the remaining ingredients and simmer for 2 to 3 minutes.

To make the garnish: Remove the leeks, carrots, and green onions from the water and scramble them together. Divide the vegetable scramble into fourths. Drain until nearly dry on paper towels. In a deep fryer or wok over high heat, heat the oil to smoking. In a frying basket or with a slotted spoon, lower one tangle of vegetables into the hot oil and fry for 15 seconds. Remove and drain on paper towels. Repeat with the remaining tangles.

To serve: Place 1 fillet in a corner of each plate. Top the fish with curried vegetables. Place a tangle of fried vegetables on top of each serving.

Steamed Onaga

Daniel Delbrel
La Cascata
Princeville Hotel
Princeville, Kauai

Serves 4

The process of pouring hot oil and soy sauce over gently steamed fish is very Hawaiian. Originally a Chinese preparation, it has become routine in many households. This technique gives fresh, delicate fish a distinctive flavor.

1 pound unpeeled Okinawan or
   regular sweet potatoes
4 ounces baby won bok
   (napa cabbage)

3 ti leaves or 1 banana leaf
Four 7-ounce onaga or red snapper
   fillets
Salt and freshly ground pepper to taste
2 ounces shiitake mushrooms,
   stemmed and thinly sliced
2 whole green onions cut into
   diagonal slivers
1 tablespoon minced fresh ginger
20 fresh cilantro leaves

1 cup peanut oil
1 cup soy sauce
2 teaspoons soy sauce for garnish

In the top of a steamer, cook the unpeeled sweet potatoes for 10 to 15 minutes, or until tender. Peel and slice in half on the diagonal. Steam the won bok for 5 minutes, or until just tender.

Cut ti leaves to fit in a steamer and line the steamer with the leaves. Season the fish with salt and pepper and place, skin-side up, in the steamer over boiling water. Cover and steam for 8 to 10 minutes, or until opaque throughout. Place the steamed fish on top of a metal rack over a shallow pan. Top the fish with the mushrooms, green onion, ginger, and cilantro. In a small saucepan, combine the oil and soy sauce and heat over high heat to almost smoking. Very carefully pour the mixture over the fish.

To serve: Arrange some steamed won bok on the bottom of each plate. Place 1 fillet on top and drizzle some of the pan drippings over the top of the fish. Stand 2 pieces of sweet potato at one end of each fish. Sprinkle ½ teaspoon soy sauce on top of each fish.

Steamed Onaga; Daniel Delbrel, La Cascata, Princeville Hotel, Princeville, Kauai

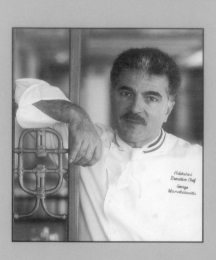

GEORGE MAVROTHALASSITIS
La Mer, Halekulani Hotel, Honolulu, Oahu

Chef Mavrothalassitis doesn't think that taking a classic French dish such as sole veronique and substituting opakapaka for the sole is the way to create a new regional cuisine. He has too much respect for Pacific cuisine and his French heritage (his Greek family emigrated to Marseilles).

The chef known as Mavro prefers to incorporate interesting flavors like tamarind, star anise and lemongrass into basic sauces rather than copy a classic French dish and replace only the main ingredient. He also finds that modern equipment has opened a world of flavor and texture, using his blender to create sauces without cream and butter.

He is adamant about freshness. Although many hotel executive chefs order their supplies over the phone, Chef Mavro will show up at the Honolulu fish auction at 7 a.m. to hand pick his selections. He goes to Chinatown to hunt for new ingredients and quizzes local farmers.

His food is some of the most elegant in the islands, earning La Mer the only Five Diamond Award for both lodging and restaurant categories from the American Automobile Association.

Mavro started out following his father's wishes. He became a mechanical engineer, but his heart wasn't in it. At twenty-eight, he entered culinary school in Marseilles. On graduation, he apprenticed at a series of three-star Michelin restaurants in Roanne, Paris, and Versailles. He then owned and operated his own restaurants, Restaurant La Presquile in Cassis and Restaurant Mavro in Marseilles.

While he was executive chef at Denver's Château Pyrénées, Mavro was discovered by Halekulani Hotel manager Urs Aeby, and brought to Hawaii.

Caroline Bates wrote in *Gourmet*, "His creative cooking and high standards have given the city (Honolulu) a dining experience comparable to a three-star restaurant in France." He was featured in the 1994 Best Hotel Chefs in America series of dinners held at the James Beard House in New York City.

Onaga Baked in Salt Crust with Herb and Ogo Sauce

George Mavrothalassitis
La Mer
Halekulani Hotel
Honolulu, Oahu

Serves 4

The crusted fish makes an impressive presentation. Be careful not to let the rock salt touch the fish when cooking or serving, as it will make the dish salty. The crust will keep the juices in as the fish cooks, making it very moist and tender. Best of all, this light preparation uses no cream, no butter, and no egg yolks.

Salt Crust Dough
6 cups all-purpose flour
2 cups (1 pound) rock salt
3 egg whites
1 cup water

3 tablespoons olive oil
3 garlic cloves, minced
1 pound fresh spinach,
    washed and stemmed
Salt and freshly ground pepper to taste

2 large ti leaves, or 1 banana leaf
One 2-pound onaga or red snapper,
  filleted with skin left on
1 egg white

Herb and Ogo Sauce
6 tablespoons olive oil
2 minced shallots
3 garlic cloves, finely chopped
½ cup dry white wine
1 tomato, peeled, seeded, and chopped
  (page 203)
1 fresh tarragon sprig
1 fresh chervil sprig
2 tablespoons minced green onion,
  green part only
½ cup ogo (seaweed)
Salt and freshly ground pepper to taste

To make the dough: Line a baking sheet with parchment paper or aluminum foil. Sift the flour into a large bowl. Add the rock salt, egg whites, and ½ cup of the water. Mix until it forms a stiff dough. Stir in the remaining ½ cup water. On a floured surface, roll the dough out into a rectangle large enough to wrap the fish. Place the dough on the prepared baking sheet.

To prepare the fish: Preheat the oven to 375°F. In a large sauté pan or skillet over medium heat, heat the oil and sauté the garlic until translucent, about 3 minutes. Add the spinach and sauté until wilted. Add salt and pepper. Cover and refrigerate until cool.

Lay the ti leaves on the dough to protect the fish from the salt. The skin will protect the top of the fish. Arrange the spinach on the ti leaves, then place the 2 fillets, skin-side up and side by side, on top of the spinach. Wrap the onaga in the rock salt dough and shape the dough like a fish. Create fins with extra pieces of dough, and use a spoon to press "eye" and "scale" marks on the dough. Brush the dough with egg white. Bake for 25 minutes, or until pastry is crisp and golden.

To make the sauce: In a medium saucepan over medium heat, heat 3 tablespoons of the olive oil and sauté the shallots until translucent, about 3 minutes. Add the garlic and white wine. Cook to reduce by half. Add the remaining sauce ingredients and the remaining olive oil.

To serve: With a wide spatula and your hands, slide the baked fish onto a platter. At the table, cut the crust lengthwise, removing only the top half. Do not let the salt crystals fall onto the fish. Remove the skin from the fish. Place a portion of fish on each plate with spinach on top of it. Pour some of the sauce around the fish on each plate.

Onaga Baked in Salt Crust with Herb and Ogo Sauce; George Mavrothalassitis, La Mer, Halekulani Hotel, Honolulu, Oahu

Opah Baked in Pistachio Crust with Ginger Essence; Corey Waite, Coast Grill, Hapuna Beach Prince Hotel, Mauna Kea Resort, Kamuela, Hawaii

Opah Baked in Pistachio Crust with Ginger Essence

Corey Waite
Coast Grill
Hapuna Beach Prince Hotel,
Mauna Kea Resort
Kamuela, Hawaii

Serves 4

Ginger and lotus root, both associated with Asian cooking, are used with this dish. Opah, or moonfish, is sealed in a crunchy pistachio crust and served on a bed of chopped vegetables. The crust is delicate and must be browned on medium, not high, heat; a two-step cooking process ensures a browned crust and completely cooked fish.

8 pieces lotus root, cut into
 ⅛-inch-thick slices
Flour for dredging
Olive oil for deep-frying
1 cup pistachio nuts, finely chopped
1 cup fresh bread crumbs
6 vine-ripened tomatoes, seeded and
 cut into ¼-inch dice (page 203)
4 green onions, green part only,
 chopped
2 tablespoons extra-virgin olive oil
1½ tablepoons minced fresh ginger
Salt and freshly ground white pepper
 to taste
Four 6-ounce opah fillets or
 salmon fillets
2 eggs, lightly beaten
2 green onions, green part
 only, chopped
Stir-fried vegetables and steamed
 jasmine rice (page 197) for serving

Dredge the lotus root in the flour to coat evenly. In a medium sauté pan or deep skillet heat 1 inch of oil until it ripples. Deep-fry the lotus root until crisp, about 1 minute. Season with salt and pepper and set aside.

Grind the pistachio nuts and bread crumbs in a blender or food processor. In a medium bowl, mix the tomatoes and green onions together.

In a large sauté pan or skillet over medium heat, heat 1 tablespoon of the olive oil and sauté the ginger for 2 or 3 minutes. Add the tomato mixture, season with salt and pepper, and heat through. Set aside and let cool.

Preheat the oven to 350°F. Season the opah or salmon with salt and pepper, dredge in flour, then egg, then coat evenly with the nut mixture. In a large ovenproof sauté pan or skillet over medium heat, heat the remaining 1 tablespoon olive oil and cook the fillets on each side for 3 minutes, or until lightly browned. Place in the preheated oven and cook for 6 minutes, or until the fish flakes easily.

To serve: Make a bed of the tomato mixture on each plate and sprinkle the entire plate, including the rim, with green onion. Place one piece of fish on each plate. Garnish with the lotus chips. Serve with stir-fried vegetables and steamed jasmine rice.

COREY WAITE
Coast Grill, Hapuna Beach Prince Hotel, Mauna Kea Resort, Kamuela, Hawaii

Corey Waite has the distinction of serving consecutively as executive chef for two luxury hotels operated by the Japan-based Prince Hotel chain: the new Hapuna Beach Prince Hotel, and the recently renovated venerable Mauna Kea Beach Hotel next door.

Waite came to Hawaii to work at the Embassy Suites hotel near Kaanapali on the island of Maui. Prior to that he cooked at the Scottsdale Princess in Arizona and the Ritz-Carlton in Washington, D.C.

He joined the Maui Prince Hotel as executive sous-chef, where he was largely responsible for the fine dining room Prince Court, which specialized in new Hawaiian regional cuisine. After six years at the Maui Prince, he was selected to open Hapuna Beach and redirect the cuisine at the beautiful Mauna Kea Beach Hotel.

Waite is a member of the American Culinary Federation and has won awards at Maui's Seven-Course Symphony competition, as well as a silver medal in the Culinary Salon for the 1985 Grand Buffet Competition in Washington, D.C. He attended the Vespar George School of Art in Boston, where he graduated in illustration and design.

Sweet and Sour Opakapaka

Sam Choy
Sam Choy's Restaurants of Hawaii
Kailua Kona, Hawaii

Serves 4

The combination of pineapple and papaya in a sweet and sour sauce is one of the oldest and most beloved island preparations. This one adds orange juice, fresh ginger, and sweet peppers to flavor the delicate pink snapper. Deep-frying the whole fish in oil is a Chinese technique.

8 ounces Okinawan or regular sweet potatoes

One 5-pound opakapaka or red snapper
Cornstarch for dusting
Salt and freshly ground pepper to taste
3 cups peanut oil

Sweet and Sour Sauce
2 cups orange juice
1 cup water
½ cup cider vinegar
One 1-inch piece fresh ginger, peeled and julienned
1 cup ketchup
1 tablespoon cornstarch dissolved in ½ cup cold water
2 tablespoons peanut oil

1 *each* red and green bell pepper, seeded, deribbed, and cut into ½-inch dice (page 196)
1 cup shiitake mushrooms, stemmed and sliced
1 cup fiddlehead ferns (pohole)
1 cup mung bean sprouts
½ fresh pineapple, diced
½ papaya, cut into ½-inch dice
5 ounces button mushrooms, sliced

1 large ti leaf (optional)

Garnish
1 medium ti leaf or small banana leaf
1 cup chopped ogo (seaweed)
1 fresh cilantro sprig
½ cup green onions, green part only, cut in ¼-inch diagonal pieces
¼ cup black sesame seeds

Bring a large pot of water to boil over high heat and add the potatoes. Boil for 15 minutes, or until a knife inserted in a potato goes in easily. Remove from heat, drain, and set aside.

Rinse the fish and pat it dry with paper towels. With a sharp knife, cut through the flesh to the bone, scoring the flesh in a criss-cross pattern. Dust the fish with cornstarch and season with salt and pepper to taste. In a large wok or deep fryer over medium-high heat, heat the oil to 350°F, or until

rippling. Place the fish in the hot oil head first, turning the tail to the back of the pan, and cook the fish for about 5 minutes, or until the meat flakes easily.

To make the sauce: In a medium saucepan, combine the orange juice, water, vinegar, and ginger. Bring to a boil and cook for 5 minutes. Add the ketchup and the cornstarch mixture. Cook and stir until thickened, about 3 minutes. Set aside and keep warm.

In a wok or medium skillet over medium-high heat, heat the oil and stir-fry the peppers, shiitake, and pohole ferns for 15 seconds. Add the bean sprouts and stir-fry for 15 seconds. Add the pineapple, papaya, and button mushrooms, and stir-fry for 30 seconds. Add the vegetables to the sauce.

To serve: Peel and mash the potatoes. Place the ti leaf on a platter. Place the scoop of potatoes on the ti leaf. Place the whole fish on top of the potatoes, pressing it into position so that it appears to be swimming. Pour the sauce and vegetables over the back and sides of the fish. Sprinkle the back of the fish with shredded ogo and top with cilantro sprig. Sprinkle the fish and vegetables with green onions and sesame seeds.

Sweet and Sour Opakapaka; Sam Choy, Sam Choy's Restaurants of Hawaii, Kailua Kona, Hawaii

Wok-seared Opakapaka with Amaranth, Hearts of Palm, and Okinawan Sweet Potatoes

Kelly Degala
Gordon Biersch Brewery Restaurant
Honolulu, Oahu

Serves 4

When assembled and piled high, this dish has the look of a miniature sci-fi forest. Bright purple Okinawan mashed potatoes form a bed for the sautéed fillets. The amaranth has three colors, and the ogo and tobiko garnishes add the final unworldly touch to this dish.

2½ pounds Okinawan or regular sweet
   potatoes
¾ cup (1½ sticks) unsalted butter,
   cut into pieces
Salt and freshly ground pepper to taste
2 cups peanut oil

Four 6-ounce opakapaka or other mild
   white-fleshed fish fillets
Salt and freshly ground pepper to taste
2 tablespoons peanut oil

Ginger Butter Sauce
1 cup dry white wine
1 teaspoon minced fresh chervil
1 teaspoon minced shallots
1 tablespoon coarsely chopped
   fresh ginger
½ cup heavy (whipping) cream
2 cups (4 sticks) cold unsalted butter,
   cut into tablespoon-sized pieces
Juice of ½ lemon
Salt and freshly ground pepper to taste

Stir-fried Amaranth and Hearts of Palm
1 cup peanut oil
4 garlic cloves, finely chopped
8 ounces hearts of palm,
   cut into julienne
1 pound fresh amaranth, or spinach,
   cleaned and trimmed
4 cups chicken stock (page 199)

Garnish
2 ounces green tobiko
2 ounces red tobiko
2 ounces black tobiko
½ cup ogo (seaweed) sprigs
12 fresh chervil sprigs

To prepare the sweet potatoes: Peel and coarsely chop half the sweet potatoes. In a large pot of salted boiling water, cook the chopped sweet potatoes until tender, about 20 to 25 minutes. Drain, reserving the cooking water. Mash the potatoes, adding the butter in pieces along with ¼ cup of the reserved cooking water. Season with salt and pepper. Set aside and keep warm.

Peel the remaining sweet potatoes and cut them into shoestrings. In a deep-fryer heat 2 cups of the oil to 350°F, or until rippling. Add the sweet potatoes and cook until they rise to the top and are lightly browned, about 1 minute. Drain on paper towels and keep warm.

To prepare the fish: Preheat the oven to 450°F. Season the flesh side of the fillets with salt and pepper. In a large ovenproof sauté pan or skillet over high heat, heat the 2 tablespoons of oil and sear the fillets, skin-side down, until crispy, about 25 seconds. Turn the fish, place in the oven, and bake for 10 minutes.

To make the sauce: In a medium saucepan, combine the wine, chervil, shallots, and ginger. Cook over medium-high heat to reduce the liquid to ⅓ cup. Add the cream and cook to reduce to ½ cup. Lower the heat and whisk the butter into the mixture 1 piece at a time to make a thick sauce. Remove the pan from heat as necessary to keep the mixture just warm enough to melt each piece of butter. Whisk in the lemon juice, salt, and pepper. Strain through a fine-meshed sieve. Set aside and keep warm over tepid water.

To prepare the stir-fry: In a wok over high heat, heat the oil to 350°F, or until rippling. Add the garlic to the oil and stir-fry for 5 seconds. Add the hearts of palm and stir-fry for 20 seconds. Add the amaranth or spinach and stir-fry for another 30 seconds, or until wilted. Add the chicken stock and stir. Set aside.

To serve: Scoop ¾ cup of the mashed potatoes onto the middle of each plate. Place ½ cup of the stir-fry on top. Top with a piece of fish, then ladle ½ cup of the sauce around it. Place 1 tablespoon of each kind of tobiko in the sauce. Scoop 2 tablespoons of the potato puree on top of the fish. Mound ¾ cup of shoestring potatoes on top. The entire structure will be 6 or 7 inches tall. Place sprigs of ogo and chervil on top of the sauce between the tobiko mounds.

Wok-seared Opakapaka with Amaranth, Hearts of Palm, and Okinawan Sweet Potatoes; Kelly Degala, Gordon Biersch Brewery Restaurant, Honolulu, Oahu

Wok-fried Opakapaka with Spicy Black Bean Sauce

Mark Ellman
Avalon Restaurant & Bar
Lahaina, Maui

Serves 4

A delicately flavored fish is paired with a piquant savory sauce of fermented black beans, garlic, ginger, and green onions. The fish is served whole surrounded by the sauce.

One 1½-pound whole opakapaka or
   other mild white-fleshed fish
Flour for dusting
4 cups soybean oil
1 tablespoon olive oil
1 tablespoon Asian sesame oil
1 tablespoon minced garlic
1 tablespoon minced fresh ginger
1 tablespoon finely chopped onion
1 tablespoon Chinese fermented
   black beans
1 tablespoon chili paste
¾ cup dry white wine
6 tablespoons unsalted butter
½ cup sliced whole green onions

    Score the outside of the entire fish into diamond shapes with a sharp knife. Dust the fish with flour. In a large wok or deep fryer over medium-high heat, heat the soybean oil to 350°F or until rippling, and fry the whole fish for 3 to 5 minutes on each side. Lift out with a pair of slotted spoons and drain on paper towels.

    In a small saucepan over medium-high heat, heat the olive and sesame oils and sauté the garlic, ginger, onion, and black beans for 1 minute. Add the chili paste, wine, and butter. Cook to reduce by half. Pour over the cooked fish and garnish with the green onion.

Seared Opakapaka with Crab Rolls

Jean-Marie Josselin
A Pacific Café
Kapaa, Kauai

Serves 4

This dish is a refreshing salad with a warm sautéed opakapaka fillet. The fresh light crab rolls combine greens and crab in a translucent rice paper wrapper. More fresh greens are caught in a bracelet of roasted potato. The opakapaka is simply sautéed to perfection and sauced with a light vinaigrette.

Potato Bracelets
4 Yukon Gold or other white potatoes
2 tablespoons peanut oil

Vinaigrette
1 cup plain rice vinegar
1 cup peanut oil
2 fresh cilantro sprigs, minced
1 garlic clove, minced
1 teaspoon red curry paste
Salt and freshly ground pepper to taste

Basil Puree
1 cup fresh basil leaves
2 tablespoons extra-virgin olive oil

Crab Rolls
4 rice paper wrappers
1 cup frisée (curly endive)
4 leaves red oak lettuce
4 leaves red romaine lettuce
1½ cups amaranth leaves or spinach
½ cucumber, cut into julienne
1 avocado, pitted, peeled, and cut
   into julienne
¼ cup radish sprouts
2 tablespoons pickled ginger
10 ounces fresh lump crabmeat

1 tablespoon peanut oil
Four 6-ounce opakapaka or other mild
   white-fleshed fish fillets
Salt and freshly ground pepper to taste

Garnish
8 Okinawan spinach leaves or regular
   spinach leaves, stemmed
1 ounce radish sprouts
2 tablespoons julienned red ginger
2 tablespoons black sesame seeds
Assorted fresh flowers

    To make the potato bracelets: Preheat the oven to 350°F. Peel the potatoes and

Wok-fried Opakapaka with Spicy Black Bean Sauce; Mark Ellman, Avalon Restaurant & Bar, Lahaina, Maui

slice into ⅛-inch slices. In a medium sauté pan or skillet over medium heat, heat the oil and sauté the potatoes until softened, about 5 minutes. Drain the potatoes on paper towels. In a cup of a nonstick muffin cup, overlap the potato slices to create a ring. Repeat with 3 more cups, using all the potato slices. Bake for 12 minutes, or until crisp and golden. Remove from the oven and let cool in the muffin cups.

To make the vinaigrette: Combine all ingredients in a blender or food processor and process until creamy. Refrigerate for 1 to 2 hours.

To make the basil puree: Place the basil and oil in a blender or food processor and puree until smooth. Pour into a squeeze bottle and set aside.

To make the crab rolls: Place the rice paper wrappers in hot water to separate. Dip the wrappers into the water only until they are translucent, and drape them over the edge of a table or work surface to drip. Divide the remaining ingredients into fourths. Place a wrapper on a work surface and fill the center with one fourth of the greens and vegetables. Divide the ginger in fourths and put one fourth on the greens. Put one fourth of the crab on top of the greens. Roll the wrapper around the filling. The filling will protrude from the open ends. Repeat with the 3 remaining wrappers.

In a large sauté pan or skillet over medium-high heat, heat the oil and sear the fillets, about 1 minute, then turn and sear on the other side, 1 minute. Reduce the heat to medium and cook for 5 minutes on each side, until the fish flakes easily and is golden brown. Season with salt and pepper.

To serve: Cut the crab rolls in half diagonally. Slice a 1½-inch-thick circle off the end of each crab roll. Lay 2 crab roll circles on the center of each serving plate. Stand 2 diagonally cut pieces of crab roll on each serving plate. Place 1 potato bracelet on each plate and stand one fourth of the spinach leaves in each bracelet. Place 1 fish fillet on each pair of crab roll circles. Drizzle the vinaigrette over the fillets and garnish with radish sprouts, red ginger, a sprinkle of sesame seeds, and flowers. Dot basil puree over the vinaigrette.

Seared Opakapaka with Crab Rolls; Jean-Marie Josselin, A Pacific Café, Kapaa, Kauai

Opakapaka with Sesame-Chili Sauce; OnJin Kim, Hanatei Bistro, Honolulu, Oahu

Opakapaka with Sesame-Chili Sauce

OnJin Kim
Hanatei Bistro
Honolulu, Oahu

Serves 4

A halo of fresh asparagus and a flavorful sauce made with ginger and chili make a healthful dish look and taste spectacular. At heart, this is a simple fillet of perfectly cooked fish.

24 asparagus stalks
Four 6-ounce opakapaka or other
  mild white-fleshed fish fillets
½ cup Asian sesame oil
1 teaspoon minced fresh ginger

1 Hawaiian or Thai chili, finely diced,
  or 1 pinch of red pepper flakes
2 tablespoons finely chopped
  green onion, white part only
¼ cup soy sauce
8 fresh cilantro sprigs, stemmed

Holding an asparagus stalk in your hands, bend it until it snaps off. Discard the tough lower end. With a sharp small knife, score the skin of the fish in a criss-cross pattern. Place the asparagus and opakapaka over simmering water in a covered steamer for 5 minutes, until the fish is opaque on the outside but translucent in the center. The asparagus will be crisp-tender.

In a sauté pan or skillet over high heat, heat the oil and sauté the ginger, chili, and 1 tablespoon of the green onions for 12 seconds. Add the soy sauce and bring to a boil.

To serve: Place a fillet in the center of each serving plate. Pour the sauce over the fish fillets. Place 6 asparagus stalks single file around each plate, overlapping the tip of one over the lower end of the next. Garnish the fish with the cilantro sprigs and remaining 1 tablespoon green onion.

Charbroiled Opakapaka with Ginger Coulis

George Mavrothalassitis
La Mer
Halekulani Hotel
Honolulu, Hawaii

Serves 4

This is a true trilogy of flavors. Ginger appears in the winey sauce and as a crispy garnish. Fennel slices braised in stock and wine serve as vegetables. And the fresh taste of watercress is concentrated in the quenelles. All three form an unusual accent to the mild taste of opakapaka.

Ginger Sauce
½ Maui or other sweet white onion, sliced
1 cup dry white wine
¼ cup grated fresh ginger
¼ cup olive oil

Braised Fennel
2 fennel bulbs
½ cup dry white wine
¼ cup water
1 ounce salt pork or fatty bacon, cut into 4 pieces

Watercress Puree
¾ cup fresh watercress sprigs
2 tablespoons olive oil
½ teaspoon fresh lemon juice

Garnish
1 cup peanut oil
¼ cup fresh ginger, cut into fine julienne

Four 6-ounce opakapaka fillets, skin on
¼ cup olive oil
Salt, freshly ground pepper, and cayenne pepper to taste

To make the ginger sauce: In a saucepan, simmer the onion and white wine for 15 minutes over medium heat. Put in a blender or food processor, add the ginger, and puree for 30 seconds. Add the olive oil and puree again until smooth.

To prepare the fennel: Preheat the oven to 350°F. Cut off any stalks and the hard outer layer of the fennel. Cut the bulbs in half. Put the fennel bulbs in a baking pan and cover with the wine and the water. Add the salt pork or bacon and bake for 15 minutes, or until tender. Slice each piece of fennel into three crosswise slices and set aside.

To make the watercress puree: Puree the watercress in a blender or food processor with the olive oil and lemon juice until smooth. The puree will be thick.

To make the garnish: In a small heavy pot over medium-high heat, heat 1 inch of the oil to 350°F, or until rippling. Add the julienned ginger and cook for 10 seconds, or until crisp. Using a slotted spoon, transfer to paper towels to drain.

To prepare the fish: Light a fire in a charcoal grill or preheat a broiler. With a sharp knife, score the skin in a criss-cross pattern. Brush the fish with the olive oil. Sprinkle lightly with the salt, pepper, and cayenne, and grill over medium-hot fire for 4 minutes on each side, until opaque throughout.

To serve: Place 3 slices of fennel evenly around each plate. Pool one fourth of the coulis on each plate. With 2 teaspoons, scoop the watercress puree and form into 12 small rounded quenelles, 3 per plate, and place quenelles between the fennel slices. Arrange the fish, skin-side up, on top of the coulis. Garnish the fish with the fried ginger.

Charbroiled Opakapaka with Ginger Coulis; George Mavrothalassitis, La Mer, Halekulani Hotel, Honolulu, Oahu

Sautéed Opakapaka with Ogo in a Crispy Taro Crust with Watercress, Tomato, and Shiso Vinaigrette

Katsuo Sugiura (Chef Suki)
Ihilani Resort & Spa
Kapolei, Oahu

Serves 4

The corm, or bulb, of Chinese taro is smaller and has a more oblong shape than Hawaiian taro root. It's also easier to find, although either taro root will do. Dry the taro well and make sure the oil is very hot before frying.

2 tablespoons minced fresh basil
3 tablespoons minced fresh parsley
6 tablespoons olive oil
Four 2½-ounce opakapaka fillets
Salt and freshly ground pepper to taste
1 Chinese or Hawaiian taro root or potato, cut into fine julienne

Watercress, Tomato, and Shiso Vinaigrette
¼ cup chopped watercress plus 1 tablespoon water
2 teaspoons minced garlic
3 tablespoons minced shiso leaves
3 tablespoons diced tomato
3 tablespoons finely chopped Maui or other sweet white onion
2 teaspoons soy sauce
2 teaspoons fresh lime juice
1 teaspoon mirin or sweet sherry
2 tablespoons olive oil
Salt and freshly ground pepper to taste

2 tablespoons ogo (seaweed), blanched, patted dry, and chopped
Olive oil for frying

To prepare the fish: In a shallow dish, combine the basil, parsley, and olive oil. Roll the fish in the marinade and let sit at room temperature for 25 minutes.

In a medium sauté pan or skillet over medium-high heat, heat the remaining 2 tablespoons olive oil and sear the fish on both sides until lightly browned. Transfer the fish to a plate and lightly salt and pepper. Let cool.

Peel the taro root or potato and cut off ¼ to ½ inch of the outside peel and flesh of the taro. Using a large chef's knife, cut the taro or potato into spaghettilike strings. Rinse in water and sprinkle with salt. Wrap the strings in a paper towel to absorb the moisture and pat very dry with more paper towels.

To make the vinaigrette: In a blender or food processor, puree the watercress with the water. In a small bowl, whisk together the watercress and remaining ingredients. Set aside.

To assemble: Lay the taro or potato strings out in a tangled strip ½ inch wide by 10 inches long. Position one-third of the fish on the strings. Place the blanched ogo on top of the fish. Roll the fish and ogo up so that the strings adhere to the fish, leaving ½ inch on either end of the roll without strings. Repeat with each fillet. In a wok or large sauté pan or skillet over high heat, heat ¼ inch olive oil. Fry the fish rolls for about 1 minute on each side, or until the taro or potato has browned. Turn the fish carefully with a slotted spatula.

To serve: Ladle vinaigrette over the bottom of each plate. Place the taro strings and fish on top.

Sautéed Opakapaka with Ogo in a Crispy Taro Crust with Watercress, Tomato, and Shiso Vinaigrette; Katsuo Sugiura (Chef Suki), Ihilani Resort & Spa, Kapolei, Oahu

Ginger-crusted Onaga with Miso-Sesame Vinaigrette

Alan Wong
Alan Wong's Restaurant
Honolulu, Oahu

Serves 4

Simple seared onaga is given an Asian touch with miso-seasame vinaigrette, stir-fried vegetables, and ginger-flavored oil. The bits of wasabe add heat.

Ginger-Scallion Oil
½ cup finely minced fresh ginger
½ cup minced whole green onion
Pinch of salt
½ cup peanut oil
1 teaspoon sesame oil

Miso-Sesame Vinaigrette
½ cup rice wine vinegar
¼ cup chicken stock (page 201)
3 tablespoons miso paste
3 tablespoons sugar
2 egg yolks
2 tablespoons chunky peanut butter
1 teaspoon minced fresh ginger

2 teaspoons Dijon mustard
1 cup vegetable oil
2 tablespoons sesame oil
2 teaspoons toasted white sesame seeds (page 196)

4 tablespoons peanut oil
Four 6-ounce 1-inch-thick onaga fillets
Salt and freshly ground pepper to taste
½ cup panko or other course bread crumbs

Stir-fried Vegetables
2 sweet white onions, chopped
12 ounces snow peas
1 zucchini, cut ½-inch dice

16 scallion curls (page 203)
2 tablespoons black sesame seeds

To make the oil: Place the ginger and onions in a deep nonaluminum bowl and season with salt. In a small saucepan heat the peanut oil over medium-high heat until rippling. Slowly pour the oil over ginger mixture; the oil will sizzle and boil up. Stir immediately. Season with sesame oil. Set aside to cool.

To make the vinaigrette: In a deep nonaluminum bowl, mix together 1/4 cup of vinegar, the stack, miso paste, and sugar. In another deep bowl whisk together the egg, peanut butter, ginger, mustard, and remaining 1/4 cup of vinegar. Slowly whisk in the vegetable oil. When the oil is blended, whisk in the sesame oil and sesame seeds. Set aside.

Stir-fried Vegetables: In a medium wok, heat the oil over high heat. Add the vegetables and stir util the onions are translucent and the vegetables are just crisp-tender, about 1 minute. Remove from heat and set aside.

To serve: Divide the vegetables among the plates. Pour the vinaigrette around the vegetables. Place one slice of fish on top of the vegetables on each plate. Drizzle with Ginger-Scallion oil and sprinkle with black sesame seeds. Top each fillet with scallion curls.

Ginger-crusted Onaga with Miso-Sesame Vinaigrette; Alan Wong, Alan Wong's Restaurant, Honolulu, Oahu

Chocolate–Macadamia Nut Toffee Torte; Rodney Weddle, The Dining Room, The Ritz-Carlton Kapalua, Kapalua, Maui

Desserts

Island desserts make use of the Hawaiian cornucopia of tropical fruits: guava, coconut, star fruit, kiwi, papaya, pineapple, mango, banana and lemon, and such exotics as lilikoi (passion fruit) and poho berries (Cape gooseberries). There's plenty of chocolate for those who think dessert's not dessert without it: A flourless chocolate cake laced with macadamia nuts, Hawaiian Vintage Chocolate whipped in a ganache, and a low-fat chocolate chip cookie ice cream sandwich.

Admittedly, many of the desserts are complex examples of the professional chef's art. They are painstakingly explained, step by step. In quite a few cases, the most complicated part of the dessert is the garnish, so you can simplify these by omitting that element, or using only one part of the garnish. Other desserts are easy and quick to prepare, like Mark Ellman's Caramel Miranda or Daniel Delbrel's Cold Tapioca with Coconut Milk, Mango, and Berries.

ED MORRIS
Hawaii Prince Hotel Waikiki, Honolulu, Oahu

The first seven years of Ed Morris' 20-year culinary career were spent as a chef. It wasn't until he discovered baking that he knew he had found what he really loved to do.

After graduation from the food service program at North Seattle Community College, Morris went to work at the Poulsbo Inn in the Puget Sound area of Washington state. In 1980, he moved to Wailea, Maui, and joined the bakery staff at the Inter-Continental Hotel, then moved to Longhi's Deli Pizzeria and Bakery in Lahaina, Maui, where he was responsible for all bakery operations, and finally to the Maui Prince Hotel as assistant pastry chef under the direction of executive chef Gary Strehl.

After three years at the Scottsdale Princess Resort and The Boulders in Arizona, Morris returned to the Prince Hotel chain in 1990 as head pastry chef of the new Hawaii Prince Hotel in Waikiki.

Coconut Crème Brûlée

Ed Morris
Hawaii Prince Hotel Waikiki
Honolulu, Oahu

Serves 8

Crème brûlée served in a nougat shell rather than the traditional ramekin has a light tropical look, especially when served over fruit on a plate decorated with colorful sauces.

Almond Sesame Nougat Shell
½ cup unsalted butter at room temperature
1½ cups sugar
1 cup light corn syrup
2 cups cake flour
¼ cup sliced almonds
2 tablespoons sesame seeds

Crème Brûlée
6 cups heavy (whipping) cream or coconut milk
1 vanilla bean, halved lengthwise
6 tablespoons sugar
12 egg yolks

Rum Syrup
¼ cup maple syrup
2 tablespoons dark rum

4 slices of white sponge cake (page 170)

1 mango, peeled, cut from the pit, and cut into ½-inch dice (page 193)
1½ cups fresh strawberries, hulled and sliced
1½ cups fresh raspberries
1 cup fresh blueberries
3 tablespoons sugar
Crème Anglaise (page 191)
Raspberry puree (page 193)
Mango puree (page 193)

To make the shells: In an electric mixer on medium speed, cream the butter and sugar together. Reduce speed to low and add the corn syrup, then add the cake flour. Stir in the nuts and seeds. Roll the mixture into a 2-inch-thick roll. Cover and refrigerate.

Preheat the oven to 350°F. Line a jelly roll pan with parchment paper or aluminum foil. Cut the roll into ¼-inch-thick slices and place 5 to 6 inches apart on the prepared pan. Bake for 15 minutes, or until golden brown. Let cool slightly. While circles are still warm and pliable, remove from pan and place on an inverted tall glass to shape into cup shapes; try to place the bottom side of the circles against the glass. Let cool on the glass. Store in an airtight container.

To make the crème brûlée: In a heavy, medium saucepan, simmer the cream or coconut milk over medium heat. Scrape the seeds from the vanilla bean halves and put the seeds and pod into the cream. In a double boiler over gently simmering water, whisk the sugar and egg yolks together until the yolks are hot and frothy. With a slotted spoon, remove the vanilla pod from the cream. Stirring constantly, add the hot cream to the egg mixture and mix thoroughly, then remove from heat and cool by setting the bottom of the pan in a bowl of ice water.

To make the rum syrup: In a small bowl, stir together the maple syrup and rum. Put into a squeeze bottle and set aside.

To serve: Preheat the broiler. Place a nougat shell on each plate. Brush the cake slices with the rum syrup and cut them into ½-inch dice. Add 2 tablespoons of the diced cake to each shell. Divide the fruit among the shells. Spoon the custard over the fruit. Sprinkle each with 1 teaspoon sugar and place under the hot broiler until the sugar bubbles, about 15 seconds. Pour ¼ cup crème anglaise on each plate. Put the raspberry sauce and mango sauce in squeeze bottles. Put 3 dots of raspberry sauce in the sauce anglaise on each plate. Squeeze a circle of mango sauce around each dot. Squeeze a larger circle of rum sauce around one mango sauce circle on each plate. With the tip of a knife, draw through the sauces from the center outward in a radial design, creating a spoke effect.

Coconut Crème Brûlée; Ed Morris, Hawaii Prince Hotel Waikiki, Honolulu, Oahu

Five Spoons of Crème Brûlée

Mark Okumura
Alan Wong's Restaurant
Honolulu, Oahu

Serves 8

The aromatic flavorings of each kind of brûlée must infuse in the cream, so each combination is brought to a very slow simmer before being added separately to egg yolks and sugar. The reward is five exotic flavors and a stunning presentation of a much-loved dessert.

Kona Mocha Crème Brûlée

1½ cup heavy (whipping) cream
2 tablespoons moist leftover Kona espresso grounds
3 egg yolks
2 tablespoons sugar
1 teaspoon unsalted butter
½ ounce milk chocolate

Thai Crème Brûlée

1½ cups heavy (whipping) cream
1 lemongrass stalk, white part only, split lengthwise
One 2-inch piece fresh ginger, peeled and cut in ⅛" slices
6 Kaffir lime leaves, minced
1 Hawaiian or Thai chili, halved and seeded
3 egg yolks
2 tablespoons sugar
1 teaspoon unsalted butter

Mango Crème Brûlée

1½ cups heavy (whipping) cream
¼ cup sliced mango, pureed
1 teaspoon fresh lemon juice
3 egg yolks
2 tablespoons sugar
1 teaspoon unsalted butter

Lilikoi Crème Brûlée

1½ cups heavy (whipping) cream
¼ cup lilikoi pulp with seeds, or passion fruit juice or puree
3 egg yolks
2 tablespoons sugar
1 teaspoon unsalted butter

Hawaiian Vintage Chocolate Crème Brûlée

1½ cups heavy (whipping) cream
2 ounces Hawaiian vintage or other good-quality bittersweet chocolate
3 egg yolks
2 tablespoons sugar
1 teaspoon unsalted butter

Garnish

½ cup granulated sugar
2 ounces chocolate, shaved
8 strips crystallized ginger
24 lilikoi seeds
¼ cup diced raw mango
8 coffee beans
8 mint sprigs

To make the Kona mocha brûlée: In a heavy, medium pan over very low heat, bring the cream to a low simmer. Add the espresso grounds and simmer for 5 minutes. Remove from heat and strain through 2 layers of cheesecloth into a small bowl, pressing down on the espresso with the back of a spoon to extract all the flavor.

In a double boiler over simmering water, whisk yolks and sugar together and cook until very thick, about 5 minutes. Place the pan in a bowl of ice water, gently stirring the egg mixture. Stir in the infused cream, butter, and milk chocolate until the chocolate is melted and the mixture is blended.

Remove from the ice bath, place in a small bowl, cover, and refrigerate.

To make the Thai brûlée: In a heavy, medium pan over very low heat, bring the cream to a low simmer. Add the lemongrass, ginger, lime leaves, and chili. Simmer for 15 minutes. Remove from heat and strain through 2 layers of cheesecloth into a small bowl, pressing down on the flavorings with the back of a spoon to extract all the liquid.

In a double boiler over simmering water, whisk yolks and sugar together and cook until very thick, about 5 minutes. Place the pan in a bowl of ice water, gently stirring the egg mixture. Stir in the infused cream and butter until blended.

Remove from the ice bath, place in a small bowl, cover, and refrigerate.

To make the mango brûlée: In a heavy, medium pan over very low heat, bring the cream to a low simmer. Add the mango puree and lemon juice and simmer for 8 to 10 minutes. Remove from heat and strain through 2 layers of cheesecloth into a small bowl, pressing down on the pulp with the back of a spoon to extract all the liquid.

In a double boiler over simmering water, whisk yolks and sugar together and cook until very thick, about 5 minutes. Place the pan in a bowl of ice water, gently stirring the egg mixture. Stir in the infused cream and butter until blended.

Five Spoons of Crème Brûlée; Mark Okumura, Alan Wong's Restaurant, Honolulu, Oahu

Remove from the ice bath, place in a small bowl, cover, and refrigerate.

To make the lilikoi brûlée: In a heavy, medium pan over very low heat, bring the cream to a low simmer. Add the lilikoi pulp and seeds, juice, or puree and simmer for 8 to 10 minutes. Remove from heat and strain through 2 layers of cheesecloth into a small bowl, pressing down on the pulp with the back of a spoon to extract all the liquid.

In a double boiler over simmering water, whisk yolks and sugar together and cook until very thick, about 5 minutes. Place the pan in a bowl of ice water, gently stirring the egg mixture. Stir in the infused cream and butter until blended.

Remove from the ice bath, place in a small bowl, cover, and refrigerate.

To make the chocolate brûlée: In a heavy, medium pan over very low heat, bring the cream to a low simmer. Remove from heat and stir in the chocolate. In the top of a double boiler over simmering water, whisk together the egg yolks and sugar and cook together until very thick, about 5 minutes. Place the pan in a bowl of ice water, gently stirring the mixture. Stir in the chocolate mixture and butter. Remove from the ice bath, place in a small bowl, cover, and refrigerate.

To serve: Preheat the broiler. Spoon each flavor of brûlée into 8 individual ceramic Chinese soup spoons. Sprinkle ½ teaspoon sugar over each. Place under the broiler for 2 or 4 seconds, or until glazed. Top each flavor with the appropriate garnish: a coffee bean on the Kona mocha, crystallized ginger on the Thai, the reserved lilikoi seeds on the lilikoi, diced mango on the mango, and chocolate shavings on the chocolate. Arrange 5 spoons, one of each flavor, side by side on a long rectangular plate and garnish the plate with mint. Repeat with remaining spoons.

MARK OKUMURA
Alan Wong's Restaurant, Honolulu, Oahu

Mark Okumura loves to eat. It's a love that propelled him into the kitchen in the first place. As a pastry chef at both Alan Wong's Restaurant and the prestigious Halekulani Hotel, Okumura is surrounded by food and can be as creative as he likes.

"It's the excitement of coming in and seeing what's been delivered from our farmers that keeps my creativity flowing," says Okumura. They bring him mountain apples, guava, passion fruit, and lychee. One farmer's pineapple mint inspired a new dessert, and the restaurant staff still drools over a creamsicle tart he made with fresh oranges from Kau.

In 1980, he received a degree in culinary arts from Kapiolani Community College in Honolulu. Two years later he added a degree in pastry making.

His practical experience includes a year in a private Hawaii bakery, as well as positions in several European and Asian restaurants, hotels, and culinary schools, among them the renowned Oriental Hotel in Bangkok.

At Alan Wong's, Okumura is stimulated most by the prospect of creating each day's special desserts. His favorite: the sorbets.

Chocolate Cake

Kathleen Daelemans
Cafe Kula
Grand Wailea Resort
Wailea, Maui

Serves 12

A rich prune taste comes through in this dense chocolate cake, made with only 1 tablespoon of oil. The bright drizzles of fruit puree add eye appeal and an intense flavor boost.

1 cup chocolate liqueur
1 cup pitted prunes
1 cup sugar
1 cup nonfat milk
1 tablespoon canola oil
1 tablespoon white wine vinegar
1 teaspoon vanilla extract
1¼ cups unbleached all-purpose flour
⅓ cup unsweetened cocoa powder
1 tablespoon ground espresso or instant espresso powder
1 teaspoon baking soda

Garnish
1 cup raspberry puree (page 193)
1 cup passion fruit puree (page 193)
4 ounces white chocolate, melted
4 ounces bittersweet chocolate, melted

Line the bottom of a 9-inch springform pan with parchment or waxed paper and coat with vegetable-oil cooking spray. In a small saucepan, combine the liqueur and prunes and simmer over low heat for 20 minutes. Set aside and let cool to room temperature. Put in a blender or food processor and blend until smooth.

Preheat the oven to 350°F. In a large bowl, combine the prune puree, sugar, milk, oil, vinegar, and vanilla. In another medium bowl, combine the flour, cocoa powder, espresso, and baking soda. Add the dry ingredients to the wet ingredients in fourths, stirring until completely blended. The batter will be thick.

Pour the batter into the prepared pan and bake for 30 to 40 minutes, or until a toothpick inserted in the center comes out clean. Remove the cake from the oven and let cool for 10 minutes. Remove the sides from the pan, set the pan on a wire rack, and let cool completely.

To serve: Place the sauces and melted chocolates in squeeze bottles. Drizzle each dessert plate with the purees and the bittersweet chocolate. Place a slice of cake on each plate. Drizzle the melted white chocolate over each slice.

Hawaiian Sweet Potato Cakes with Pineapple Ice Cream and Coconut Crème Fraîche

Mark Hetzel
Four Seasons Resort Maui
Wailea, Maui

Serves 4

Hawaii knows how to make the most of sweet potatoes, combining two different colors for these sautéed cakes. Pineapple and coconut add more tropical tastes. Start the ice cream at least two days ahead.

Pineapple Ice Cream
¾ cup diced dried pineapple
3 tablespoons Japanese bourbon or other good bourbon
3 tablespoons water
1½ cups heavy (whipping) cream
3½ cups pineapple juice
½ vanilla bean, halved lengthwise
Four 1-inch pieces ginger, peeled and sliced
9 egg yolks
½ cup granulated sugar
⅔ cup simple syrup (page 202)

Coconut Crème Fraîche
2½ cups heavy (whipping) cream
1½ cups (12 ounces) coconut milk
2 tablespoons buttermilk

Sweet Potato Cake
1 sweet potato
1 Okinawan sweet potato
¼ cup Maui natural sugar or other raw sugar
2 eggs
½ vanilla bean, halved lengthwise
2 tablespoons all-purpose flour
½ teaspoon ground cinnamon
4 tablespoons clarified butter (page 186)
4 strips Candied Ginger (recipe follows)

To make the ice cream: In a medium bowl, stir together the dried pineapple, bourbon, and water (if using a bourbon other than Japanese bourbon, dilute it by adding 1 tablespoon water). Cover and refrigerate overnight.

The next day, put the pineapple in a fine-meshed sieve over a bowl to drain. In a heavy medium saucepan, bring the cream, 1½ cups of the pineapple juice, the vanilla bean, and ginger to a boil over medium-high

Hawaiian Sweet Potato Cakes with Pineapple Ice Cream and Coconut Crème Fraîche; Mark Hetzel, Four Seasons Resort Maui, Wailea, Maui

Chocolate Cake; Kathleen Daelemans, Cafe Kula, Grand Wailea Resort, Wailea, Maui

heat. Set aside. In a small bowl, whisk together the yolks and sugar until pale in color. Stir a large spoonful of the hot cream mixture into the egg yolks, and then add the egg mixture to the pan. Stirring constantly, cook over medium heat for 1½ minutes, or until the mixture thickens and coats the spoon. Strain through a fine-meshed sieve into a medium bowl. Cover and refrigerate overnight.

Whisk the remaining 2 cups pineapple juice and the simple syrup into the chilled custard. Freeze in an ice cream maker according to the manufacturer's instructions When the ice cream is partially frozen but still can be stirred, fold in all but ½ cup of the soaked dried pineapple and return to the freezer. Reserve the ½ cup pineapple for garnish.

To make the crème fraîche: In a medium bowl, blend all the ingredients together and let sit in a warm place (85° to 90°F) overnight.

To make the cake: Grate the sweet potatoes with the coarse holes of a grater or grate in a food processor. Rinse quickly in cold water. In a medium bowl, stir the sugar and eggs together. Scrape the seeds from the

vanilla bean into the flour (discard the pod). Add the flour and cinnamon to the eggs and stir to make a smooth batter. Stir in the grated sweet potatoes.

In a medium sauté pan or skillet, melt the butter over medium-high heat. Place a 3-by-½-inch ring mold in the pan. Spoon ¼ cup of the sweet potato batter into the ring, pressing it together and smoothing the top. Cook for 1½ minutes, or until a light golden crust forms. With a metal spatula, turn the mold, running a knife around the inside of the ring after turning. Cook for 1½ minutes, or until golden on the second side. Using the spatula, remove the pancake in the mold and drain on a paper towel. Remove the mold. Repeat to make 4 pancakes.

To serve: Place each pancake on a dessert plate and dust with confectioners' sugar. Place 2 large tablespoons of coconut crème fraîche beside each cake. Add a scoop of ice cream to each. Scatter the reserved pineapple pieces in 3 small groups of 4 to 5 pieces on each plate, and stand a strip of candied ginger to one side of the cake.

Candied Ginger
Makes 1 cup

10 inches fresh ginger, peeled and
  cut in julienne
½ cup sugar
¼ cup water
1 tablespoon corn syrup
Granulated sugar for dusting

In a heavy, medium saucepan, cover the ginger with water and bring to a boil. Drain, leaving the ginger in the pan. In another heavy, medium saucepan, combine the sugar, water, and corn syrup and bring to a boil over medium-high heat, stirring constantly. Cook for 2 minutes, then pour the mixture over the ginger. Cook the ginger and sugar mixture over low heat for 1 hour. Cover and let stand overnight.

Bring the mixture to a boil, reduce heat to low, and simmer 1 hour. Place a wire rack over a baking pan lined with parchment paper or aluminum foil. Lift the ginger out of the syrup with tongs and place on the rack to dry completely. Roll in granulated sugar and store in an airtight container for up to 1 month.

Flourless Macadamia Nut–Chocolate Cake; Gerard Reversade, Gerard's at the Plantation Inn, Lahaina, Maui

Flourless Macadamia Nut–Chocolate Cake

Gerard Reversade
Gerard's at the Plantation Inn
Lahaina, Maui

Serves 8

This dense cake can be baked a day ahead and finished on the day you plan to serve it. The chocolate, coffee, and macadamia nuts bring the Big Island to mind.

5 ounces bittersweet chocolate
1 cup macadamia nuts
¾ cup granulated sugar
8 eggs, separated
1 cup unsalted butter at
     room temperature
Pinch of salt

Coating and Garnish

1½ cups heavy (whipping) cream
4 ounces bittersweet chocolate
⅔ cup (3 ounces) macadamia nuts,
     chopped and toasted (page 196)
1 tablespoon coffee extract
1 tablespoon Kahlúa or other coffee-
     flavored liqueur
8 fresh strawberries, hulled

Preheat the oven to 375°F. Place a round of parchment or waxed paper in the bottom of an 8-inch round cake pan or springform pan, and tie a collar of parchment or waxed paper around the sides to extend 2 inches over the top of the pan. Butter and flour the

paper. Soften the chocolate by leaving it in a warm place for 10 minutes. Put the nuts and sugar in a blender or food processor and pulverize the nuts.

In a double boiler, beat the egg yolks until very pale in color. Place over barely simmering water to warm. Melt the chocolate in a double boiler over simmering water. Stir in the butter until blended. With a wire whisk, gently stir the chocolate into the yolks. With the same whisk, stir in the nut mixture until the sugar has melted.

In a large bowl, beat the egg whites with the salt until they form stiff peaks. Stir ½ cup of the egg whites into the chocolate mixture to lighten it; then gently fold all of the egg whites into the chocolate mixture. Transfer the batter to the prepared cake pan. Bake for 45 minutes, or until a toothpick inserted in the center comes out clean. Let cool in the pan until just warm to the touch, then invert onto a wire rack and let cool completely to room temperature. The cake will deflate slightly as it cools. It can be covered and set aside overnight at this point.

To make the coating and garnish: In a heavy, medium saucepan, warm 1 cup of the cream over medium heat and stir the chocolate into the cream until completely melted. Place the cake on a wire rack over a baking sheet and pour the chocolate mixture over the cake, completely coating the top

and sides. Smooth with a spatula. Let cool to firm slightly, then press the chopped macadamia nuts into the chocolate. Using a broad spatula, transfer the cake to a plate.

In a deep bowl, beat the remaining ½ cup cream until soft peaks begin to form. Beat in the coffee extract and Kahlúa until stiff peaks form. Put the cream in a pastry bag fitted with a large star tip and pipe rosettes on and around the cake. Garnish with strawberries.

Lemon Cream Cappuccino

Jeff Walters
La Mer
Halekulani Hotel
Honolulu, Oahu

Serves 6

It helps to have a cool kitchen and cool hands when you create chocolate pieces like these little cups. Once you have mastered them, the cups can be used to hold a variety of fillings. Here they are used to present coffee-flavored sabayon and tart lemon cream. The cups, lemon cream, and sabayon should all be made 1 day ahead. You can simplify the preparation by substituting pieces of lady-finger or sponge cake for the bisquit. You'll find the mocha paste at bakers' supply stores.

Chocolate Cups

4 ounces couverture chocolate

Lemon Cream

4 whole eggs
1 cup sugar
1 cup (2 sticks) unsalted butter at
     room temperature, cut into pieces
Grated zest and juice of 4 lemons

Cappuccino Sabayon

3 egg yolks
¼ cup sugar
½ envelope plain gelatin
½ cup brewed cold
     decaffeinated espresso
¼ cup Kahlúa
1 tablespoon mocha paste
1¼ cups heavy (whipping) cream

St. Marc Bisquit

¾ cup almonds
2 tablespoons sugar
11 egg whites
⅞ cup plus 1¼ cups sugar
1 cup cake flour

¼ cup brewed cold
  decaffeinated espresso
⅓ cup heavy (whipping) cream
Cocoa powder for dusting

To make the cups: Cut 6 heavy flexible plastic strips 8¾ inches long and 4 inches wide. In a double boiler over simmering water, melt the chocolate and heat to 100°F. Let the chocolate cool to 90°F and place on a heating pad set on low to maintain that temperature. Lay the strips on a work surface and use a brush or thin spatula to spread a layer of chocolate less than ⅛ inch thick on a strip. When the chocolate has firmed slightly but before it is hard, lift the strip with both hands and curve it, chocolate-side in, to fit inside a 3-inch ring mold or PVC pipe ring. Slip the strip inside the mold, making sure the ends of the strip just meet. Repeat with the remainder of the strips. Roll 1 tablespoon chocolate between your palms and the work surface until it forms a 10-inch-long stick. Make 6; refrigerate to set.

Lay a piece of parchment or waxed paper on a work surface and spread a layer of chocolate ⅛ inch thick or less on the paper. Let set until firm, then lay a second layer of paper over the chocolate, grasp both layers of paper, and flip the entire stack. Remove the first layer of paper, exposing a smooth chocolate surface. Using a 3½-inch-diameter glass or ring mold, cut through the chocolate with the point of a sharp knife to make six 3½-inch-diameter circles. Pull the remaining chocolate away from the circles and set aside.

When the chocolate molds are completely set, lift the plastic circles out of the ring molds and gently peel off the plastic strips, exposing the chocolate cylinders. Lift the chocolate discs from the parchment and place 1 on each serving plate. Warm a sheet pan in a 200°F oven. Put the warm pan on a work surface. With cool hands, gently lift one of the chocolate cylinders, touch one end of it briefly to the warmed pan until it starts to melt, then place immediately in the center of one of the chocolate circles, forming a cup. Repeat with the remaining cylinders. Place in the refrigerator or freezer until set, or store overnight.

To make the lemon cream: In a large bowl, beat the eggs and sugar together until smooth. Add the butter and zest and beat until smooth again. Put in a double boiler over barely simmering water and cook until the mixture thickens, about 12 minutes, stirring constantly. Stir in the lemon juice and cook for 2 to 3 more minutes, stirring constantly. Remove from heat and let cool slightly until it begins to set. Strain through a fine-meshed sieve into a bowl, cover, and refrigerate overnight.

To make the sabayon: In a double boiler over barely simmering water, combine the egg yolks and sugar and beat until it gets thick and foamy, about 1 minute. Sprinkle the gelatin over the espresso. Stir in the Kahlúa and mocha paste. Stir the mixture into the sabayon and place the pan in a bowl of ice water to chill, stirring occasionally. In a deep bowl, beat the cream until soft peaks form and gently fold in the sabayon, blending well. Cover and refrigerate overnight.

To make the bisquit: In a food processor or nut grinder, combine the almonds and sugar and process to a fine meal. In a large bowl, beat the egg whites and the ⅞ cup sugar until stiff peaks form. Sift the almond meal, remaining sugar, and cake flour and gently fold into the meringue.

Preheat the oven to 400°F. Line one half of a jelly roll pan with parchment or waxed paper and spray with vegetable-oil cooking spray. Spread the mixture evenly over the paper and bake for 5 to 7 minutes, until firm. Let cool and cut into 2½-inch circles to fit inside the chocolate cups.

To serve: Remove the cups, lemon cream, and sabayon from the refrigerator. Whip the lemon cream and the sabayon to restore their light texture. With an iced tea spoon or similar small spoon, place a dot of lemon cream in the bottom of each cup to anchor the bisquit. Gently press a bisquit circle inside the cup and soak it with a 2 teaspoons of espresso. Spoon in more lemon cream until the cup is half filled, then fill to within ⅛ inch of the top with the cappuccino sabayon. Repeat with the remaining cups. In a deep bowl, whip the cream until it just starts to thicken. Spoon the cream over the sabayon to the top of each cup. Garnish each cup with a chocolate stick and dust the cup and plate with cocoa powder.

Lemon Cream Cappuccino; Jeff Walters, La Mer, Halekulani Hotel, Honolulu, Oahu

Caramel Miranda

Mark Ellman
Avalon Restaurant & Bar
Lahaina, Maui

Serves 4

This is a dessert to share with others. One large dish is prepared and presented at the table with dessert spoons and forks for everyone. If you prefer, you may divide the ingredients among individual plates.

Caramel Sauce
1 cup plus 6 tablespoons sugar
⅔ cup water
1 teaspoon cream of tartar
1 cup heavy (whipping) cream
1 teaspoon butter

4 ounces Hawaiian Vintage or other fine-quality bittersweet chocolate, broken into small pieces

Fruit
Select 11 fruits from the following fruits, or a total of 2¾ cups of any combination:
¼ cup sliced star fruit
¼ cup sliced peeled kiwi fruit
3 coquitos, or ¼ cup grated fresh coconut
¼ cup sliced peeled mango
¼ cup sliced peeled papaya
¼ cup sliced peeled lychees
¼ cup sliced peeled apple banana or regular banana
¼ cup sliced fresh strawberries
¼ cup fresh or frozen blueberries
¼ cup fresh raspberries
¼ cup fresh blackberries
¼ cup fresh marionberries or boysenberries
¼ cup cubed Maui or other pineapple

2 scoops Macadamia Nut Ice Cream (page 194, 195)

To make the sauce: In a heavy saucepan, combine the sugar, water, and cream of tartar and cook over high heat until coppery brown. Remove from heat and whisk in the cream, continuing to whisk until the mixture has cooled to room temperature. Whisk in the butter. Set aside.

To serve: Preheat the broiler. On a large ovenproof shallow bowl, drizzle the caramel sauce in a lacy design. Sprinkle the chocolate pieces over the caramel and spoon the fruit over the caramel and chocolate. Place the plate under the broiler for 3 to 5 minutes, or until the fruit is heated. Mound the ice cream in the center and serve immediately.

Papaya and Cheese Charlotte with Coconut-Vanilla Sauce

Gerard Reversade
Gerard's at the Plantation Inn
Lahaina, Maui

Serves 6 to 8

Strawberry papaya provides a richer color to the custard, but regular papaya can be used. The coconut milk can be fresh or canned. Make the charlotte a day ahead and refrigerate overnight.

Custard Base
1 cup milk
1 vanilla bean, halved lengthwise
1 envelope plain gelatin
¼ cup cold water
3 egg yolks

¼ cup sugar
3 dozen ladyfingers
1 strawberry or regular papaya, peeled, seeded, and chopped
½ cup heavy (whipping) cream, slightly whipped (no peaks)

Mascarpone Filling
½ envelope plain gelatin
2 tablespoons plus ½ cup cold water
1 cup sugar
3 egg whites

Caramel Miranda, Mark Ellman, Avalon Restaurant & Bar, Lahaina, Maui

Pinch of salt
Grated zest of 1 lemon
1 cup (8 ounces) mascarpone cheese
    at room temperature

Coconut-Vanilla Sauce
1½ cups coconut milk
1 tablespoon vanilla extract

Garnish
2 ounces coconut, flaked
Fresh edible flowers

To make the custard base: In a heavy, medium saucepan, combine the milk and vanilla bean and heat the milk to scalding over medium-high heat. Sprinkle the gelatin over the water and let sit for 3 minutes. Meanwhile, in a small bowl, whisk the egg yolks with the sugar. Whisk a little of the hot milk into the egg yolks, then whisk this mixture into the milk in the pan. Cook over medium heat, stirring constantly, until the mixture is thick enough to coat the spoon, about 2 minutes. Remove from heat. Stir in the gelatin mixture until completely dissolved. Strain the custard through a fine-meshed sieve into a bowl. Set the custard bowl in a bowl of ice water and stir to cool.

Dip the back of each ladyfinger in the custard base. Stand ladyfingers around the sides of an 8-cup charlotte mold, fitting them tightly together. Cover the bottom of the mold with ladyfingers, cutting to fit if necessary.

To finish the custard: Puree the papaya in a blender or food processor. Strain the puree through a fine-meshed sieve. Beat the strained puree into the cooled custard. Fold in the whipped cream. Pour the custard into the mold; the mold will be half full. Refrigerate the mold for at least 15 minutes.

To make the mascarpone filling: Sprinkle the gelatin over the 2 tablespoons water. In a heavy, medium saucepan, combine the sugar and the ½ cup water and boil over medium-high heat to 240°F, or until a small amount dropped into a glass of cold water forms a soft pliable ball. Stir in the gelatin mixture until dissolved. In a large bowl, beat the egg whites with the pinch of salt until soft peaks form. Gradually add the sugar mixture in a small stream, while beating to stiff, shiny peaks. Let cool.

In a medium bowl, beat the lemon zest into the mascarpone. Gently fold the mascarpone into the cooled meringue. Fill the remainder of the charlotte mold with the mascarpone filling and smooth the top. Refrigerate overnight.

To make the sauce: Just before serving, whisk the coconut milk and vanilla together in a small bowl.

To serve: Using a long knife, loosen the charlotte from the side of the mold and invert the mold onto a serving plate. Spoon the sauce around the charlotte. Sprinkle flaked coconut on top of the charlotte and sauce. Garnish with edible flowers.

Papaya and Cheese Charlotte with Coconut-Vanilla Sauce; Gerard Reversade, Gerard's at the Plantation Inn, Lahaina, Maui

MARK HETZEL

The Four Seasons Resort Maui, Wailea, Maui

Mark Hetzel entered the Culinary Institute of America to become a chef, but under the influence of one of his instructors, Albert Kumin, he decided he wanted to specialize in pastry. At Kumin's International Pastry Arts Center, he learned to create desserts that thrilled and excited. Later, at Lenôtre in Paris, he further developed his skills.

Hetzel worked as pastry chef at the Four Seasons Inn on the Park in Houston and set up the pastry program for Rock Resorts on the island of Lanai. At The Four Seasons Resort he uses local fruits, and loves working with chocolate. "I'm not an artist," he says with a laugh, "but I seem to have good luck with chocolate." Hetzel also works to reduce the sugar content of his desserts, keeping them as light as possible.

Kona Coffee–Chocolate Cheesecake with Macadamia Nut Crust

Mark Hetzel
The Four Seasons Resort Maui
Wailea, Maui

Serves 8

A rich mocha flavoring from Hawaii-grown chocolate and coffee is blended with macadamia nuts and bananas in this dessert. The finished cheesecake resembles an individual torte, surrounded by a sea of caramel sauce. Other fruits and sauces can be used for variation.

Crust

2 cups unbleached all-purpose flour
¼ teaspoon salt
¼ teaspoon sugar
7 tablespoons cold unsalted butter, chopped
3 ounces bittersweet chocolate, grated
¾ cup lightly packed brown sugar
½ cup macadamia nuts, finely chopped
½ cup pecans, finely chopped
3 ounces freshly brewed double-strength Kona coffee
¼ teaspoon vanilla extract

Cheesecake Filling

6 ounces bittersweet chocolate, chopped
1 cup heavy (whipping) cream
3 tablespoons ground Kona coffee
1 pound cream cheese at room temperature
½ cup plus 2 tablespoons granulated sugar
4 eggs
¼ cup heavy (whipping) cream
2 tablespoons crème de cacao

Sautéed Bananas

3 tablespoons unsalted butter
2 tablespoons packed brown sugar
2 ripe bananas, peeled
2 tablespoons Tia Maria liqueur

Banana-Caramel Sauce

3 bananas, peeled and diced
3 tablespoons orange juice
1 cup plus 2 tablespoons heavy (whipping) cream
2 cups granulated sugar
½ cup water
5 tablespoons dark rum

Chocolate Ganache

1 cup plus 2 tablespoons heavy (whipping) cream
4 tablespoons unsalted butter
3/8 cup granulated sugar
3 tablespoons unsweetened cocoa powder
5 tablespoons water
9½ ounces bittersweet chocolate, chopped

Macadamia Nut Brittle

2 cups plus 2 tablespoons granulated sugar
1 cup simple syrup (page 202)
1 cup water
¼ teaspoon salt, dissolved in 2 tablespoons warm water
2 cups macadamia nuts
1 tablespoon unsalted butter
¼ teaspoon baking soda, dissolved in 2 tablespoons warm water
¼ teaspoon finely ground coffee

To make the crust: In a medium bowl, blend the flour, salt, sugar, and butter with a pastry blender or your fingers until it is the texture of cornmeal. Add the chocolate, brown sugar, and nuts, and work with your fingertips until all ingredients are blended. Add the coffee and vanilla and mix to form a soft dough. Wrap in plastic wrap and refrigerate for 4 to 6 hours.

When ready to bake, preheat the oven to 350°F. Remove the dough from the refrigerator and roll out ¼ inch thick on a lightly floured surface. Using a 4-inch ring mold as a cutter, cut out 8 circles. Press the remaining dough into eight 4-inch fluted tart shells. Place the shells and circles on a baking sheet and bake in the oven for 8 minutes, or until partially set. Let cool.

To make the filling: In a double boiler over barely simmering water, melt the chocolate and heat to 100°F. In a small saucepan, bring the cream and coffee to a boil over medium heat. Strain through a fine-meshed sieve into the chocolate. Whisk until smooth and shiny.

Preheat the oven to 350°F. In a food processor or electric mixer, beat the cream cheese and sugar together until light and fluffy. Beat in the eggs one at a time, scraping down the sides of the bowl with a rubber spatula and beating the mixture between each addition. Add the cream and liqueur and blend. Mix in the melted chocolate. Pour the mixture into the crust. Bake until the center is just firm, about 15 minutes.

To prepare the bananas: In a medium sauté pan or skillet, melt the butter and brown sugar over medium-high heat. Cut the bananas into thin diagonal slices. Add the bananas to the caramel. Add the liqueur and sauté, tossing or stirring to coat all sides, until the bananas are just tender, about 1 minute. Remove from heat, pour out onto a plate, and let cool.

To make the sauce: Puree the bananas and orange juice in a blender or food processor. In a deep saucepan over medium-high heat, bring the cream to a boil. Remove the cream from the heat and stir in the puree. In a medium sauté pan or skillet, combine the sugar and water and cook over medium-high heat to a golden caramel color. Carefully pour in the hot cream mixture and cook for 3 to 4 minutes, stirring to blend. Strain the mixture through a fine-meshed sieve into a small bowl. Peel and cut the remaining banana into fine dice; you should have ¼ cup. Stir in the rum and diced bananas.

To make the ganache: In a heavy, medium saucepan, combine the cream, butter, and sugar, and bring to a boil. In a small bowl, stir the cocoa and water to blend, then add to the cream mixture. Return the cream to a boil. Place the chocolate in a medium heatproof bowl and pour the boiling cream mixture over the chocolate to melt it. Gently stir the cream mixture and chocolate together. Keep warm over barely simmering water.

To make the brittle: Oil a piece of marble or a baking sheet. In a heavy, medium saucepan, combine the sugar, simple syrup, and water and cook over medium heat to 236°F, or until a small amount dropped into a glass of cold water forms a soft pliable ball. Stir the salt water into the mixture. Continue heating to 265°F, or until the same test yields a hard, pliable ball. Add the

macadamia nuts and continue to cook to a light caramel color, 320°F. Remove from heat, stir in the butter, baking soda mixture, and coffee, and pour out onto the prepared marble or baking sheet. Let cool. Break into large pieces and store in an airtight jar until ready to use.

To assemble: Line a baking sheet with parchment or waxed paper and place a wire rack on top. Place 4 sautéed banana slices on top of each cheesecake. Cover each with one of the baked cookies and press them firmly into place. Unmold the cakes onto the wire rack, sealed-side down. Pour ganache over the tarts to coat them completely. Let set, then carefully lift with a spatula and place on dessert plates. Surround each cake with sauce and stand a 5-by-3-inch piece of macadamia nut brittle in the top of each cake.

Kona Coffee–Chocolate Cheesecake with Macadamia Nut Crust; Mark Hetzel, The Four Seasons Resort Maui, Wailea, Maui

Sam Choy's Pineapple Cheesecake

Robert Eng
Sam Choy's Diamond Head
  Restaurant
Honolulu, Oahu

Makes one 9-inch cheesecake, serves 8

Pineapple flavors the rich filling and dresses the plates in this island version of cheesecake. The simple candylike crust features macadamia nuts, another island touch.

Macadamia Nut Crust
1 cup macadamia nuts
½ cup sugar
3 tablespoons unsalted butter, melted

Filling
1¾ pounds cream cheese at
  room temperature
1 cup sugar
1 teaspoon grated orange zest
1 teaspoon grated lemon zest
4 large eggs
1¼ cups sour cream
5 tablespoons heavy (whipping) cream

1 pineapple, peeled, cored, and finely
  diced

Midori Syrup
1 cup Midori liqueur
¼ cup sugar

Garnish
1 cup crème anglaise (page 191)
½ cup heavy (whipping) cream,
  whipped to stiff peaks
8 fresh mint sprigs

To make the crust: Preheat the oven to 375°F. Line the bottom of an 8-inch springform or cake pan with a circle of parchment paper or aluminum foil. In a blender or food processor, grind the nuts to the texture of coarse meal. Add the sugar and blend. Add the melted butter gradually and blend until all the nut-sugar mixture is moistened. With your fingers, press the mixture evenly into bottom of the prepared pan to create a ¼-inch-thick crust. Bake the crust for 5 minutes, or until lightly browned. Let cool.

Sam Choy's Pineapple Cheesecake; Robert Eng, Sam Choy's Diamond Head Restaurant, Honolulu, Oahu

To make the filling: Reduce the oven temperature to 350°F. In a food processor or an electric mixer on slow speed, cream the cheese, sugar, and zests together until fluffy. Scrape the bowl and beaters with a rubber spatula at each stage of preparation. Add the eggs one at a time, beating thoroughly after each addition. Mix in the sour cream. Add the heavy cream and mix thoroughly. Pour half of the batter into the cooled crust in the pan.

Place the pineapple in a towel, roll up the towel, and wring as much juice as possible out of the pineapple pieces. Sprinkle about ½ cup pineapple evenly over the filling, avoiding the center and outside edge of the batter. Reserve the remaining pineapple for garnish. Pour in the rest of the filling to within ⅛ inch of the top. Press down any pineapple that has floated to the surface so that it does not burn. Set the filled pan in a deeper pan and fill the outer pan halfway up the cake pan with hot water. Place in the oven and bake for 60 to 75 minutes, or until a knife inserted in the center comes out clean.

To make the syrup: In a heavy, small saucepan over medium-high heat, blend the Midori and sugar. Bring to a boil, lower heat to medium, and cook until reduced to a thick syrup, 5 to 7 minutes.

To serve: Place 2 tablespoons of crème anglaise on each dessert plate and spread to cover the plate. Unmold the cheesecake and cut into 8 slices, dipping the knife into hot water to clean it between each cut. Center a slice on each plate. Place the whipped cream in a pastry bag fitted with a medium star tip and pipe a rosette of cream onto the wide portion of each slice. Garnish with a mint leaf. Place 2 tablespoons of reserved chopped pineapple next to each slice. Place the Midori syrup in a squeeze bottle and squeeze in small loops around the plate in the crème anglaise. With the point of a sharp knife, pull through the syrup to form a pleasing design.

ROBERT ENG

Sam Choy's Diamond Head Restaurant, Honolulu, Oahu

Doing what he loves to do, and doing it on an everyday basis, is what drives pastry chef Robert Eng. At Sam Choy's on the slopes of Diamond Head, Eng feels he can take his passion to any level he wants. The potential for creativity is endless.

Quite a switch for a young man who in 1992 graduated from Hampshire College in Amherst, Massachusetts, with a B.A. in history and international relations. While in college, he got a taste of the kitchen as a crew member one summer at the local Burger King. He also worked in a small bakery in the Hampshire Mall, where he tested, baked, and sold baked goods.

Eng found he liked the work enough to return to school in Honolulu at Kapiolani Community College and earn an Associate in Science degree in culinary arts. He graduated with honors and went on to positions as a baker's helper, chef's assistant, and bakery manager.

At Sam Choy's he specializes in cheesecake and crème brûlée, but says he has no favorites. It's the potential for creativity that keeps him going.

Kathleen's Low-Fat Chocolate Chip Ice Cream Sandwich

Kathleen Daelemans
Cafe Kula
Grand Wailea Resort
Wailea, Maui

Makes 8 cookies; serves 4

Hard to believe, but each of these cookies has only 2 grams of fat. Sucanot, which is evaporated cane juice, gives a distinctive molasseslike taste to the cookies. The ice cream should be made a day ahead; purchased low-fat frozen yogurt or sorbet can also be used.

2½ cups whole-wheat flour
1½ teaspoons baking soda
1 teaspoon salt
½ cup (1 stick) unsalted butter
   at room temperature
1 banana, pureed in a blender or food
   processor (½ cup puree)
¾ cup Sucanot (available at natural
   foods stores)
¾ cup lightly packed light
   brown sugar
1 teaspoon vanilla extract
4 egg whites
8 ounces non-dairy chocolate chips
   (available at natural foods stores)

Kathleen's Low-Fat Chocolate Chip Ice Cream Sandwich; Kathleen Daelemans, Cafe Kula, Grand Wailea Resort, Wailea, Maui

4 scoops Kathleen's Virtually
   No-Fat Chocolate Ice Cream
   (recipe follows)
4 ounces bittersweet chocolate,
   melted, or cocoa for dusting
   (optional)

Preheat the oven to 280°F. Line a baking sheet with parchment paper or aluminum foil. In a medium bowl, stir the flour, baking soda, and salt together. Set aside. In another medium bowl, beat the butter, banana puree, Sucanot, and brown sugar until fluffy. Beat in the vanilla, egg whites, and chips. Stir in one fourth of the reserved dry ingredients, then fold in the remainder until blended. The batter will be thick and chunky.

Scoop about 2 tablespoons of batter for each cookie and drop 3 inches apart on the prepared baking sheet. Bake 12 to 15 minutes, until golden brown. Let cool before removing from pan. The cookies will be chewy; if you prefer them crunchy, bake them at 320°F.

To serve: Place a cookie on each serving plate and top with a scoop of ice cream. Lean another cookie against the ice cream. Drizzle with melted chocolate or dust with cocoa if desired.

Kathleen's Virtually No-Fat Chocolate Ice Cream
Makes 2 quarts

4 pounds slightly overripe bananas,
   peeled (10 to 15 bananas)
⅓ cup unsweetened cocoa powder

Line a baking sheet with parchment or waxed paper and place the bananas on the paper. Freeze overnight. Remove from the freezer and place in the bowl of a food processor. Add the cocoa powder. Pulse until smooth and creamy. If necessary, this can be done in two batches. Freeze in an ice cream freezer according to the manufacturer's instructions.

Variations

• Add 1 teaspoon flavor extract such
   as almond or peppermint.

• Add 1 teaspoon liqueur such as
   Grand Marnier or crème de menthe.

• Add the grated zest of ½ orange and
   1 cup almonds, crushed.

Sweet Dim Sum Box

Gale E. O'Malley
Hilton Hawaiian Village
Honolulu, Oahu

Serves 4

This elaborate South Seas dessert sampler was created for President and Mrs. George Bush during one of their visits to Hawaii, where it was spectacularly presented in a bamboo steamer over dry ice.

Marzipan and Azuki Bean Paste Egg Rolls
8 ounces marzipan
½ cup azuki bean paste

Candied Kumquat Pot Stickers
Four 2-inch circles puff pastry dough
4 candied kumquats

Prune Wontons
Peanut oil for deep-frying
4 wonton wrappers
4 tablespoons prune puree

Papaya and Mango Beggar's Purses
½ cup ¼-inch-diced papaya
¼ cup mango puree
2 tablespoons cake or cookie crumbs
Four 6-inch egg roll wrappers

Cream Puffs with Orange Filling
Four 2-inch cream puffs (page 191)
½ cup heavy (whipping) cream
1 tablespoon orange concentrate
½ tablespoon (½ envelope) plain
   gelatin
1 tablespoon water
¾ cup plain fondant
Red paste food coloring

Phyllo Tartlets
3 sheets phyllo dough
½ cup fresh bread crumbs
6 tablespoons unsalted butter, melted

Pistachio Sauce
1 cup crème anglaise (page 191)
3 tablespoons pistachio paste

Garnish
1½ tablespoons confectioners' sugar,
   sifted
½ cup blackberry sauce (page 194)
½ cup chocolate sauce (page 188)
4 small scoops green tea ice cream
   (page 194, 195)
Pastillage fans (optional)
2 cups dry ice chips (optional)

To make the marzipan and azuki bean paste egg rolls: Preheat the broiler. Divide the marzipan in half and roll between 2 sheets of waxed paper into 2 strips, each 1½ inches wide and 8 inches long. Fill a pastry bag fitted with a plain ½-inch tip with the azuki bean paste. Pipe a ½-inch strip of paste along each strip. Roll up lengthwise into a long slender strip and cut into 2-inch-long rolls. Decoratively score the tops of each on the diagonal, making a ropelike effect. Place on a baking pan close under the broiler for a few seconds, or until lightly browned.

To make the candied kumquat pot stickers: Preheat the oven to 375°F. Gently roll the puff pastry rounds on a lightly floured board. Place a kumquat on each, centered on one half of the circle. Fold the dough over, press together, and use a 2-inch round cutter to trim the excess dough. Bake for 10 to 15 minutes, or until puffed and golden brown.

To make the prune wontons: Pour oil to a depth of 2 inches in a heavy pot or skillet. Heat to 375°F, or until almost smoking. Meanwhile, lay out the wonton wrappers and place 1 tablespoon prune puree in the center of each. Fold up 2 opposing corners toward each other, but do not press them together. Grasp the other 2 opposing corners in your fingers and twist them, clockwise, around the two standing corners. Twist until the filling is enclosed and the packet holds its shape, and then turn back the points of each corner like a petal.

Fry the wontons, turning frequently, until golden and crisp, 2 to 3 minutes. Using a slotted spoon, remove from the oil and drain on paper towels. Reserve the oil.

To make the papaya and mango beggar's purses: In a small bowl, combine the diced papaya, mango puree, and cake or cookie crumbs. Lay out the egg roll wrappers and place about 2 tablespoons of the papaya mixture in the center of each. Pull up the edges, gathering at the top, and tie each gently with an 8-inch piece of white string. Reheat the wonton oil to 375°F, or until almost smoking. Fry the purses in the hot oil, turning frequently, until golden and crisp, 2 to 3 minutes. Using a slotted spoon, remove from the oil and drain on paper towels.

To make the cream puffs: In a deep bowl, whip the cream until stiff peaks form. Fold in the orange concentrate.

Sweet Dim Sum Box; Gale E. O'Malley, Hilton Hawaiian Village, Honolulu, Oahu

In a small saucepan, combine the gelatin and water. Heat over low heat until the gelatin is dissolved. Let cool, then fold into the cream mixture. Place the mixture in a pastry bag fitted with a small tip. Make a small X in the bottom of each cream puff and fill the puffs with the cream mixture. Refrigerate until chilled.

In a double boiler over simmering water, heat the fondant until it is liquid enough to coat. Insert a skewer in the bottom of a cream puff and dip the puff into the fondant to coat it. Remove and place on a baking sheet lined with parchment paper or waxed paper to dry. Repeat with the remaining cream puffs. Place 1 dot of paste food coloring on top of each, in the center. Refrigerate.

To make the phyllo tartlets: Preheat the oven to 375°F. Place 1 sheet of the phyllo dough on a sheet of parchment paper or waxed paper. Sprinkle lightly with some of the bread crumbs and drizzle 2 tablespoons of the butter over using a pastry brush. Repeat with another sheet, then place the final sheet on top. Brush the top with the final 2 tablespoons of butter. Using a 3-inch round cutter, cut out 8 circles. Press the circles into eight 2-inch fluted shell tins. Bake 10 to 12 minutes, or until golden and crisp. Let cool.

To make pistachio sauce: In a small bowl, whisk together the crème anglaise and pistachio paste. Set aside.

To serve: Preheat the oven to 350°F. and reheat the pot stickers, beggar's purses, and wontons for 6 to 8 minutes. Dust the beggar's purses with confectioners' sugar. Place the blackberry puree and pistachio and chocolate sauces in squeeze bottles. Divide the serving plates down the center with an elongated S of chocolate sauce. Fill one side with blackberry puree and the other with pistachio sauce. Place 1 beggar's purse in the center of each plate, then alternate the egg rolls, pot stickers, wontons, and puffs around the plates. Place green tea ice cream in the phyllo shells at the last moment and place 2 on each plate.

To duplicate the chef's presentation, top the ice cream with a pastillage fan or similar wafer. Place ½ cup of the dry ice chips in the bottom of each of 4 lacquer boxes (handle the dry ice chips with small tongs; do not touch them with your fingers). Add a small amount of hot water. Place a small bamboo steamer on top of each box and place the plated dessert in the steamer. The hot water will activate the dry ice and steam will pour out.

Jeff Walters
La Mer, Halekulani Hotel, Honolulu, Oahu

Chocolate, marzipan, pastillage, pulled sugar, cinnamon rolls, popovers — Jeff Walters does it all and loves it.

Walters joined Honolulu's top-ranked Halekulani Hotel in August of 1985 as pastry sous-chef, and has been creating spectacular desserts for La Mer as well as the hotel's other facilities ever since.

Originally from Charlotte, Michigan, Walters has made his home in Hawaii for thirteen years. He attended the three-year apprenticeship program for pastry chefs offered by the Hawaii Hotel and Restaurant Industry Employment and Training Trust. He furthered his pastry knowledge by learning the art of sugar pulling and blowing from noted Swiss chef Ewald Notter.

Walters has worked at the Hyatt Regency Waikiki and at the Hilton Hawaiian Village Hotel. He was assistant manager at Honolulu's trendsetting Bakery Europa and a baker at Pâtisserie Le Bon before joining the Halekulani.

Floating Island

Jeff Walters
La Mer
Halekulani Hotel
Honolulu, Oahu

Serves 6

The spun sugar crowns are so ethereal this dessert might be called Floating Clouds. The spun sugar puffs are the most challenging part of the dessert, and can be done ahead of time. The compounds listed in the recipe are pastes, not purees, and are very concentrated. They are available from bakers' supply stores. For a variation, the meringues can be floated in fruit sauce.

Meringue
6 egg whites
⅓ cup sugar
2 tablespoons raspberry compound
1 tablespoon reduced raspberry juice
   (page 193)

Pistachio Sauce
2½ cups milk
¾ cup sugar
½ vanilla bean, halved lengthwise
8 egg yolks, beaten
1 tablespoon pistachio compound

Caramelized Pistachios
⅓ cup sugar
1 tablespoon water
¼ teaspoon fresh lemon juice
¾ cup pistachios, toasted (page 196)
1 tablespoon butter
2 tablespoons reduced raspberry juice
   (page 193)

Angel Hair Swirl
1 cup sugar
½ cup corn syrup
¼ cup water

To make the meringue: Cut six 3-inch squares of parchment paper or aluminum foil. In a large bowl, combine the egg whites and half of the sugar. Beat until frothy, then gradually add the remaining sugar while beating until stiff glossy peaks form. Beat in the raspberry compound and the reduced raspberry juice.

In a large pot bring the water to a boil, then reduce to a simmer. Place the meringue in a large pastry bag fitted with a large plain tip and pipe the meringue onto the parchment paper squares in 6 mounds. Lift a parchment square by the corner and place in the water, meringue-side down. Let the meringue poach for 3 minutes, then lift it by grasping a corner of the paper with tongs. Peel off the paper by pressing gently on the meringue with the back of a spoon or a knife. Flip the meringue with a slotted spoon and poach on the other side for 3 minutes. It will begin to expand when it is done. Remove from water with a slotted spoon and let dry on paper towels. Repeat with the remaining meringues. Place all the meringues in the refrigerator to chill.

To make the sauce: In a medium saucepan, combine the milk and sugar. Scrape the seeds out of the vanilla pod pieces into the milk, then add the pods as well. Bring the mixture to a boil. Remove the pods with a slotted spoon and lower heat to medium. Stir a large spoonful of the hot milk mixture into the eggs, then gradually add this mixture to the hot milk, stirring constantly, and cook until the sauce thickens and coats the spoon. Immediately strain through a fine-meshed sieve into a medium bowl, stir in the pistachio compound, cover, and refrigerate.

To make the caramelized pistachios: Oil a large baking sheet. In a small, heavy saucepan, combine the sugar, water, and lemon juice and cook over medium-high heat until the sugar starts to caramelize around the edges. Remove from heat, stir in the pistachios, and return to medium heat until the sugar is golden brown, stirring constantly. Remove from heat and stir in the butter and raspberry juice. Pour the mixture onto the prepared sheet pan and separate the pistachios with a fork. Let cool.

To make the sugar swirl: Cover a work surface with newspaper. Place 2 long oiled wooden dowels, each ½-inch in diameter, 16 inches apart on the work surface so that they extend over the edge. Cover the floor under the dowels with newspaper. In a double boiler over boiling water, combine all the ingredients and cook to 295°F, or until a small amount dropped into a glass of cold water separates into hard, brittle threads. Use a wet pastry brush to wash the crystals that form on the sides of the pan back into the cooking sugar. When the sugar has reached 295°F, remove from the heat and let cool until the syrup has thickened to the consistency of thick honey. Using a wire whisk that has been cut off to leave long straight wires sticking out of the handle, dip the whisk into the syrup and wave it quickly back and forth over the dowels. Thin sugar strands will spin off the whisk wires and fall across the dowels. Dip and repeat 3 more times. Lift the spun sugar off the dowels with your hands and shape gently into a loose 3-inch beehive of sugar strands. Cut off any straggling strands with scissors. Set aside in a cool dry place. Repeat to form 5 more beehives.

To serve: Pool ½ cup sauce into each of 6 cream soup plates and arrange a meringue in the center of each. Place 6 caramelized pistachios in the sauce around each meringue and crown each meringue with a spun sugar puff.

Floating Island; Jeff Walters, La Mer, Halekulani Hotel, Honolulu, Oahu

Tropical Fruits with Passion Fruit Sabayon and Balsamic Syrup; Jeff Cabiles, Kea Lani Hotel Suites & Villas, Wailea, Maui

Tropical Fruits with Passion Fruit Sabayon and Balsamic Syrup

Steve Amaral with Jeff Cabiles
Kea Lani Hotel Suites & Villas
Wailea, Maui

Serves 4

A syrup made from balsamic vinegar is a light and refreshing accent for tropical fruits. The syrup could be used by itself over ice cream or other desserts. Kula raspberries are grown on the slopes of Maui's Haleakala volcano; any tart red raspberries may be substituted.

Balsamic Syrup

1 cup balsamic vinegar
3 tablespoons packed brown sugar

Sabayon

2 egg yolks
4 tablespoons passion fruit jelly
2 tablespoons sugar
1 cup Prosecco or other dry
   sparkling wine
2 lilikoi (passion fruit), peeled, seeded,
   and diced
1 jackfruit, peeled and diced
1 pineapple, peeled, cored, and diced
2 star fruit, cut in ¼-inch slices
12 fresh strawberries, hulled
4 kiwi fruit
4 cups fresh Kula or other raspberries

To make the syrup: In a heavy, small saucepan, combine the vinegar and the sugar, and cook over medium-high heat to reduce by half, or until syrupy. Cover and refrigerate.

To make the sabayon: In a double boiler, combine the egg yolks, jelly, and sugar, and whisk until smooth. Place over simmering water and add the wine. Whisk the mixture constantly until it thickens and coats a spoon. Set aside.

To serve: Divide the fruit among 4 serving plates and arrange attractively on each plate. Spoon 3 tablespoons warm sabayon over the fruit on each plate, and 3 more tablespoons of sabayon around the side of each plate. Drizzle 2 tablespoons balsamic syrup over the fruit on each plate.

JEFF CABILES
Kea Lani Hotel Suites & Villas, Wailea, Maui

Lanai-born Jeff Cabiles learned to bake by baking. After graduating from Honolulu Community College's commercial baking program in 1980, he became a baker and dietary worker delivering food to hospital patients at the Queen's Medical Center in Honolulu.

When the Maui Marriott Hotel needed a production baker who could handle the baking for three in-house restaurants and a catering department that served five thousand people at one seating, Cabiles was their man.

From Maui he transferred to the Marriott on Marco Island, Florida, then to the Torrance, California, Marriott, where he was part of the opening culinary team. From there he moved to the Marriott Host International in Los Angeles. By then he was managing a bakery with forty-six employees who produced baked products for such outlets as Pizza Hut and Dunkin' Donuts.

Cabiles began creating signature desserts with a tropical flavor when he joined the Royal Lahaina Resort & Tennis Club at Kaanapali on the island of Maui.

When the Kea Lani Hotel opened he took his talents over to the resort located on Maui's south shore.

Cabiles has also taught baking at Maui Community College and instructed seminars on wedding cakes, bread sculptures, and gingerbread villages.

Heather Carlin
David Paul's Lahaina Grill, Lahaina, Maui

Heather Carlin has always loved to bake. Even as an accountant, pushing figures around on a spreadsheet, she knew she'd rather be whipping up a sweet dessert.

The twenty-six-year-old approached David Paul Johnson, owner of David Paul's in the old whaling port of Lahaina, Maui, and he took her on as his pastry chef. For him she has created such desserts as Red Chili Carrot Cake, Triple Berry Pie, and Chocolate Macadamia Nut Flan.

Carlin worked for a short time with pastry chef Casey Lodgson at Roy's Kahana Bar & Grill. She also has a degree from Virginia Tech's Hotel and Restaurant Management School, where she worked as the assistant manager of the catering department.

Fresh Fruit in Vanilla-infused Balsamic Vinegar

Heather Carlin
David Paul's Lahaina Grill
Lahaina, Maui

Serves 4

A Hawaiian twist on the Italian dessert of simple fresh fruit with balsamic vinegar. Here the vinegar is infused with vanilla and fresh fig, served with tropical fruit. Any variety of fresh fruit can be used. The vinegar can be infused with vanilla alone if you wish.

Vanilla-infused Balsamic Vinegar
1 cup balsamic vinegar
1 vanilla bean, halved lengthwise
1 ripe fig, chopped

1 ripe papaya, peeled, seeded, and
   cut into ½-inch dice
4 to 5 ripe figs, cut into pieces
3 cups fresh strawberries, hulled and
halved
1 cup fresh raspberries
¼ cup sugar

Garnish
4 fresh strawberries, sliced and fanned
4 fresh mint sprigs

To make the vinegar: In a medium non-aluminum saucepan or skillet, heat the vinegar until nearly boiling over medium-high heat. Add the vanilla bean to the vinegar. Reduce heat to low and simmer for 5 minutes. Remove the vinegar from the stove and add the fig. Let sit for at least 4 hours or up to overnight at room temperature. Cover and refrigerate before serving.

To serve: Strain the vinegar. In a large bowl, toss the papaya, figs, and berries together with the sugar and vinegar. Divide among 4 glasses and garnish with strawberries and mint sprigs.

Honey and Hawaiian Vintage Chocolate Ganache with Gold-dusted Chocolate Leaves and Poha Berry Sauce

Philippe Padovani
The Manele Bay Hotel
Lanai City, Lanai

Serves 4

A rich-as-Croesus dessert combines the melting texture and taste of honey ganache with bittersweet chocolate frills garnished with gold leaf. The slightly tart sauce provides counterpoint to the richness of the chocolate. It can, of course, be made without the touch of gold; sprinkle just a little confectioners' sugar on each frill if you prefer.

Kiawe Honey Ganache
¼ cup heavy (whipping) cream
½ Polynesian or other vanilla bean,
   halved lengthwise
2 tablespoons Kiawe or other fragrant
   honey
2 ounces Hawaiian vintage or other
   fine-quality bittersweet chocolate,
   chopped
2 tablespoons unsalted butter

Poha Berry Sauce
1 cup milk
½ Polynesian or other vanilla bean,
   split lengthwise
3 egg yolks
¼ cup sugar
1 cup fresh poha berries or Cape
   Gooseberries or raspberries

Chocolate Leaves
9 ounces Hawaiian vintage or other
   high-quality bittersweet chocolate
2 tablespoons canola or other light
   vegetable oil
2 sheets gold leaf (optional), or
   confectioners' sugar for dusting

To make the ganache: In a heavy saucepan, bring the cream to a boil over medium-high heat. Add the vanilla bean and honey. Set aside for 15 minutes to infuse the flavors. Remove the vanilla bean and add the chocolate, stirring until the chocolate has melted and the ganache is smooth. Pour into a small bowl and stir in the butter. Set aside and let cool.

To make the sauce: In a medium saucepan, bring the milk to a boil over medium-high heat and add the vanilla bean. Set aside for 15 minutes to infuse the flavors. Remove the vanilla bean. In a medium bowl, combine the egg yolks and sugar and whisk until smooth. Pour the hot milk over the mixture, stirring constantly. Pour the egg mixture into the pan and cook over medium heat, stirring constantly, until the sauce is thick enough to coat the spoon. Be careful not to let it boil. Place the berries or raspberries in a medium bowl and strain the sauce through a fine-meshed sieve into the bowl over the berries. With a mixer, blend until smooth. Place the bowl in a bowl of ice water to chill the sauce quickly. Cover and refrigerate.

To make the chocolate leaves: In a double boiler over simmering water, melt the chocolate and heat to 100°F. Add the oil to the chocolate and blend well. Let cool to 90°F. Using 2 ungreased jelly roll pans, pour half of the melted chocolate evenly over the surface of each pan, spread it out, and let cool completely. With a spatula, putty knife, or your thumbnail, scrape the chocolate off the pan in 1½-inch frilled strips and pinch the loose pieces at one end for a leaflike design. Make 6 leaves for each plate. Using the point of a knife, with very light strokes, brush off the gold from the back of half of a gold sheet until the gold attaches to the chocolate. Set aside.

To serve: Use 4 chilled dessert plates. Fill a pastry bag with the ganache and pipe 5 dots about 1 inch in diameter near the edge of each plate. Attach 1 leaf per dot in a pleasing pattern. If using confectioners' sugar instead of gold, dust with confectioners' sugar. Divide the sauce among the plates and pour a border of sauce around each leaf pattern.

Honey and Hawaiian Vintage Chocolate Ganache with Gold-dusted Chocolate Leaves and Poha Berry Sauce; Philippe Padovani, The Manele Bay Hotel, Lanai City, Lanai

Fresh Fruit in Vanilla-infused Balsamic Vinegar; Heather Carlin, David Paul's Lahaina Grill, Lahaina, Maui

Lilikoi Cheesecakes; Lisa Siu, 3660 on the Rise, Honolulu, Oahu

Lilikoi Cheesecakes

Lisa Siu
3660 on the Rise
Honolulu, Oahu

Serves 6 to 8

The silky, colorful lilikoi filling contrasts with the crunchy macadamia crust and crisp coconut tuiles. Although it's simple to do, the presentation is spectacular.

Macadamia Crust

½ cup (1 stick) cold unsalted butter
¼ cup packed brown sugar
½ cup macadamia nuts, finely chopped
1 cup unbleached all-purpose flour

Lilikoi Filling

1 envelope plain gelatin
¼ cup room temperature water
1 pound cream cheese at room temperature
1 cup granulated sugar
5 egg yolks
¼ cup lilikoi puree (page 193)
1½ cups heavy (whipping) cream

Glaze

1 cup apricot jam
⅓ cup lilikoi puree (page 193)

Garnish

4 Coconut Tuiles (recipe follows)
½ cup lilikoi puree (page 193)
⅓ cup raspberry puree (page 193)
Confectioners' sugar for dusting
8 fresh mint sprigs

To make the crust: Preheat the oven to 350°F. Butter eight 4-inch tart tins and line the bottom of each with parchment or greased waxed paper. In a food processor with a paddle attachment or using a pastry cutter, cut together the butter, brown sugar, and nuts. Blend in the flour and mix until it resembles coarse meal. Place the dough in the pan and, using your fingers, lightly press the pastry evenly over the bottom of the pan and one fourth of the way up the side. Bake for 10 to 12 minutes, or until it just starts to brown. Let cool.

To make the filling: Sprinkle the gelatin over the water and let sit. In a medium bowl beat together the cheese and ½ cup of the sugar. In a double boiler over barely simmering water, whisk the egg yolks and remaining ½ cup sugar together until pale in color, about 3 to 4 minutes. Cook the mixture until it thickens and coats the spoon. Stir in the gelatin mixture until completely dissolved. Stir in lilikoi puree. Beat the egg mixture into the cheese mixture, scraping down the sides of the bowl occasionally. In a deep bowl, whip the cream until it forms soft peaks. Gently fold the whipped cream into the custard. Pour into the cooled crust or tart shells, level the top, and refrigerate until chilled and firm.

To make the glaze: In a small pan, warm the apricot jam over low heat until melted. Strain through a fine-meshed sieve and stir in the lilikoi puree. With a spoon, spread the glaze over the chilled cheesecakes. Refrigerate for 1 hour to set the glaze.

To serve: Unmold the tarts and cut each in half. Offset 2 halves on each plate, sliding 1 half halfway past the other. Add 1½ teaspoons of lilikoi sauce to each side and dot with 1 teaspoon of raspberry sauce. Pull through the dots with the point of a knife from the center to the outside to create a radial design. Set a coconut tuile half vertically between the tart halves. Dust the plate with confectioners' sugar. Garnish with mint.

Coconut Tuiles
Makes 9

½ cup (1 stick) unsalted butter at
   room temperature
¾ cup sugar
1⅓ cups cake flour
½ cup shredded coconut
1 egg, beaten
2 egg whites, slightly beaten
1 teaspoon vanilla extract

Preheat the oven to 325°F. Butter and lightly flour 2 baking sheets. In a medium bowl, cream the butter and sugar together. Gradually stir in the cake flour until smooth. Stir in the coconut. Stir in the egg, egg whites, and vanilla. Spread on the prepared pan in 6- to 8-inch circles 4 inches apart. Bake for 10 to 12 minutes until the edges are browned and the centers are cooked through. Cut 3 to 4 of the warm cookies in half and transfer all the cookies to wire racks to cool. Store in an airtight container.

LISA SIU
3660 on the Rise, Honolulu, Oahu

Lisa Siu's desserts are a good reason to keep your head when ordering the main meal at 3660 on the Rise. Siu, wife of chef Russell Siu, is a "local" who attended high school at Honokaa on the Hamakua Coast of the Big Island of Hawaii.

In 1978, she enrolled in the food service program at Maui Community College. This led to positions at the Plaza Club in Honolulu and a series of private clubs in Texas and California.

3660 is located in the Kaimuki neighborhood of Honolulu. The quality of its food and its location between two affluent parts of town have made it a solid favorite with residents. Siu's crème brûlée at 3660 and her vanilla bread pudding at the new Kakaako Kitchen near downtown Honolulu have earned her raves.

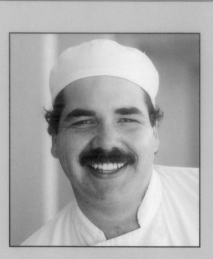

MANUEL GARCIA

La Cascata, Princeville Hotel, Princeville, Kauai

Manuel Garcia came to Princeville as pastry chef under the direction of Judy Capertina and continued when Daniel Delbrel joined the resort as executive chef. The Southern California native previously worked as chef tournant at The Lodge at Pebble Beach and as an assistant baker at the Inn at Spanish Bay.

Garcia received his Associate of Culinary Arts degree from Cypress College in California. In 1993 he won the Richard T. Keating Award from the Culinary Institute of America.

White Chocolate–Mango Mousse

Manuel Garcia
La Cascata
Princeville Hotel
Princeville, Kauai

Serves 8

Fresh fruit and featherweight mousse create beautiful little cakes circled with a band of mango petals. The chocolate garnish can be used on almost any dessert; the dark and light contrasting bands of chocolate are particularly pretty against the golden mango.

Cake

1½ cups (7 ounces) macadamia nuts, coarsely chopped
1½ cups confectioners' sugar
⅔ cup unsifted cake flour
4 whole eggs
3 egg whites
3 tablespoons granulated sugar
3 tablespoons unsalted butter, melted

Mousse

2½ ounces white chocolate, chopped
1¼ cups mango puree (page 193)
2 egg whites
2½ cups heavy (whipping) cream
2 egg yolks
⅓ cup granulated sugar
1 envelope plain gelatin
¼ cup cold water

Garnish

4 mangos, peeled, cut from pit, and cut into thin slices
1½ tablespoons apricot jelly
8 fresh strawberries, hulled and cut into crosswise slices
24 fresh blackberries
¼ cup ganache (page 188)
Chocolate Coils (recipe follows)

To make the cake: Preheat the oven to 375°F. Line a jelly roll pan with parchment paper or aluminum foil. In a blender or food processor, grind the nuts and the confectioners' sugar to a fine powder. Combine with the cake flour in a large bowl and sift. Regrind and resift particles that do not go through the sifter. Add the whole eggs, beating until the batter is thoroughly blended. Set aside.

In a large bowl, beat the egg whites until foamy. Gradually beat in the sugar until the meringue forms stiff peaks. Stir a large spoonful of batter into the meringue to lighten it, then fold the remaining meringue into the batter. Stir a large spoonful of batter into the melted butter, then pour the butter into the batter and blend. Spread the batter evenly in the prepared pan and bake for 10 minutes, or until just set. Let cool.

To make the mousse: Melt the white chocolate in a double boiler over barely simmering water. Strain the chocolate through a fine-meshed sieve and return to the double boiler to keep warm. Put one half of the mango puree in a medium bowl and place the bowl in a larger bowl of ice water. In a deep bowl, beat the cream until soft peaks form. Cover and refrigerate.

In a medium bowl over hot water, beat the egg yolks and the ⅓ cup sugar together until foamy. Place the egg mixture in a mixer and set to beat at medium-high speed.

Sprinkle the gelatin over the cold water and let set for 3 minutes. Meanwhile, in a small saucepan over low heat, warm the other half of the mango puree. Do not overheat; it should just be tepid. Stir in the gelatin mixture and whisk gently until completely dissolved. Stir in the melted chocolate until smooth. Pour into the cool mango puree and stir to blend the warm and cool mixtures; you want to cool the puree to add the remaining ingredients, but not so much that it sets up in the bowl.

When the mixture is cooled and starting to thicken, remove the egg mixture from the mixer; it should be pale yellow in color and thick enough that a slowly dissolving ribbon forms when some of it is dribbled on the surface. Stir a large spoonful of the mango mixture into the egg mixture, blending well. Pour the egg mixture into the mango mixture and whisk gently to blend. Stir a large spoonful of mixture into the meringue, then gently fold the meringue into the mixture. Stir a large spoonful of mixture into the whipped cream, then gently fold the whipped cream into the mixture. Chill in refrigerator.

To serve: Using eight 4-inch ring molds, cut cake circles and leave them in the bottoms of the molds. Reserve

24 mango slices. Line the inside walls of the molds with a ring of overlapping mango slices, slipping the last slice under the first to complete the circle. Ladle the mousse into mango-lined molds. Level off with the back of a knife.

In a small pan over medium heat, slightly warm the jelly and stir to blend. Remove the molds from the refrigerator and cover the top of each with the jelly glaze. Place the molds on a baking sheet and refrigerate until the glaze sets.

Fan 3 of the reserved mango slices on each dessert plate. Add a ring of overlapping strawberry slices and 3 blackberries. To remove the molds, lift each mold from the baking sheet with a wide metal spatula. With a thin-bladed knife, cut around the mold between the mousse and the mold to loosen. Using your fingers, set the mold on an inverted glass or other flat-bottomed object that is slightly smaller than the ring mold and press the mold down gently. Carefully lift the entire mousse assembly and place it on the plate next to the mango slices. Place the ganache in a squeeze bottle or pastry bag fitted with a very small tip and pipe a spiral around one side of the dish. Garnish each mousse with a chocolate coil.

Chocolate Coils
Makes 8 coils

2 ounces white chocolate
2 ounces milk chocolate
2 ounces dark bittersweet chocolate

You will need a Styrofoam block about 15 inches square, push pins, and eight 9-by-2-inch heavy flexible plastic strips. Pin one end of each strip to the Styrofoam. Separately melt each chocolate in a double boiler over barely simmering water. Put each chocolate in a squeeze bottle. Squeeze stripes of the chocolates over the plastic strips, letting them overlap in places. Spread the chocolate out slightly to a ⅛-inch thickness with a long thin spatula. When the chocolate has cooled slightly but is still pliable, twist the strips of plastic with the chocolate into a spiral shape and pin the other end of each strip to the Styrofoam to keep the coils in place. Keep in a cool place until set. When ready to use, unpin the strips and gently peel away the plastic, leaving the chocolate coils.

White Chocolate–Mango Mousse; Manuel Garcia, La Cascata, Princeville Hotel, Princeville, Kauai

The Nobleman's Dessert Box

Gale E. O'Malley
Hilton Hawaiian Village
Honolulu, Oahu

Serves 4

Gale O'Malley's desserts are never simple, but the stunning presentations are worth the effort. For his Dessert Box he nestles a shiny Chinese hat and sorbets in a lacquer box, then provides a lid of decorated chocolate. The mounds of chestnut pastry cream and ganache are a treat even without the box.

Dessert Box Lid

2 ounces white chocolate, chopped
4 ounces bittersweet chocolate, chopped
12 pastillage flowers (optional)

Mandarin Orange Sauce

½ cup mandarin orange slices, or
  1 tablespoon Grand Marnier
1 cup crème anglaise (page 191)
4 Chinese Hats (recipe follows)
4 small scoops mango sorbet
  (page 195)
4 small scoops pineapple sorbet
  (page 195)
4 small scoops lilikoi sorbet (page 195)
4 pastillage fans (optional)
12 fresh raspberries
4 fresh mint sprigs

To make the lids: Select four 6-inch by 1½-inch-deep lacquer boxes to hold the desserts. Lay a piece of heavy flexible plastic over a work surface. In a double boiler over simmering water, melt the white chocolate and heat to 100°F. Let cool to 90°F. Pour the chocolate onto the plastic. Using a wood-grain tool (available at home

painting centers), "walk" the tool across the chocolate, spreading it into a wood-grain pattern. Place the plastic in the refrigerator to chill and set the chocolate.

In a double boiler over simmering water, melt the bittersweet chocolate and heat to 100°F. Let cool to 90°F. Remove the plastic from the refrigerator and place on the work surface. Pour the dark chocolate at one end of the wood-grain pattern. With a long, thin spatula, quickly spread the dark chocolate across the wood-grain design, being careful not to disturb the design. Spread more dark chocolate beside the first strip, making a piece large enough to form the lids for the boxes. Build up the chocolate until it is slightly thicker than ⅛ of an inch. Return to the refrigerator to chill and set. Using the box as a pattern, outline

The Nobleman's Dessert Box; Gale E. O'Malley, Hilton Hawaiian Village, Honolulu, Oahu

four box lids on the chocolate. With a sharp knife, cut out the shape of the box lid. Pull away the extra chocolate from around the lids. Place a second piece of plastic over the cut-out lids. Holding the two plastic pieces together with your hands, flip them over. Peel the plastic from the tops of the lids, revealing the wood-grain design. If using the pastillage flowers, with a spoon place 3 dots of warm chocolate on one area of each lid and press 3 pastillage flowers into the chocolate. Place the lids in the freezer.

Put the leftover chocolate back in a double boiler and remelt over simmering water. Place in a pastry bag fitted with a fine tip and pipe 3 large free-form closed loops in the bottom of each of the lacquer boxes. Place in the freezer to set.

To make the sauce: Finely dice the mandarin orange slices and stir into crème anglaise. Set aside. Or, add 1 tablespoon Grand Marnier to the crème anglaise and stir until smooth.

To serve: Remove the lacquer boxes from the freezer. Using a spoon, carefully fill in the chocolate loops with orange sauce. Place one Chinese hat in one end of a lacquer box. Place 1 small scoop of each sorbet to the side of the center of the box. Affix the pastillage fan, if using, to the sorbets and lean it against the side of the box. Scatter raspberries in the box and garnish with a mint sprig. Repeat with the other boxes. Place each box on a lacquer tray. Remove the chocolate lids from the freezer and tilt a lid against each box. Serve immediately.

Chinese Hat
Makes 4

Chocolate Cake
4 eggs
⅔ cup sugar
¼ cup cocoa
Pinch of salt
¾ cup sifted cake flour
3 tablespoons unsalted butter, melted

Chestnut Pastry Cream
2 cups milk
½ cup sugar
2 eggs
1¼ tablespoons cornstarch
1¼ tablespoons all-purpose flour
2 tablespoons sugar
½ cup chestnut puree
2 tablespoons rum

Ganache
1 cup heavy (whipping) cream
1 pound semisweet chocolate, chopped

¼ cup raspberry jam
3 ounces bittersweet chocolate
4 candied violets

To make the cake: Preheat the oven to 350°F. Line the bottoms of two 9-inch round cake pans with parchment paper. Warm a deep bowl: fill the bowl with warm water, empty it, and dry thoroughly. In the warmed bowl, beat the eggs and sugar together until the mixture thickens and a ribbon forms when a spoonful is drizzled on the surface. Fold the cocoa powder into the egg yolk mixture. Gradually fold the salt and two thirds of the flour into the egg yolk mixture. Blend a large spoonful of the mixture into the butter, then gently fold the butter and the remaining one third of the flour into the mixture. Pour into the prepared pans and bake 10 minutes, or until a toothpick inserted in the center comes out clean. Let the pan cool for 10 minutes, then remove the cakes from the pans and cool completely on a wire rack. You will have two ½-inch-thick cakes.

To make the pastry cream: In a heavy, medium pan, scald the milk over medium heat, add the sugar, and whisk gently until the sugar dissolves. In a medium bowl, mix the eggs, cornstarch, flour, sugar, and the chestnut puree together. The mixture will be gray in color. Pour one half of the milk mixture slowly into the egg mixture, stirring constantly. Place the remaining milk mixture over medium heat and

stir the egg mixture into it. Heat, stirring constantly, until it thickens, about 10 minutes. Remove from heat and stir in the rum. Place the pan in a bowl of ice water and let cool. Cover and refrigerate. When the pastry cream is thoroughly chilled, beat the heavy cream in a deep bowl until soft peaks form. Gently fold the whipped cream into the pastry cream.

To make the ganache: In a heavy pan bring the cream to a boil over medium-high heat. Remove from heat. Add the chocolate and stir until melted. Let cool thoroughly.

To assemble: Place the sponge cake circles on a work surface and cut each into 4 4-inch circles (reserve leftover pieces for other uses). Spread 4 circles with a thin layer of raspberry jam and a thin layer of ganache. Top each with a second circle. Place in the freezer to set, 2 to 3 hours.

In a double boiler over simmering water, gently warm the ganache to pouring consistency. Remove the cakes from the freezer and place them on a work surface. Mound the chestnut pastry cream into a smooth cone on top of each cake. Set a wire rack over a baking pan lined with waxed paper and place the shaped cakes on the rack. Pour ganache over the cones to completely cover. Chop 1 ounce of the chocolate very fine. Press the chopped chocolate pieces around the bottom edge of the cakes. Place in the refrigerator until the ganache has set, 2 to 3 hours.

Chop the remaining 2 ounces of chocolate. In a double boiler over simmering water, melt the chocolate. Put the chocolate in a pastry bag fitted with a small plain tip. Pipe chocolate in narrow loops from the center of each cone down around the sides. Place a dot of warm chocolate on the peak and press a candied violet into the chocolate. Refrigerate until firm, about 5 minutes.

Black Sesame Nougatines with Green Tea Mousse and Glazed Chestnuts

Katsuo Sugiura (Chef Suki)
Ihilani Resort & Spa
Kapolei, Oahu

Serves 4

These napoleonlike desserts blend the Asian tastes of black sesame seeds and green tea with the old world flavor of caramelized chestnuts. Star fruit lends a tropical look and taste, although other fruit could be used.

Nougatines
¾ cup plus 2 tablespoons unsalted butter
1¼ cup granulated sugar
¼ cup honey
⅓ cup heavy (whipping) cream
2 cups black sesame seeds
¾ cup bread flour

Green Tea Mousse
15 egg yolks
1⅓ cups granulated sugar

2 tablespoons green tea powder
4 cups heavy (whipping) cream
2 tablespoons Grand Marnier
8 egg whites

36 Glazed Chestnuts in Caramel Sauce (recipe follows)
Confectioner's sugar for dusting
3 star fruits, cut into ⅛-inch slices
½ cup raspberry puree (page 193)
48 fresh raspberries
8 fresh mint sprigs

To make the nougatines: Line a baking sheet with aluminum foil, or spray with vegetable-oil spray. In a heavy saucepan, combine the butter, sugar, honey, and cream and bring to a strong boil over medium-high heat, stirring constantly. Cook until the mixture reaches 240°F, or until a small amount dropped into a glass of cold water forms a soft, pliable ball. In a small bowl, mix together the sesame seeds and flour, then stir it into the sugar mixture and mix well. Drop by heaping tablespoonfuls 3 inches apart onto the prepared baking sheet. Bake for 12 minutes, or until golden. Let cool. Makes about 38 pieces; store in an airtight container.

To make the mousse: In a large bowl, beat the yolks until foamy. Gradually add one cup of the sugar, beating continually, until fluffy. Beat the green tea powder into the egg mixture until thoroughly blended. Stir in the cream and Grand Marnier until blended. Cover and refrigerate. In a large bowl, beat the egg whites until foamy. Gradually add the remaining ⅓ cup sugar while beating until the egg whites form stiff, glossy peaks.

To assemble: Lay 1 nougatine on a serving plate. Put the mousse in a large pastry bag fitted with a large plain tip and pipe a ¾-inch-thick mound of mousse on the nougatine. Pour 1 large spoonful of caramel sauce on the mousse and press 3 glazed chestnuts into the caramel. Place another nougatine on top of the mousse. Repeat with a second layer of mousse, caramel, and 3 more chestnuts. Dust a nougatine heavily with confectioners' sugar and place on the top. Heat a metal skewer over high heat and lay it across the sugar in a criss-cross design, letting the heat melt and caramelize the sugar. Repeat with the remaining nougatines and mousse. Cut each star fruit slice in half. Garnish each plate with 3 teaspoons raspberry puree, three star fruit halves, 6 raspberries, 3 chestnuts, and a mint sprig.

Glazed Chestnuts in Caramel Sauce
Makes 3 cups

36 canned chestnuts, drained
2 cups water
1 cup sugar

Pat the chestnuts dry with paper towels. In a heavy saucepan, combine the water and sugar and stir over low heat just until the sugar dissolves. Increase the heat to medium-high and continue to cook, brushing away the crystals that form on the sides of the pan with a damp brush. Do not stir. Let the mixture boil until the sugar turns golden brown. Remove from heat immediately and place the pan in a bowl of ice water. When the caramel has cooled slightly, dip the chestnuts in the caramel to coat, and set aside on aluminum foil or waxed paper. If the caramel thickens too much before use, warm it gently to melt.

Black Sesame Nougatines with Green Tea Mousse and Glazed Chestnuts; Katsuo Sugiura (Chef Suki), Ihilani Resort & Spa, Kapolei, Oahu

Chilled White Nougat with Candied Fruits and Guava Coulis

Jeff Walters
La Mer
Halekulani Hotel
Honolulu, Oahu

Makes 8

A cool dessert of molded nougat flavored with candied fruit, sliced almonds, and crunchy nougatine. The guava coulis adds color and flavor.

Crushed Nougatine
1 cup sliced almonds, toasted
  (page 196)
⅓ cup corn syrup
½ cup granulated sugar

White Nougat
1 cup granulated sugar
¼ cup water
4 egg whites
¼ cup confectioners' sugar, sifted
⅔ cup candied fruit, marinated
  overnight in kirsch and drained
½ cup sliced almonds, finely chopped
  and sifted
Crushed Nougatine, above
1 cup heavy (whipping) cream

Guava Coulis
1 cup guava puree (page 193)
½ cup sugar

Garnish
6 fresh mint sprigs
6 nougatine curls or wafer cookies

To make the nougatine: Lightly oil a piece of marble or a baking sheet. In a blender or food processor, grind the almonds to a fine powder. Sift the powder, regrind the large pieces to a powder. In a heavy, medium saucepan over low heat, warm the corn syrup and add the sugar, stirring slightly to dissolve. Increase the heat to medium-high and cook for about 10 minutes, or until it turns a light caramel color. Do not stir. Use a pastry brush to brush the sugar crystals down the sides of the pan as the sugar cooks, and lift the pan occasionally and roll the contents around. Remove from heat, stir in the ground almonds, and pour onto the prepared surface. Let cool slightly, then roll the mixture out with an oiled rolling pin to approximately 14 by 14 inches. Cut six ½ by 7 inch strips. While they are still warm and pliable, twist each strip around a pen, spoon-handle, or other small cylinder shape

in a spiral. Set the spirals aside to cool. Let the remainder of the nougatine sheet cool completely, then crush with the rolling pin and sift the pieces, recrushing as necessary until the texture is uniform.

To make the nougat: Line a baking sheet with parchment paper or aluminum foil. Set eight 3-inch ring molds or PVC pipe pieces on the sheet. In a heavy, medium saucepan, combine the granulated sugar and water and bring to a boil over medium-high heat. Continue boiling until it reaches 240°F, 5 to 6 minutes, or until a small amount dropped in a small glass of water forms a small pliable ball. While the sugar is boiling, beat the egg whites in a large bowl until frothy. Gradually beat in the powdered sugar until soft peaks form. When the sugar reaches temperature, slowly pour it into the meringue in a thin stream, beating constantly until the sugar is absorbed and the meringue is thick and cold, about 4 minutes. Fold in the candied fruit, almonds, and crushed nougatine.

In a deep bowl, whip the cream until soft peaks form and fold gently into the meringue mixture. Place the mixture in a large pastry bag fitted with a large plain tip and pipe into the molds, filling tightly. Smooth off the tops with the back of a knife and put the sheet with the filled molds in the freezer for 2 hours.

To make the coulis: In a heavy, medium saucepan, combine the puree and sugar, stir to blend, and bring to a boil over medium-high heat. Remove from heat, cool, and refrigerate.

To serve: With a broad spatula, loosen the molds from the baking sheet and place 1 mold off center on each plate. Run the tip of a thin knife around the inside of each mold to loosen the nougat and lift off the molds. Pour 3 tablespoons guava coulis on each plate, and garnish with a mint sprig and a nougatine curl or wafer cookie.

Chilled White Nougat with Candied Fruits and Guava Coulis; Jeff Walters, La Mer, Halekulani Hotel, Honolulu, Oahu

Oheloberry Dessert in Tulip Cookies

Peter Chilla
Coast Grill
Hapuna Beach Prince Hotel,
Mauna Kea Resort
Kamuela, Hawaii

Serves 8

The tart red oheloberry, said to be a favorite of the goddess Pele, grows only on the volcano side of the Big Island of Hawaii. Other small berries like cranberries, currants, gooseberries, or blueberries can be substituted. Bread flour, with its higher gluten content, is specified for the cookies; all-purpose flour can be used, but the cookies will break more easily.

2 envelopes plain gelatin
½ cup cold water
1 cup oheloberries or other small fresh
  berries
1½ cups sugar
½ cup Riesling or other sweet
  white wine
1 cup heavy (whipping) cream
2 tablespoons plain yogurt
8 Tulip Cookies (recipe follows)

1 cup heavy (whipping) cream
4 star fruit, sliced
4 kiwi fruit, peeled and cut into
  ⅛-inch-thick slices
4 pear apple (Asian pear), peeled and
  cut into ⅛-inch-thick slices

Garnish
Chocolate curls (see page 189)
8 fresh mint sprigs

Sprinkle the gelatin over the water and let soak for 3 minutes. Meanwhile, combine the berries, sugar, and wine in a medium saucepan. Bring to a boil over medium-high heat, stirring until sugar dissolves. Cook for 2 to 3 minutes. Remove from heat and add the softened gelatin. Process in a blender or food processor to make a coarse puree. Let cool completely.

In a deep bowl, beat the cream until it forms soft peaks. Fold three fourths of the berry mixture and the yogurt into the whipped cream; reserve the remaining berry mixture. Fill the tulip cookies with the mixture and chill in the refrigerator for 45 minutes to 1 hour before serving.

To serve: In a deep bowl, beat the cream until it forms stiff peaks. Place 3 slices of star fruit, 1 kiwi slice, and 2 small fans of pear apple slices on each serving plate. Spoon one eighth of the reserved berry mixture around fruit on the edge of each plate. Place a filled tulip cookie in the center of each plate. Fill a pastry bag fitted with a medium star tip with the whipped cream and pipe cream onto the oheloberry filling. Sprinkle chocolate curls over the cream and garnish each plate with a mint sprig.

Tulip Cookies
Makes 8 cookies

7 tablespoons unsalted butter
7 tablespoons sugar
½ cup bread flour
3 egg whites
2 ounces bittersweet chocolate,
  chopped

Preheat the oven to 350°F. Invert a large baking sheet and spray the back very lightly with vegetable-oil cooking spray. In a medium saucepan or skillet, melt the butter and sugar over low heat. Transfer the mixture to a medium

Oheloberry Dessert in Tulip Cookies; Peter Chilla, Coast Grill, Hapuna Beach Prince Hotel, Mauna Kea Resort, Kamuela, Hawaii

bowl, stir in the flour, and add the egg whites. Whisk until the batter is smooth.

Using a large serving spoon, drop circles of batter on the prepared baking sheet. With a spatula or table knife, spread the batter into triangles. Bake until golden brown, about 12 minutes.

Quickly remove the cookies from the pan and, while they are still warm, place them over an inverted glass or cup and bend them into a cupped tulip shape. Let them cool in this position. If they become too stiff to bend before you are finished, return them momentarily to the oven to warm them slightly again.

When the cookies are cool, set them upright. In a double boiler over barely simmering water, melt the chocolate. Use a small pastry brush to paint the inside of each cookie with the chocolate. Let set. The cups can be made early in the day and kept in a cool (not refrigerated) area until ready to fill.

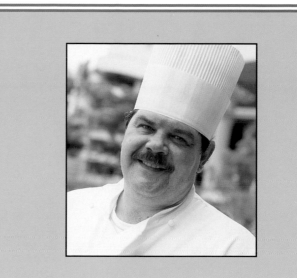

PETER CHILLA

Coast Grill, Hapuna Beach Prince Hotel, Mauna Kea Resort, Kamuela, Hawaii

Peter Chilla's father wanted him to become a chef, but Peter was more interested in engineering. Today he does both, for his desserts are constructed in such as way as to dazzle even the most fanatic dieter.

In both the pastry kitchen of the Mauna Kea Beach Hotel, and in its sister hotel the Hapuna Beach Prince, located next door, Chilla incorporates the bounty of the islands into his desserts. He loves using macadamia nuts, fresh island pineapple, papaya, poha berries, and guava.

Trained in the classical European tradition, Chilla apprenticed in West Germany and Canada before moving to the Biltmore Hotel in Coral Gables, Florida. From there he went to Turnberry Isle Yacht and Country Club and the Jockey Club in Miami. In 1990 he joined the prestigious old Mauna Kea.

Chilla is a member of the Chaîne des Rôtisseurs.

Panna Cotta and Exotic Fruit with Lilikoi-Apricot Sauce

Philippe Padovani
The Manele Bay Hotel
Lanai City, Lanai

Serves 4

A simple dessert of molded cream topped with fruit becomes exotic when the fruits are Hawaiian and lilikoi turns up in the sauce. The mild citrus taste of the panna cotta and the cinnamon-flavored sauce blend well with many fruits. The recipe is easily adapted to whatever fruits are at their peak in your market.

Lilikoi-Apricot Sauce
½ cup water
¼ cup sugar
1 clove
½ vanilla bean, halved lengthwise
1 cinnamon stick
3 apricots, peeled, pitted, and diced
¼ cup lilikoi pulp

Panna Cotta
2½ cups heavy (whipping) cream
½ cup sugar
2½ tablespoons butter
1 vanilla bean, halved lengthwise
1 tablespoons lemon zest, grated
½ envelope (½ tablespoon) plain gelatin
2 tablespoons cold water
3 tablespoons Cointreau

Hawaiian Fruits
1 mango, peeled, and sliced
1 papaya, peeled, seeded and sliced
1 small pineapple, peeled, cored, and cubed
1 banana, peeled and sliced
12 lychees, peeled

4 fresh mint sprigs

To make the sauce: In a small saucepan, combine the water, sugar, clove, vanilla bean, and cinnamon stick over medium-high heat and bring to a boil. Add the apricots and lilikoi pulp and simmer over low heat until the apricots are tender. When cooked, blend the sauce until smooth, then strain through a fine-meshed sieve into a bowl and set aside to chill.

To make the panna cotta: In a small saucepan, combine the cream, sugar, butter, vanilla bean and lemon zest over medium-high heat and bring to a boil. Remove from heat and let sit, covered, for 15 minutes to infuse the flavors. Sprinkle the gelatin over the water and let set for 3 minutes. Add the Cointreau and gelatin mixture to the infused cream, whisking well to combine. Strain through a fine-meshed sieve into a bowl. Pour an equal amount into each of 4 dessert bowls. Place in the refrigerator until set.

To serve: In a large bowl toss the fruit with the sauce. Arrange the fruit attractively on top of each bowl of panna cotta. Garnish each with a sprig of mint.

Panna Cotta and Exotic Fruit in Lilikoi-Apricot Sauce; Philippe Padovani, The Manele Bay Hotel, Lanai City, Lanai

Bittersweet Chocolate Pie

Kathleen Daelemans
Cafe Kula
Grand Wailea Resort
Wailea, Maui

Serves 6

Guiltless, silky smooth, and rich-tasting—this may be the perfect chocolate pie. The basic recipe can be garnished with different kinds of fruit and different colors of chocolate. Silken tofu is available in the Asian foods section of grocery stores; it is creamier than firm tofu. Fruitsource is a liquid sweetener.

Crust

10 low-fat graham crackers, broken
2 tablespoons maple syrup
2 tablespoons canola oil
2 tablespoons water

Filling

½ cup Fruitsource (available at natural foods stores), or honey
¼ cup maple syrup or honey
21 ounces silken tofu
1 tablespoon vanilla extract
¾ cup unsweetened cocoa powder

Garnish

¾ cup raspberry puree (page 193)
½ cup banana slices
18 fresh raspberries
6 fresh mint sprigs
Unsweetened cocoa powder
    for dusting
6 tablespoons grated white chocolate

To make the crust: Preheat the oven to 350°F. In a food processor, grind the crackers to fine crumbs. Pour into a medium bowl, add the remaining ingredients, and mix together until it forms a mass. Or, to make by hand, combine all the ingredients in a small bowl and stir together until the mixture forms a mass. Put the dough in an 8-inch pie pan and press with your fingers to form a ¼-inch-thick shell. Bake for 8 minutes, or until set and lightly browned. Let cool in the pan.

To make the filling: In a medium saucepan over medium heat, combine the Fruitsource and maple syrup or honey and cook for 5 minutes. Combine this mixture and all the remaining filling ingredients in a blender or food processor and blend until smooth. Pour the mixture into the cooled pie crust. Refrigerate for at least 2 hours, or until firm but puddinglike.

To serve: Cut the pie and place slices on individual dessert plates. Sprinkle 2 tablespoons of raspberry puree on each plate and garnish with a few banana slices, 3 fresh raspberries, and a mint leaf. Sprinkle the rim of the plate with cocoa powder, and sprinkle 1 tablespoon white chocolate over the pie.

Bittersweet Chocolate Pie; Kathleen Daelemans, Cafe Kula, Grand Wailea Resort, Wailea, Maui

Deep-Dish Banana-Coconut Cream Pie; Mark Hetzel, The Four Seasons Resort Maui, Wailea, Maui

Deep-Dish Banana Coconut Cream Pie

Mark Hetzel
The Four Seasons Resort Maui
Wailea, Maui

Serves 6 to 8

Mounded high in a sugar crust, resting on a thick layer of chocolate and nougat, caramel mousse and coconut cream support arches of chocolate-glazed bananas that are hidden by whipped cream until the pie is cut. Plan ahead; the dough for the crust must be made the day before, and the nougat can be made several days ahead. You can save time by using ready-made peanut brittle.

Sugar Crust Dough
1 cup (2 sticks) unsalted butter
½ cup confectioners' sugar
2¼ cups unbleached all-purpose flour
1 egg white

Chocolate Glaze
7¼ ounces bittersweet chocolate, chopped
18 ounces coating chocolate
5 tablespoons peanut oil

Peanut Nougat (recipe follows)

6 finger bananas or other small bananas, peeled

Caramel Cream
4 teaspoons plain gelatin
½ cup plus 3 tablespoons cold water
1 cup plus 6 tablespoons sugar
3 egg whites
5 egg yolks
1¾ cup heavy (whipping) cream, whipped to stiff peaks

Coconut Mousse

2 teaspoons plain gelatin
2 tablespoons Coco Lopez or other
    coconut syrup
1 cup heavy (whipping) cream
½ cup coconut milk
¼ cup flaked fresh coconut (page 190)

Topping

2 cups heavy (whipping) cream
1 tablespoon sugar

To make the dough: In a medium bowl, mix the butter and the sugar together. With a pastry blender or your fingers, work the flour into the butter mixture until it resembles coarse meal. Stir in the egg white and stir until it forms a ball. Wrap the dough in plastic wrap and refrigerate overnight.

The next day, bake the crust: Preheat the oven to 350°F. Line the bottom of a 10-inch springform pan with parchment paper or butter the pan. Roll the dough out ¼-inch thick on a lightly floured board. Using the bottom of the springform pan as a template, cut a circle out of the dough and place it in the bottom of the pan. Cut a strip of dough 3 inches wide and long enough to circle the inside of the pan, and roll it up into a spiral. Place it on end in the pan, and unroll it around the inside of the pan. Press the ends and bottom seam together to seal. Bake until light golden, 8 to 10 minutes. Let cool.

To make the glaze: In a double boiler, melt the chocolate over barely simmering water and stir in the coating chocolate. Cook until the chocolate melts and reaches 100°F. Stir in the oil and blend thoroughly.

Remove the crust from the pan, place it on a plate, and brush it with the chocolate glaze. Crumble the

peanut nougat with a small mallet or other heavy object. Reserve ¼ cup and sprinkle the remaining ¾ cup in a thin layer over the bottom of the crust. Line a baking sheet with aluminum foil or waxed paper. With a small fork, dip the bananas in the chocolate glaze and place on the prepared pan to set.

To make the caramel cream: In a small bowl, sprinkle the gelatin over ¼ cup of the water. In a heavy medium saucepan, cook ½ cup plus 2 tablespoons of the sugar over medium heat to a pale amber, 320°F. Slowly pour in ¼ cup of the water, stirring, and continue cooking to 250°F, or until a small amount dropped into a glass of cold water forms a soft pliable ball. Meanwhile, in a large bowl, beat the egg whites with 2 tablespoons of the sugar on high speed until they form stiff peaks. When the caramelized sugar is at the proper temperature, slowly add it to the whites, beating the whites continually as you pour. Add the gelatin mixture and beat until the mixture cools to room temperature.

In a deep bowl, beat the egg yolks until pale in color. In a heavy medium saucepan, combine the remaining ½ cup plus 2 tablespoons sugar and the remaining 3 tablespoons water. Cook over medium heat to 250°F, or until the mixture is thick and bubbling but has not browned. Gradually beat the sugar into the egg yolks, continuing to beat until the mixture cools. Fold the yolk and egg white mixtures together, then gently fold into the whipped cream. Pour into the crust.

To make the coconut mousse: In a small pan, sprinkle the gelatin over the coconut syrup and let sit for 3 minutes. Place over low heat water and stir until gelatin is dissolved. In a deep

bowl, beat the cream until soft peaks form. Slowly add the coconut milk and continue to beat until soft peaks form. Stir in the gelatin mixture and blend, then fold in the flaked coconut. Pour into the crust.

To make the topping: In a deep bowl, beat the cream and sugar until stiff peaks form.

To assemble: Stand the glazed bananas, curved side facing the center, on top of the pie, in a circle with the tips touching at the center. Pile the cream onto the top of the pie, mounding it into a pyramid covering the bananas. With a long thin spatula, press grooves into the cream all around the pie from the top center down to the outside rim. Sprinkle with the reserved chopped nougat. Chill for 3 to 4 hours before serving.

Peanut Nougat
Makes 1 pound

2 cups granulated sugar
¼ teaspoon fresh lemon juice
2½ cups (1 pound) raw peanuts

Lightly oil a piece of marble or a baking sheet. In a medium bowl, toss the sugar with the lemon juice. In a heavy medium saucepan, cook 1 cup of the sugar over medium heat, stirring, until it turns pale amber. Add ½ cup of the remaining sugar and cook until it dissolves and turns a pale amber. Repeat with the remaining ½ cup sugar. When the sugar turns a pale amber, add the peanuts and stir until they are lightly toasted. Spread out onto the prepared surface and let cool. Break into large pieces with your hands or a small mallet and store in an airtight jar until ready to use.

Molokai Sweet Bread Pudding

Derek Langlois
The Plantation House Restaurant
Kapalua, Maui

Serves 8

Molokai bread is an unspiced sweet Hawaiian yeast bread usually served for breakfast, but it also makes wonderful desserts. It is available in many Hawaiian groceries; brioche may be substituted elsewhere. For this pudding the bread is densely packed with custard, spices, and fruit, and served with a sweet rum sauce.

Bread Pudding
6 eggs
2 cups sugar
2½ cups heavy (whipping) cream
1 tablespoon cinnamon
1 tablespoon ground nutmeg
2 cups fresh pineapple chunks
2 cups sliced banana
1 cup macadamia nuts
1½ pounds Molokai sweet bread or brioche

Hana Bay Rum Sauce
6 egg yolks
2 cups confectioners' sugar, sifted
4 tablespoons butter, melted
½ tablespoon Hana Bay or other dark rum

Garnish
1 cup heavy (whipping) cream
1 tablespoon granulated sugar
4 fresh mint sprigs

To make the pudding: Preheat the oven to 325°F. Grease and flour an 8-inch round cake pan. In an electric mixer, beat the eggs on medium speed for 5 minutes, or until pale in color and doubled in volume. Reduce the speed to low and gradually add the sugar, then add the cream, cinnamon, nutmeg, pineapple, and banana. Add the nuts. Cut the bread into slices, then cut the slices in half Add the bread pieces to the fruit mixture and let soak for 15 minutes. Pour the mixture into the prepared cake pan, pressing it into the corners. Cover with aluminum foil. Bake for 1 hour, or until firm and golden. Let cool.

To make the sauce: In a electric mixer bowl, beat the eggs on high speed for 3 minutes, or until pale in color. Reduce speed to low and gradually add the confectioners' sugar and melted butter. Stir in the rum until blended.

To serve: Beat the cream until it thickens. Sprinkle in the sugar and continue beating until stiff peaks form. Pool the sauce in the center of 8 dessert plates, and place a slice of pudding in each pool of sauce. Place the cream in a pastry bag fitted with a large star tip and pipe a rosette of cream on top of each slice. Garnish with a mint sprig.

DEREK LANGLOIS
The Plantation House Restaurant, Kapalua, Maui

If it comes from the sea, Derek Langlois will cook it.

His appreciation for everything from the ocean may reach back to his Cape Cod roots. The New England native graduated in Culinary Arts from Johnson & Wales University in Providence, Rhode Island, and started out as the breakfast kitchen manager during the summer in Van Rensaelear's Restaurant in South Wellfleet, Massachusetts.

Today, he works as *garde manger* and does ice carvings at the fashionable Plantation Restaurant on the west side of the island of Maui. In his spare time he hits the surf and enjoys the sun.

Hot Lilikoi Soufflés

Amy Ferguson-Ota
The Dining Room
The Ritz-Carlton Mauna Lani
Kohala Coast, Hawaii

Serves 4 to 6

These featherweight desserts are drenched in fruit flavor—and you can change the flavor just by changing the fruit puree. The moist soufflés need no additional sauce.

4 tablespoons unsalted butter
6 tablespoons lilikoi (passion fruit) puree, strained
⅔ cup sugar
4 egg yolks
Grated zest of 2 lemons
5 egg whites
Confectioners' sugar for sprinkling

Preheat the oven to 425°F. Butter the inside of 4 to 6 individual soufflé dishes and sprinkle with granulated sugar; rotate the dishes to cover the sides and bottom with sugar, and pour out the excess. Place the dishes on a baking sheet. In a heavy medium saucepan over medium heat, melt the butter and stir in the lilikoi puree and ⅓ cup of the sugar. Whisk in the egg yolks one at a time. Continue stirring over medium heat, frequently scraping down the sides with a rubber spatula; the mixture will thicken. Stir in the zest. Set aside and let cool to room temperature.

In a large bowl, whip the egg whites until frothy, then gradually beat in the remaining sugar until stiff, glossy peaks are formed. Stir a large spoonful of the beaten whites into the yolk mixture to lighten it, then fold in the remaining whites.

Very gently spoon the soufflés into the prepared cups, mounding the centers slightly to ¼ inch above the top of the cups. Bake for 5 minutes. Reduce heat to 350°F and continue baking 5 to 7 more minutes, or until puffed and browned. Remove from the oven, sprinkle with confectioners' sugar, and serve immediately.

Hot Lilikoi Soufflés; Amy Ferguson-Ota, The Dining Room, The Ritz-Carlton Mauna Lani, Kohala Coast, Hawaii

Molokai Sweet Bread Pudding; Derek Langlois, The Plantation House Restaurant, Kapalua, Maui

Big Island Vintage Chocolate Surprise; Jeff Walters, La Mer, Halekulani Hotel, Honolulu, Oahu

Banana Split

Kathleen Daelemans
Cafe Kula
Grand Wailea Resort
Wailea, Maui

Serves 2

This healthful banana split is a riot of fruit. Any pleasing combination of fruits can be used. The chef suggests using up leftover fruit by cutting out any bruises or spots and freezing the fruit until enough is accumulated to make the sorbet.

2 firm ripe bananas, peeled
½ cups mixed sliced fresh fruit such as oranges, raspberries, pineapple, mangoes, and kiwi fruit
4 scoops Fruit Sorbet (recipe follows)
Raspberry puree for topping (page 193)

Slice the bananas lengthwise and place 2 halves along the sides of each serving dish. Place the fresh fruit between the banana halves. Place 2 scoops of sorbet on each bed of fresh fruit. Drizzle with the raspberry puree.

Fruit Sorbet
Makes 1 quart

This extremely flexible recipe can be made with nearly any amount of fruit; just keep the amount of apple juice in proportion to the quantity of fruit.

About 2 pounds fresh or frozen peeled fruit pieces and/or berries
About ½ cup unsweetened apple juice or other juice as preferred
Liqueur and/or flavor extracts to taste (optional)

Let the fruit thaw slightly if frozen. Put the fruit and juice in a blender or food processor and puree. Freeze in an ice cream maker according to the manufacturer's instructions. If the mixture is too thick, thin by adding a little more juice; if too runny, add more fruit. Liqueurs and flavor extracts can be added in combination with the fruit. Add any liqueur to the mixture when it is partially frozen, then return it to the freezer.

Banana Split; Kathleen Daelemans, Cafe Kula, Grand Wailea Resort, Wailea, Maui

Big Island Vintage Chocolate Surprise

Jeff Walters
La Mer
Halekulani Hotel
Honolulu, Oahu

Serves 4

These beautiful chocolate tortes spill warm ganache when pierced by a fork at the table. Carefully seal the ganache in the center of each mold before baking so that it stays intact until the proper moment.

Ganache

4 ounces bittersweet chocolate, chopped
9 tablespoons heavy (whipping) cream

Cookie Dough

6 tablespoons unsalted butter
½ cup granulated sugar
¾ teaspoon vanilla extract
⅛ teaspoon salt
6 tablespoons unsweetened cocoa powder
¾ cup plus 2 tablespoons unbleached all-purpose flour

Garnish

Unsweetened cocoa powder for dusting
Confectioners' sugar for dusting

To make the ganache: Put the chocolate in a small bowl. In a small saucepan, bring the cream to scalding and pour over the chocolate. Stir until the chocolate melts and the mixture is smooth. Let cool to room temperature.

To make the cookie dough: In a large bowl, combine the butter, sugar, vanilla, and salt and beat just until blended. Do not overbeat. The dough should be moist; if it is too dry, moisten with a little water. Sift the cocoa powder and flour together on top of the batter and mix slowly until blended.

To assemble: Brush the interior of 4 individual soufflé dishes with melted butter and coat with cocoa powder. Reserve one fourth of the dough. Divide the remaining dough among

KATHLEEN DAELEMANS
Cafe Kula, Grand Wailea Resort, Wailea, Maui

Kathleen Daelemans was determined that the guests at Cafe Kula, one of the hotel's restaurants, would not only dine on spa food, but that they would love what they tasted. She liked the idea of big plates of big food with plenty of color, texture, and flavor.

Daelemans was a good thirty pounds overweight when she agreed to open the restaurant in 1991, but she did it and took off the weight at the same time. She came to Maui from San Francisco's Zuni Cafe where she worked with Judy Rodgers. On the island, Daelemans developed a repertoire of dishes that were low in cholesterol, fat, sugar, and sodium, but still pleased the palate and all the other senses.

The beautiful ripe fruits and vegetables available from local farmers inspired her to create breakfasts of island fruits such as blood oranges infused with rosemary and maple syrup.

Daelemans has appeared on national television on "The Home Show," and in magazines such as *Bon Appetit, Self, McCall's,* and *Time*.

the dishes, pressing it into the bottom and sides of the dishes. Tamp down firmly in the center with a dowel, leaving a hollow. Pour the ganache into the hollow to within ¼ inch of the top of the dish. Refrigerate for 30 minutes.

Preheat oven to 375°F. Cover the top with the reserved dough, and seal. Bake for 15 minutes, or until set and lightly browned.

To serve: Dust 4 dessert plates with cocoa powder and confectioners' sugar. Unmold the hot cookie shells onto the plates. Be careful not to break the shells. Dust the confectioners' sugar over the tops.

Cold Tapioca with Coconut Milk, Mango, and Berries; Daniel Delbrel, La Cascata, Princeville Hotel, Princeville, Kauai

Cold Tapioca with Coconut Milk, Mango, and Berries

Daniel Delbrel
La Cascata
Princeville Hotel
Princeville, Kauai

Serves 4

Tapioca is such an old dessert it seems new again, especially when it's made with palm sugar and coconut milk. This dish can be served hot, but it is particularly refreshing when served cold.

4 cups water
½ cup tapioca pearls
Pinch of salt
¼ cup sugar
2 tablespoons palm sugar or
   simple syrup (page 202)
⅔ cup coconut milk

Garnish
1 mango, peeled, cut from the pit,
   and sliced (page 193)
4 fresh strawberries, hulled and
   cut into thin slices
20 fresh blackberries
Seasonal fresh berries (optional)
4 ti leaves or other decorative large
   leaves (optional)

In a large saucepan, bring the water to a boil over medium-high heat and add the tapioca. Boil for 25 to 30 minutes, or until the tapioca pearls are translucent. Add the salt, sugar, and palm sugar and stir together, then add the coconut milk. Bring to a boil, stirring constantly until the sugar is dissolved and the milk comes to a boil, about 45 seconds. Remove from heat and let cool to room temperature, about 1 hour.

To serve: Spoon into parfait or champagne glasses and place a glass on each dessert plate. Garnish each glass of tapioca with 5 fresh mango slices. Arrange the strawberry slices into a flower and place a blackberry in the center. Garnish each with 4 more blackberries. Remove the central rib from each ti leaf or other decorative leaf, tie a knot in the center of each leaf, and place at the base of each glass, if you like.

Lilikoi Custard Tart

Beverly Gannon
Haliimaile General Store
Haliimaile, Maui

Makes one 9-inch tart; serves 12

Macadamia nuts and lilikoi puree give Hawaiian flavor to this rich tart. The unusual crust is bound with egg white. The baking intensifies the flavor of the nuts.

Macadamia Nut Crust

1½ cups macadamia nuts, toasted
　(page 196)
3 tablespoons sugar
3 tablespoons all-purpose flour
1 egg white

Lilikoi Filling

3 large eggs
1 cup sugar
1 teaspoon grated lemon zest
1 cup lilikoi (passion fruit) puree
　(page 193)
¼ cup heavy (whipping) cream

Garnish

1 cup heavy (whipping) cream
Raspberry puree (page 193)
Mango puree (page 193)

To make the crust: Preheat the oven to 375°F. Generously spray vegetable-oil cooking spray in a 9-inch tart pan with a removable bottom. In a food processor, process the nuts and sugar until the nuts are finely chopped. Add the flour and egg white and process until the mixture holds together. Or, in a medium bowl, cut together the nut mixture and flour. Add the egg and stir with a fork until it forms a mass. The dough will be sticky. With wet fingertips, press the dough over the bottom and up the sides of the prepared pan.

Bake for 15 minutes, or until the crust slightly pulls away from the sides of the pan. Let cool.

To make the filling: In a medium bowl, combine the eggs, sugar, and lemon zest and whisk just until blended. Stir in the lilikoi puree and cream. Pour into the prepared crust and bake for 25 to 30 minutes, or until the custard is puffed and golden and a knife inserted near the center comes out clean.

To serve: In a deep bowl, beat the cream to stiff peaks. Cut the tart into 12 pieces and place them on serving plates. Put the purees in squeeze bottles and drizzle the plates with them. Place the whipped cream in a pastry bag fitted with a medium star tip and garnish each slice with rosettes of whipped cream.

Lilikoi Custard Tart; Beverly Gannon, Haliimaile General Store, Haliimaile, Maui

Kona Coffee and Hawaiian Vintage Chocolate Mousse Torte; Gale E. O'Malley, Hilton Hawaiian Village, Honolulu, Oahu

Kona Coffee and Hawaiian Vintage Chocolate Mousse Torte

Gale E. O'Malley
Hilton Hawaiian Village
Honolulu, Oahu

Makes one 9-inch torte; serves 8

This masterpiece is an exotic version of a layer cake: chocolate layers, a meringue layer, two flavors of mousse, and marzipan, garnished with Hawaiian poho berries. Standing the cake wedges up vertically makes a dramatic presentation. The meringue mushrooms could garnish almost any dessert.

Marzipan disc
½ pound marzipan
3 drops green food coloring

Meringue Disc and Mushrooms
6 egg whites
½ teaspoon cream of tartar
1½ cup confectioners' sugar, sifted
¾ cup macadamia nuts, finely ground
Unsweetened cocoa powder
    for dusting

Chocolate Cake
4 eggs
⅔ cup sugar
¼ cup cocoa powder
Pinch of salt
¾ cup cake flour, sifted
3 tablespoons unsalted butter, melted

¼ cup apricot jam
1 cup ganache (page 188)

Kona Coffee Mousse
3 envelopes plain gelatin
4 tablespoons instant coffee powder
½ cup water
2 cups heavy (whipping) cream
5 egg yolks
¾ cups confectioners' sugar, sifted

¼ cup Kahlúa

Hawaiian Vintage Chocolate Mousse
6 ounces Hawaiian Vintage Chocolate
    or other fine-quality bittersweet
    chocolate
3 envelopes plain gelatin
½ cup water
2 cups heavy (whipping) cream
5 egg yolks
¾ cup confectioners' sugar, sifted

4 ounces bittersweet chocolate, melted
½ cup raspberry puree (page 193)
24 fresh poho berries or raspberries
8 fresh mint sprigs

To make the marzipan disc: Knead the marzipan until pliable. Dot with 3 drops of green food coloring, fold the marzipan over the coloring, and knead until the color has spread evenly throughout the marzipan. On a piece of parchment paper or aluminum foil, roll the marzipan into a 9-inch round disk that is ⅛-inch thick. Press with the back of a large knife to score the disk with parallel lines ¼ inch apart. Refrigerate.

To make the meringue disc and mushrooms: Preheat the oven to 200°F. Line a baking sheet with parchment or buttered heavy brown paper. Trace around a 9-inch round cake pan to draw a circle on the paper. In a large bowl, beat the egg whites and cream of tartar together until stiff peaks form. Gradually add the confectioners' sugar, beating until stiff peaks form. Place one fourth of the meringue in a pastry bag fitted with a medium plain tip. On the edges of the prepared baking sheets, outside the traced circle, pipe sixteen ¾-inch puffs (for the mushroom caps) and 16 thin 1½-inch lines (for mushroom stems) on the prepared pan. Put any leftover meringue back into the bowl with the reserved meringue and fold in the macadamia nut flour. Place the nut meringue in a large pastry bag fitted with a large plain tip and pipe in a tight spiral on the circle drawn on the prepared baking sheet. Fill in the circle with meringue and smooth the top slightly with a spatula or table knife. Bake for 1 to 1½ hours, or until crisp but not browned. Remove from oven, lift the paper with the meringues, and place on a wire rack to cool right on the paper.

When cool, lift from the paper. With a sharp knife, trim the meringue circle to fit inside the cake pan. Set aside. With the tip of a sharp knife, scrape a small hole in the bottom of each mushroom cap. Use the same sharp knife to shave one end of each stem into a small point. Press a stem point into each cap. Dust the caps with a little cocoa powder and set aside.

To make the cake: Preheat the oven to 350°F. Line the bottoms of two 9-inch round cake pans with parchment paper. Warm a deep bowl: fill the bowl with warm water, empty it, and dry thoroughly. In the warmed bowl, beat the eggs and sugar together until the mixture thickens and a ribbon forms when a spoonful is drizzled on the surface. Fold the cocoa powder into the egg mixture. Gradually fold the salt and two thirds of the flour into the egg mixture. Blend a large spoonful of the mixture into the butter, then gently fold the butter and the remaining one third of the flour into the mixture. Pour into the prepared pans and bake 10 minutes, or until a toothpick inserted in the center comes out clean. Let the pan cool for 10 minutes, then remove the cakes from the pans and cool completely on a wire rack. You will have two ½-inch-thick cakes.

Line a 9-by-2½-inch round cake pan with a circle of parchment paper or greased waxed paper. Cut a strip of heavy flexible plastic 4 inches wide and 30 inches long. Place the plastic strip around the inside of the cake pan, letting it extend above the top.

In a small pan melt the jam over medium heat. Strain the jam through a fine-meshed sieve. Spread a thin layer of about one third of the apricot jam on one cake circle and place in the prepared pan, jam-side up. Place the ganache in a pastry bag fitted with a large plain tip and pipe a spiral of ganache over the jam.

To make the coffee mousse: In a small bowl, sprinkle the gelatin and instant coffee over the water and set aside. In a deep bowl, beat the cream until it forms soft peaks and set aside. In a large bowl, whip the egg yolks and sugar until the mixture thickens and a slowly dissolving ribbon forms when a spoonful is drizzled on the surface. Stir in the gelatin mixture and blend until completely dissolved. Stir one fourth of the whipped cream into the egg mixture to lighten the mixture, then fold in the remaining cream. Pour over the ganache in the cake pan and smooth the top.

Place the meringue disc over the coffee mousse, pressing it slightly into the mousse to bond. Sprinkle the Kahlúa over the meringue disc.

To make the chocolate mousse: In a double boiler over simmering water, melt the chocolate. Set aside in the pan. In a small bowl, sprinkle the gelatin over the water and set aside. In a deep bowl, whip the cream until it forms soft peaks and set aside. In a large bowl, whip the egg yolks and sugar until the mixture thickens and a slowly dissolving ribbon forms when a spoonful is drizzled on the surface. Stir in the gelatin mixture and blend until completely dissolved. With a rubber spatula, gently stir in the warm chocolate. Stir one fourth of the whipped cream into the egg mixture to lighten the mixture, then fold in the remaining cream. Pour over the meringue disc in the cake pan and smooth the top.

Spread the second cake circle with one third of the apricot jam and place, jam-side down, over the mousse, pressing it slightly into the mousse to bond. Spread the remaining apricot jam over the top of the cake. Press the marzipan disc into the jam, scored-side up. Place the cake in the freezer for 1 to 2 hours, or until frozen.

To serve: Remove the cake from the freezer. Turn the cake out of the pan and remove the paper from the bottom. Place the cake on a serving plate. Gently pull the plastic strip off the side. With a heavy sharp knife, cut the cake into wedges, dipping the knife into hot water and wiping the blade between cuts. With a pastry brush or small spoon, cover one half of the top of each wedge with melted chocolate. Place 2 dots of melted chocolate off-center on each plate and stand a meringue mushroom on each dot, holding the mushrooms until the chocolate cools and they stand upright on their own. With a spatula and your hand, lift each cake wedge and place it upright on its spine on each serving plate next to the mushrooms. Spoon a little raspberry puree on each plate. Remove the husks from 16 poho berries and spread open the husks on the remaining 8 poho berries. Garnish each plate with 2 husked berries, 1 berry with the husk still attached, and 1 mint sprig.

Chocolate Macadamia Nut–Toffee Torte

Rodney Weddle
The Dining Room,
The Ritz-Carlton Kapalua
Kapalua, Maui

Serves 8

Begin in the hardware store: Chef Weddle uses a metal mesh screen door insert as a stencil for his genoise, a squeegee designed for cement work as the perfect scraper for the stencil, and ordinary PVC pipe cut into rings for molds. Look for heavy flexible plastic which is sold in rolls, a masonry comb, and wood-grained paint rollers: they are all tools for the imaginative chef. This torte uses nearly every pastry-making skill, but it can be simplified by eliminating the patterned design on the cake and by using fresh fruit alone for garnish.

Pâte Cigarette

2 cups (4 sticks) unsalted butter at room temperature
4 cups (1 pound) confectioners' sugar, sifted
16 egg whites
3¼ cups unbleached all-purpose flour
Dash of vanilla extract
⅔ cup unsweetened cocoa powder

Sablé Cookie Dough

¼ cup plus 3 tablespoons unsalted butter
¼ cup plus 2 tablespoons confectioners' sugar, sifted
1 cup unbleached all-purpose flour
1 egg yolk
½ teaspoon vanilla extract
Dash of salt

Macadamia Nut–Toffee Filling

½ cup granulated sugar
¼ cup (½ stick) butter, cut into pieces
¼ cup heavy (whipping) cream
½ cup macadamia nuts, coarsely chopped

Ganache Filling

2 ounces bittersweet chocolate, chopped
1 tablespoon heavy (whipping) cream
1 tablespoon Grand Marnier

Milk Chocolate Mousse

2 ounces milk chocolate, chopped
½ cup heavy (whipping) cream

Dark Chocolate Mousse

4 ounces bittersweet chocolate, chopped
1 cup heavy (whipping) cream

Glazed Bananas

½ cup granulated sugar
1 drop fresh lemon juice
½ cup heavy (whipping) cream
1 tablespoon unsalted butter
1 banana, peeled and sliced

Caramelized Banana Sabayon

6 egg yolks
½ cup sugar
¼ cup crème de banana liqueur
¼ cup heavy (whipping) cream, whipped to soft peaks
Glazed Bananas, above

Dark Chocolate Glaze

2 ounces bittersweet chocolate, chopped
¼ cup simple syrup
¼ cup nappage (apricot jam blended with pectin)

Garnish

2 ounces bittersweet chocolate, chopped
1 cup fresh raspberries
8 Striped Chocolate Garnishes (page 189)
8 pulled sugar leaves (page 202)
8 pulled sugar spirals (page 202)

To make the pâte cigarette: Preheat the oven to 375°F. Lay a sheet of parchment paper or buttered aluminum foil on a work surface. Lay a 24-inch-by-14-inch piece of patterned metal mesh on top of the paper or foil as a stencil. In a large bowl, cream the butter and sugar until fluffy. Gradually beat in the egg whites until well blended. Gradually beat in the flour and mix to a smooth batter. Blend in the vanilla. Pour half of the batter into a large bowl and stir in the cocoa powder until completely blended.

With a long thin spatula, spread the chocolate batter across the stencil in a very thin layer. Use a squeegee to scrape across the back of the stencil, leaving the chocolate batter in the holes. Carefully lift the stencil. Lift the paper or foil and place on baking sheet pan. Put the pan in the freezer for 8 to 10 minutes, or until the design is set.

Put the pan on a work surface. Using a clean spatula, quickly spread the white batter in a ⅛-inch layer over the chocolate design, taking care not to disturb the chocolate layer. Bake for 7 minutes, or until very light brown. Set aside to cool slightly. Lay a sheet of parchment paper or waxed paper over the top of the cake and, grasping the top and bottom layers of paper, flip the cake over. Peel off the paper or foil to reveal the design. Let cool completely. Do not refreeze.

Line a baking sheet with parchment paper and place 2-inch-tall by 4-inch-diameter ring molds or PVC pipe sections on the paper. Cut flexible heavy plastic into 8 strips, each 3½ inches wide and 12½ inches long. Line each mold with a strip, which will stand 1½ inches above the top of the molds. Make sure the ends meet.

Cut 8 strips of cake 12 inches long and 3½ inches wide to fit the inside of the prepared ring molds. Gently roll the cake strip, pattern-side out, and place it in the ring mold, unrolling it around the side of the mold. Make sure the ends meet but do not overlap.

To make the sablés: Line a baking sheet with parchment paper or lightly buttered aluminum foil. Preheat the oven to 350°F. In a large bowl, cream the butter and sugar until light and fluffy. Gradually stir in the flour to blend. Add the egg yolk, stirring to blend completely. Stir in the vanilla and salt. Roll the dough out on a lightly floured board to a ⅛-inch thickness. Cut out eight 2¾-inch-diameter discs. With a thin spatula, transfer the discs to the baking sheet and place in the oven. Bake for 8 to 9 minutes, or until golden. Let cool. Remove the cookies from the pan with a spatula and press one into the bottom of each mold. They should fit snugly.

To make the macadamia nut–toffee filling: In a medium, heavy saucepan, melt the sugar over medium-high heat, swirling until it turns a light golden brown. Remove from heat and swirl in the butter. Return to heat and stir in the cream. Add the nuts and stir to coat. Let cool. Place 1 tablespoon of filling in the bottom of each mold to cover the cookie.

To make the ganache: Put the chocolate in a medium bowl. In a heavy saucepan bring the cream to a boil. Pour the cream over the chocolate and stir together until melted. Stir in the Grand Marnier. Spoon 1 tablespoon in each mold over the filling.

To make the milk chocolate mousse: Melt the milk chocolate in a large double boiler over barely simmering water. In a deep bowl, whip the cream until it forms soft peaks. Stir a large spoonful of whipped cream into the warm chocolate, mixing thoroughly. Gently fold the remainder of the cream and chocolate together. Put the mousse in a pastry bag fitted with a medium tip and pipe a ¼-inch layer in each mold.

To make the dark chocolate mousse: Melt the dark chocolate in a large double boiler over barely simmering water. In a deep bowl, whip the cream until it forms soft peaks. Stir a large spoonful of whipped cream into the warm chocolate, mixing thoroughly. Gently fold the remaining cream into the chocolate. Fill the molds completely with the mousse and smooth the top with a thin spatula. The molds should now be filled to the tops of the plastic collars. Refrigerate for 30 minutes.

To make the glazed bananas: In a small, heavy saucepan, melt the sugar over medium-high heat and swirl in the

lemon juice. Continue to cook the mixture until it is a light golden brown. Gradually pour in the cream, stirring constantly. Swirl in the butter and stir until melted. Remove from heat and fold in the banana, stirring gently until coated.

To make the sabayon: In a double boiler over barely simmering water, whisk the egg yolks and sugar together. Stir in the liqueur. Cook, stirring constantly, until the mixture thickens and coats the spoon. Let cool completely. Fold in the cream. Gently fold in the glazed banana slices.

To make the glaze: Melt the chocolate in a double boiler over simmering water. Add the syrup and nappage and stir until smooth.

To serve: Remove the molds from the refrigerator. With a thin spatula, loosen the bottom of each mold from the paper. Lift the rings off the molds. Gently peel away the plastic collars

With a small spoon, spread 1½ teaspoons glaze on the top of each torte, being careful not to let the glaze drip down the sides (if the glaze drips, skim it off with a kitchen knife or spatula). Return the tortes to the refrigerator to firm.

To garnish and serve: Melt the chocolate in a double boiler over simmering water. Put the chocolate in a pastry bag fitted with a fine plain tip. Pipe 2 thin intersecting chocolate lines on the top border of the serving plate. With a spatula or your fingers, place a torte in the center of each plate. Pool 2 tablespoons sabayon on one side of each torte. Pipe a dot of chocolate at the bottom edge of the torte and press one striped chocolate garnish into the chocolate, holding it for a few seconds until it holds firmly. Garnish with a few raspberries, a pulled sugar leaf, and a pulled sugar spiral.

Chocolate–Macadamia Nut Toffee Torte; Rodney Weddle, The Dining Room, The Ritz-Carlton Kapalua, Kapalua, Maui

RODNEY WEDDLE
The Dining Room, The Ritz-Carlton Kapalua, Kapalua, Maui

Pastry chef Rodney Weddle commands a staff of bakers, manages the pastry operations at the Ritz-Carlton Kapalua, and assists with menu planning for four restaurants and special events. He makes a chocolate chip cookie with macadamia nuts so good you weep. And Weddle has learned it all "on the job."

He credits much of his knowledge to executive pastry chef Gale O'Malley, with whom he trained for two years at the Hilton Hawaiian Village Hotel in Waikiki. Prior to joining the Ritz-Carlton, he worked at the Stouffer Wailea Beach Resort on Maui and the Sheraton Royal Hawaiian Hotel.

A native of Kansas City, Missouri, Weddle is a member of the Honolulu chapter of Chefs de Cuisine and the Maui chapter of the Chefs' Association.

Warm Pineapple Tart with Coconut Sauce

Jeff Walters
La Mer
Halekulani Hotel
Honolulu, Oahu

Serves 4

A spiral of pineapple wedges turns into a flowerlike tart when the wedges are stacked against one another as they are applied. The tips of the pineapple pieces caramelize slightly as the tart is broiled.

Coconut Sauce
1 cup granulated sugar
8 egg yolks
1 cup coconut milk
1 cup pineapple puree (page 193)
2 tablespoons rum

Tart
8 ounces frozen puff pastry dough
2 egg yolks
¼ cup confectioners' sugar, sifted
1½ pineapples, peeled, cored, and cut in 1½-inch wedges
4 tablespoons granulated sugar

Garnish
½ cup guava puree (page 193)
4 fresh mint sprigs (optional)

To make the sauce: In a large bowl, beat the sugar and egg yolks until creamy. Gradually beat in the coconut milk and pineapple puree. Place in a double boiler over barely simmering water and cook, stirring constantly, until the mixture thickens and coats the spoon, about 3½ minutes. Remove from heat and strain through a fine-meshed sieve into a bowl. Stir in the rum and let cool, stirring occasionally.

To make the tart: Preheat the oven to 350°F. Line a baking sheet with parchment paper or grease it. On a lightly floured surface, roll the puff pastry out ⅛-inch thick and cut into four 7-inch circles. Place the circles on the prepared pan and bake for 16 minutes, or until crisp and golden brown. Remove from the oven and prick a few small holes in each circle. In a small bowl, beat the egg yolks and confectioners' sugar until smooth. Spread a thin, even coat of the egg mixture over the baked pastry and return the pastry to the oven for 2 minutes, or until the mixture is set. Remove from the oven and set aside.

Cut each pineapple wedge crosswise into ¼-inch-thick slices. In a large dry nonstick sauté pan or skillet over high heat, sauté the pineapple wedges on one side until golden brown, 30 to 40 seconds. Arrange the pineapple wedges, browned-side up, to cover the pastry circles from the rim to the center, overlapping the slices. As you work toward the center, the slices will stand up slightly against one another. Preheat the broiler. Sprinkle each tart with 1 tablespoon granulated sugar. Broil the tarts 5 inches from the heat for 5 minutes, or until the sugar is caramelized.

To serve: Center the tarts on individual dessert plates. Pour the coconut sauce around the tarts. Put the guava puree in a squeeze bottle and squeeze dots of puree 1 inch apart in the coconut sauce around the tarts. Garnish each plate with a mint leaf if you like.

Warm Pineapple Tart with Coconut Sauce; Jeff Walters, La Mer, Halekulani Hotel, Honolulu, Oahu

Banana Lumpia and Macadamia-Sapote Ice Cream

Gerard Kaleohano
Mid-Pacific Country Club
Lanikai, Oahu

Serves 4

Lumpia are potstickers, tiny packages enclosing intense bursts of flavor. These are filled with spiced bananas and served with a bright orange macadamia-sapote ice cream.

Lumpia
2 cups panko or coarse bread crumbs
1 cup macadamia nuts, finely chopped
½ cup packed brown sugar
1 teaspoon ground cinnamon
1 egg
8 wonton wrappers
8 bananas, peeled
3 cups vegetable oil

Sauce
¾ cup heavy (whipping) cream
2 cups (15 ounces) lychees, peeled and seeded
1 teaspoon packed brown sugar
1 teaspoon ground cinnamon
2 egg yolks
½ cup sapote juice
½ cup macadamia nuts, coarsely chopped
½ cup crème de menthe

Garnish
8 fresh strawberries, thinly sliced to the hull and fanned
Macadamia-Sapote Ice Cream (recipe follows)
¼ cup chocolate sprinkles, or ½ cup chocolate curls (page 189)
4 fresh mint sprigs
¼ cup edible flowers, torn into small bits

To make the lumpia: In a shallow bowl, mix together the panko, macadamia nuts, brown sugar, and cinnamon. In another shallow bowl, beat the egg lightly. Spread the wrappers on a work surface and brush with the beaten egg. Roll each banana in a wrapper, folding in the ends after one roll to encase the banana. Dip in the beaten egg and roll in the crumb mixture. Dip again in the beaten egg, and roll again in the crumbs.

In a large wok over high heat, heat the oil to almost smoking. With tongs or a slotted spoon, place 4 of the lumpia in the hot oil and cook quickly until golden brown, about 35 to 40 seconds. Do not overcrowd the pan. Using tongs or a slotted spoon, transfer the lumpia to paper towels to drain. Return the oil to almost smoking and repeat with remaining lumpia. Cut the lumpia crosswise into halves.

To make the sauce: In a medium, heavy saucepan bring the cream to a low boil over medium heat, add the lychees, and cook for 30 seconds.

Banana Lumpia with Macadamia-Sapote Ice Cream; Gerard Kaleohano, Mid-Pacific Country Club, Lanikai, Oahu

Add the brown sugar and cinnamon and stir to blend. Stir in the egg yolks and cook until slightly thickened. Stir in the juice and return to low boil. Stir in the macadamia nuts and cook for 30 seconds. Add the crème de menthe and return to low boil, stirring to blend. Cook until slightly thickened, about 1 minute.

To serve: Spoon one fourth of the sauce on each of 4 serving plates. Arrange the lumpia, cut-side out, in a cross shape, leaving space in the center. Place 1 strawberry fan between each 2 lumpia. Place a scoop of ice cream in the center. Sprinkle the ice cream with chocolate sprinkles or curls. Garnish each plate with a mint sprig and flower bits.

Macadamia-Sapote Ice Cream
Makes 1 quart

1 sapote, peeled and pureed
2 cups heavy (whipping) cream
2½ cups macadamia nuts,
   coarsely chopped

In a heavy, medium saucepan, bring the sapote and heavy cream to a boil over high heat. Reduce heat to medium and cook for 2 minutes, stirring constantly. Let cool, then cover and refrigerate until completely chilled, 1 to 2 hours. Freeze in an ice cream maker according to manufacturer's instructions. When the ice cream is partially frozen, stir in the macadamia nuts. Return to the freezer.

GALE E. O'MALLEY
Hilton Hawaiian Village, Honolulu, Oahu

Gale O'Malley likes seeing young, aspiring pastry chefs make it on their own. He was the youngest and the first American-born pastry chef to receive a Grand Prize for excellence from the French government, in 1981.

Today, O'Malley presides over the pastry kitchens at the rambling Hilton Hawaiian Village. Much of his work involves doing community service for events such as the Fantasies in Chocolate benefit for the Hawaiian Humane Society, the Dessert Fantasy for United Cerebral Palsy, and the Chef and the Child benefit presented by the Honolulu Chapter of Chefs de Cuisine.

O'Malley's real dedication is to Hawaii's young chefs, and he is active as an apprenticeship instructor. He participates in the Hawaii Student Culinary Show held annually at the Kapiolani and Leeward community colleges, and is part of the Work Study for Special Education program run by the State of Hawaii department of education.

The Unforgettable Torte

Gale E. O'Malley
Hilton Hawaiian Village
Honolulu, Oahu

Serves 4

This beautiful torte of chocolate cake, hazelnut meringue, and flavored fillings is unforgettable, both for its taste and its presentation. The torte could be served by itself, of course. But try the adventure of creating the dramatic chocolate petals and wings; the reward is a piece of art.

Chocolate Garnishes
8 ounces bittersweet chocolate
8 striped chocolate wings (page 189, 190)
4 dark chocolate wings (page 189)
Eight 4½-inch dark chocolate discs (page 189)
24 striped chocolate tulip petals (page 189, 190)

Hazelnut Meringues
6 egg whites
½ teaspoon cream of tartar
1½ cups confectioners' sugar, sifted
1 cup hazelnuts, finely ground

The Unforgettable Torte; Gale E. O'Malley, Hilton Hawaiian Village, Honolulu, Oahu

Chocolate Cake
4 eggs
⅔ cup sugar
¼ cup cocoa
Pinch of salt
¾ cup sifted cake flour
3 tablespoons unsalted butter, melted

White Cake
4 eggs
⅔ cup sugar
2 teaspoons vanilla
Pinch of salt
1 cup sifted cake flour
3 tablespoons unsalted butter, melted

Chocolate Buttercream
3 ounces bittersweet chocolate, chopped
2 egg yolks
⅓ cup granulated sugar
¼ cup water
½ cup (1 stick) unsalted butter at room temperature

¼ cup raspberry jam
36 fresh raspberries
1½ cups ganache (page 188)
¼ cup Chambord or other raspberry liqueur
1 cup heavy (whipping) cream,

whipped to soft peaks
1 tablespoon unsweetened cocoa powder
½ pound marzipan

2 ounces bittersweet chocolate, melted
1 tablespoon unsweetened cocoa powder
4 lattice dark chocolate leaves (page 190)

To assemble the chocolate garnishes:

To assemble the wings: Line a sheet pan with waxed paper. In the top of a double boiler over simmering water, melt 4 ounces of dark chocolate. Lay four striped chocolate wings, stripe-side up, on the waxed paper. Place the melted chocolate in a pastry bag or paper cone with a fine tip and pipe a quarter-sized dot of hot chocolate on the lower fourth of each wing. Press a plain chocolate wing onto each dot and hold if necessary until the chocolate sets enough to hold the wing. Pipe another quarter-sized dot of hot chocolate onto the lower fourth of the plain wings, and press another striped wing onto each. Place in the refrigerator to set, 5 to 7 minutes.

Line another sheet pan with waxed paper. Place four discs on the waxed paper. Pipe a 2-inch dot of hot chocolate on a circle, mounding the dot. Place an assembled wing upright on the dot of chocolate and hold until it sets. Pipe additional hot chocolate at the base of the wing to secure it firmly. Place in the freezer. Repeat with the others wings. The wings can remain in the freezer for 2 days.

To assemble the tulip cups: Line a sheet pan with waxed paper. In the top of a double boiler over simmering water or in a microwave, melt 4 ounces of dark chocolate. Place four discs on the waxed paper. Place the melted chocolate in a pastry bag or paper cone with a fine tip and pipe a 1-inch strip of chocolate on the rim of the disc. With the tips of your fingers lift a striped tulip petal and place it, striped-side in and point-side up, into the chocolate. Adjust with a slight outward lean and hold gently until it sets firmly enough to stay. Repeat with five more tulip petals. Place in the freezer. Repeat with the remaining three discs. The cups can remain in the freezer for 2 days.

To make the meringues: Preheat the oven to 200°F. Line a baking pan with parchment paper or heavy brown paper. Trace around a 4-inch ring mold to draw 4 circles on the paper. In a large bowl, beat the egg whites and cream of tartar together until foamy. Gradually beat in the confectioners' sugar until the meringue forms stiff peaks. Fold in the ground hazelnuts. Place the meringue in a pastry bag fitted with a medium plain tip and pipe a tight solid spiral on a circle drawn on the prepared baking sheet. Fill in the circle completely. Repeat with the remaining circles and smooth the tops slightly with a spatula or table knife. Bake for 1 to 1½ hours, or until crisp but not browned. Remove the paper with the meringues and place on a wire rack to cool on the paper.

When cool, lift the meringues from the paper. With a sharp knife, trim the edges of each meringue circle to fit inside a 4-inch ring mold. Set aside at room temperature until ready to use.

To make the chocolate cake: Preheat the oven to 350°F. Line the bottoms of two 9-inch round cake pans with parchment paper. Warm a deep bowl: fill the bowl with warm water, empty it, and dry thoroughly. In the warmed bowl, beat the eggs and sugar together until the mixture thickens and a ribbon forms when a spoonful is drizzled on the surface. Fold the cocoa into the egg mixture. Gradually fold the salt and two thirds of the flour into the egg mixture. Blend a large spoonful of the mixture into the butter, then gently fold the butter and the remaining one third of the flour into the mixture. Pour into the prepared pans and bake for 10 minutes, or until a toothpick inserted in the center comes out clean. Let the pan cool for 10 minutes, then remove the cakes from the pans and cool completely on a wire rack. You will have two ½-inch thick cakes.

To make the white cake: Preheat the oven to 350°F. Line the bottoms of two 9-inch round cake pans with parchment paper. Warm a deep bowl: fill the bowl with warm water, empty it, and dry thoroughly. In the warmed bowl, beat the eggs and sugar together until the mixture thickens and a ribbon forms when a spoonful is drizzled on the surface. Stir the vanilla into the egg mixture. Gradually fold two thirds of the flour into the egg mixture. Blend

a large spoonful of the mixture into the butter, then gently fold the butter and the remaining one third of the flour into the mixture. Pour into the prepared pans and bake for 10 minutes, or until a toothpick inserted in the center comes out clean. Let the pan cool for 10 minutes, then remove the cakes from the pans and cool completely on a wire rack. You will have two ½-inch thick cakes.

To make the buttercream: In a double boiler over barely simmering water, melt the chocolate. Strain the chocolate through a fine-meshed sieve into a small bowl and set aside to cool slightly. In a medium bowl, beat the egg yolks until light and fluffy. In a heavy, medium saucepan, stir the sugar and water together. Bring to a boil over medium heat, using a pastry brush to brush down any crystals that form on the sides of the pan. Do not stir the mixture while it is heating. Boil to 240°F, or until a small amount dropped into a glass of cold water forms a soft, pliable ball. Remove from heat. While beating the eggs yolks on medium speed, gradually pour a thin stream of the sugar mixture into the yolks. Increase the speed to high and continue pouring until all the sugar has been absorbed and the mixture has cooled. It will be light and fluffy.

In a small deep bowl, cream the butter. Add the butter 1 tablespoon at a time to the mixture, beating constantly, until the butter is incorporated. While beating, gradually pour the chocolate into the buttercream until completely blended and smooth. The buttercream will keep up to 2 months in the freezer.

To assemble: Line a baking sheet with parchment paper or aluminum foil. Place four 4-inch ring molds on the sheet. Cut 4 strips of heavy flexible plastic 4 inches wide and 12¾ inches long to fit the inside of the ring molds. Place a plastic strip around the inside of each mold, letting it extend above the top.

Cut four 4-inch circles from the chocolate sponge. Trim each sponge circle to ½-inch thick. Spread a thin layer of raspberry jam on each sponge circle and place one in each prepared mold, jam-side up. Put the buttercream into a pastry bag fitted with a large plain tip and pipe a layer over each sponge. Press 6 of the raspberries into

the buttercream of each torte. Put the ganache in a pastry bag fitted with a medium plain tip and pipe a layer of ganache over the raspberries. Reserve the remaining ganache for the final assembly.

Place a meringue disc over each layer of ganache, pressing it down slightly. Sprinkle the meringue with Chambord. Press the juice from the remaining 12 raspberries, strain through a fine-meshed sieve, and gently fold the raspberry juice into the whipped cream. Spoon 2 to 3 tablespoons of the raspberry cream over each meringue.

Cut the white sponge into four 4-inch circles. Trim the sponge circles to ½-inch thick and press one on top of the whipped cream in each mold. Fold the cocoa powder into the raspberry cream and spoon 2 to 3 tablespoons over each cake. Smooth the tops with the back of a kitchen knife and place the molds in the freezer until firm, 2 to 3 hours.

Line a baking sheet with parchment or aluminum foil. Place a wire rack on the baking sheet. Roll the marzipan into a ⅛-inch-thick sheet and cut four 4-inch circles. In a double boiler over barely simmering water, warm the ganache to pouring consistency. Remove the molds from the freezer and gently warm the outsides of the molds with warm towels. Run the tip of a thin sharp knife around the inside of each mold to loosen the rings. Unmold the tortes onto the wire rack. Strip off the plastic. Press a skewer or fork into each torte and dip completely in the ganache, then place on the rack to drip. Press a marzipan disc onto the top of each torte while the ganache is still soft.

To serve: Place a petal cup slightly off center on a dessert plate and carefully center a torte in the cup. Place the melted chocolate in a pastry bag fitted with a small plain tip. Pipe a small pool of melted chocolate on the plate and place a wing garnish in the melted chocolate, holding it in place until the chocolate cools and firms. Dust the top of the marzipan disc with cocoa powder. Pipe a ½-inch mound of ganache in the center and lean a chocolate lattice leaf against the ganache. Repeat with the remaining tortes.

Lilikoi Truffle

Mark Hetzel
The Four Seasons Resort Maui
Wailea, Maui

Serves 8

There are two kinds of lilikoi, a light yellow variety and the more intensely colored Tangier variety. In this dessert the light variety is used for the custard and the ganache, and the Tangier variety is used for the garnish. You may, of course, use only one variety in the dessert; it will still taste wonderful.

Lilikoi Custard

6 eggs
1 cup sugar
¾ cup lilikoi puree (page 193)
Grated zest of 1 orange
½ cup (1 stick) plus 1 tablespoon
    unsalted butter
1 envelope plain gelatin
¼ cup cold water
¾ cup heavy (whipping) cream
1 tablespoon sugar

Bittersweet Chocolate Cake

6 ounces bittersweet chocolate,
    chopped
4 ounces unsweetened chocolate,
    chopped
1 cup (2 sticks) unsalted butter, cut up
5 whole eggs
4 egg yolks
½ cup sugar
¾ cup unbleached all-purpose flour

6 ounces bittersweet chocolate,
    chopped

Lilikoi Ganache

12 ounces bittersweet chocolate,
    chopped
9 ounces milk chocolate, chopped
6 tablespoons heavy (whipping) cream
4 tablespoons unsalted butter
¾ cup sugar
⅔ cup lilikoi puree (page 193)

Garnish

Unsweetened cocoa powder
    for dusting
1 cup Tangier lilikoi juice and seeds
4 lilikoi, halved lengthwise
24 lilikoi leaves

To make the custard: In a double boiler over barely simmering water, stir together the eggs and sugar and let warm to 100°F. In a heavy saucepan, bring the lilikoi puree, zest, and butter to a boil over medium-high heat. Meanwhile, sprinkle the gelatin over the cold water and let sit for 3 minutes. Add a large spoonful of the hot puree to the egg mixture and blend, then whisk the egg mixture into the hot puree. Reduce heat to low and cook, stirring constantly, for 2 minutes, until the mixture thickens and coats the spoon. Remove from the heat and add the gelatin, stirring until it is completely dissolved. Set the pan in a bowl of ice water and stir until cold. In a deep bowl, whip the cream until it forms soft peaks, adding the sugar gradually as you beat. Fold the custard into the whipped cream, cover with plastic wrap, and refrigerate at least 1 hour or overnight.

To make the cake: Preheat the oven to 350°F. Line a jelly-roll pan with parchment paper or aluminum foil. In the top of a double boiler set over barely simmering water, melt the chocolates and butter, and bring the temperature of the mixture to 100°F. Stir to blend. Set aside.

In a medium bowl, whisk the eggs, egg yolks, and sugar until foamy, about 2 minutes. Stir the warm chocolate into the egg mixture, then stir in the flour. Pour into the prepared

Lilikoi Truffle; Mark Hetzel, The Four Seasons Resort Maui, Wailea, Maui

pan and spread with a spatula to fill the pan evenly. Bake for 10 minutes, or until just firm; do not overbake. Let cool to the touch, remove from the pan, and let cool completely. Using a 2½-inch diameter cookie cutter or glass, cut eight circles from the cake. Cut the remaining cake into ½-inch dice.

To make the chocolate cups: In a double boiler over barely simmering water, melt the chocolate. Brush eight 2½-inch-diameter half-sphere molds with the chocolate to form a thin shell and put in the freezer to set.

To make the ganache: In a large double boiler over barely simmering water, melt the chocolates together. In a heavy saucepan, stir the cream, butter, sugar, and lilikoi puree together and bring to a boil over medium-high heat. Gradually add the hot cream mixture to the melted chocolate, stirring constantly, until smooth and shiny. Remove the pan from heat and let cool until slightly firm.

To assemble: Line a jelly-roll pan with parchment or waxed paper and place a wire rack on top. Fold the diced cake into the custard. Fill the chocolate cup molds with the custard mixture. Place the cake circles over the custard mixture, sealing the chocolate cups. Unmold the chocolate cups, warming the molds slightly with a warm towel to loosen the chocolate, and invert onto the wire rack. With a small spatula or flat knife, spread the ganache over the cups to coat. Allow to set slightly, then touch a spatula or the back of a spoon to the ganache and pull it away, leaving a tiny lifted curl of ganache. Repeat randomly all over each truffle to make each look prickly. Place in the refrigerator to set, about 15 minutes.

To serve: With a metal spatula, lift the truffles and place one on each dessert plate. Dust lightly with cocoa powder. Spoon 2 tablespoons of lilikoi juice with seeds around each truffle. Place 1 lilikoi half on each plate and garnish with 3 leaves.

Pineapple Tart

Dominique Jamain
The Maile Restaurant
Kahala Hilton
Honolulu, Oahu

Serves 4

Small round tarts show off pineapple wedges which have been seared to caramelize some of their sugar. The ice cream and piña colada sauce that finish the tarts could stand on their own as a refreshing dessert.

Four very thin 5-inch circles of puff pastry dough
1 large pineapple, peeled, cored, and cut into 4 equal wedges, small leaves reserved

Piña Colada Sauce

1 cup pineapple juice
1¼ cups crème anglaise (page 191)
⅓ cup dark rum
¼ cup coconut milk

Garnish

¾ cup Crème Légère (recipe follows)
2 tablespoons apricot jelly mixed with 1 tablespoon water
4 scoops Macadamia Nut Ice Cream (page 194, 195)
Reserved small pineapple leaves

Preheat the oven to 350°F. Line a baking sheet with parchment paper or aluminum foil. Place the puff pastry circles on the sheet and prick the pastry liberally with a fork. Bake for 10 to 15 minutes, or until lightly browned and slightly puffed. Let cool.

Meanwhile, cut each pineapple wedge into ¼-inch-thick slices. Heat a dry large nonstick sauté pan or skillet over high heat. Sear each pineapple slice until golden brown, about 1 minute. Turn with tongs and sear the other side. Set aside on a wire rack and let cool.

To make the sauce: In a small saucepan, boil the pineapple juice over medium-high heat until reduced to ¼ cup. Pour into a medium bowl and set the bowl inside a larger bowl filled with ice. Stir to cool. Stir the crème anglaise, rum, and coconut milk into the reduced pineapple juice.

To serve: Spoon ¼ cup sauce into each of 4 serving plates. Place a pastry circle on each plate and spread each evenly with the crème légère. Overlap the pineapple slices in a circle on top of the cream, tucking the last slice under the first. Brush the jelly mixture over the top of the pineapple slices. Place a scoop of ice cream in the center of each tart and garnish by standing tiny pineapple leaves upright in the ice cream.

Crème Légère

Makes 4 cups

Hot Mixture

3 cups milk
¾ cup sugar
1 tablespoon butter
Pinch of salt

Cold Mixture

1 cup milk
1 teaspoon vanilla extract
4 eggs
½ cup cornstarch

1 cup heavy (whipping) cream, whipped to soft peaks

To make the hot mixture: In a heavy, medium saucepan, combine all ingredients and bring to a boil over medium-high heat, stirring occasionally.

To make the cold mixture: In a medium saucepan, whisk together all the ingredients. Stir the boiling hot mixture into the cold mixture. Pour the combined mixtures back into the pot and cook for 2 to 3 minutes. Place the custard in a bowl and let cool.

In a deep bowl, whip the cream until it forms stiff peaks. Gently stir a spoonful of whipped cream into the custard, then fold the remaining whipped cream into the custard until smooth. Cover and store in the refrigerator for up to 1 day.

Pineapple Tart; Dominique Jamain, The Maile Restaurant, Kahala Hilton, Honolulu, Oahu

The Traditional Luau Feast

"Fish and poi, fish and poi. All I need is fish and poi ..."

Those words from a childhood song come immediately to mind whenever the subjects of luau and traditional Hawaiian food come up.

The luau is a feast that celebrates important events such as weddings, graduations, housewarmings, anniversaries, or a baby's first birthday. Whatever the occasion, it means lots of food, good feeling among friends and family, and often music and dance.

Today there are two kinds of luau: the kind given for tourists, and the kind given by locals in backyards, church halls, and community centers.

Tourist luau are blatantly commercial, with food that only remotely resembles real Hawaiian food. You are likely to find teriyaki steak, tossed green salad in large quantities, and almost no poi or raw seafood. Hawaiians, on the other hand, love raw black crab, opihi (limpets) and limu (seaweed), poke (marinated raw fish), and wana (sea urchin).

A luau put on for visitors usually has a stagey hula show and is often set near the sand at a beachfront resort hotel, or sometimes in the hotel's garden. There will be lei and flowers on the tables, and the event will be very pretty, if not terribly authentic.

But the real thing is all about cementing the bonds of friendship and family. A luau can last the entire weekend, with people arriving on Friday afternoon to begin the preparation. Aunties arrive from the Big Island with orchids and anthuriums for decoration. All the "calabash" (extended family related by marriage or affection) relatives are there to pitch in and help (and start partying before the actual event).

By early morning on the day of the event, the imu, or luau pit, is dug and filled with hot rocks and ti leaves. A pig, often wrapped in chicken wire to hold it together after cooking, is lowered into the pit. Other foods — turkeys, laulau (ti leaf bundles of meat and fish), sweet potatoes, fish — are added, then everything is covered with leaves, burlap, and soil, and left to steam all day.

Opihi and limu will have been gathered from the seaside, or purchased at great expense in a local market.

Now the preparation of the other food begins. The day proceeds with a lot of chopping, stirring, and laughter. The side dishes, such as poke, squid luau (squid cooked with taro tops and coconut milk), lomi lomi salmon (a salad of salted salmon, tomatoes, onions and chili peppers), chicken long rice (a Chinese dish of chicken and bean thread noodles), and haupia or kulolo (coconut or taro puddings) are made ahead.

And there is always poi. Originally poi was made by peeling, cooking, and pounding taro roots into a paste. Today poi is purchased from regional factories, and the product is superior for its smoothness and consistency. For all the joking by tourists about its similarity to wallpaper paste, poi continues to be a favorite with locals. This healthy staple starch is the basis of the traditional Hawaiian diet.

Now the younger family members decorate the tables and the hall. Often long picnic tables are covered with rolls of paper. Family members and friends then decorate with ti leaves, lauae ferns, and flowers down the center. A fancier luau might have tapa or pareu-designed fabric tablecloths.

Just before the luau begins, flavored soda water in bottles, a square piece of coconut cake, red alae salt (coarse sea salt mixed with clay), raw onions, and other condiments are placed at each seat.

The guests arrive in their finest muumuu and aloha shirts. Children are always included and show up scrubbed clean and wearing their best jeans or shorts.

The music strikes up as the guests arrive — not tourist music, but the "cha-lang a-lang" variety that has been played by backyard bands for as long as anyone can remember. The hula dancers aren't uniformly slender and the dances aren't perfectly coordinated, but the dancers are the granddaughters, mothers, or uncles of the people in the group. They may forget some of the movements, but they know the meaning of the dance. It is a gift to their family — their *ohana*.

The party often continues on Sunday. The kalua pig is reheated on top of the stove with cabbage and onions. Other leftovers are heated up and laid out, or left on the stove for people to help themselves.

By early afternoon, everyone is headed home for the other side of the island, or for the airport to catch a late plane home to their own island. Now the luau-givers can collapse—and gather up their memories.

If you decide to give a luau yourself, remember that the food should be fresh and plentiful, the preparation shared, and the spirit open and loving.

"Fish and poi. Fish and poi. All I need is fish and poi . . ."

Sam Choy Throws a Luau

Sam Choy was just a lad when he began helping out with his father's luau, the first of those native feasts given expressly for island visitors. Now Sam's son helps out with *his* luau. If you want to hold your own luau, invite your family and friends, and follow Sam's example.

The perfect *imu,* or baking pit, is dug into the earth and lined with volcanic rocks or other rocks that will not split when heated to a high temperature, such as granite (slate, shale, and other sedimentary rocks won't work). A fire is built over the rocks and allowed to burn down until the rocks themselves are extremely hot. The rocks are then spread on the bottom of the pit and pulled to the sides; after the food is added the rocks will be piled on top of the food and the pit covered for slow cooking. The process is similar to that used for a New England clambake.

Ti leaves and banana leaves are prepared. The midrib can be cut away slightly on the back of the leaf so the leaf will bend more easily.

A cleaned pig is rubbed with sea salt inside and out, wrapped in banana leaves and then ti leaves, and trussed in chicken wire so it can easily be lifted from the pit when it is finished.

Hot rocks are placed in the body cavity, and the pig is lowered into the pit, covered, and slow cooked for about 6 hours. Toward the end of the cooking, other items to be baked, such as sweet potatoes, are added to the pit.

The finished pig is lifted from the *imu*, and the meat is pulled into serving pieces. The side dishes are removed from the pit and placed on the table to be eaten.

While the pig is cooking, the tables are readied. Sam sets out dishes of other foods such as poi, several kinds of fish such as opakapaka (simplified versions of Sam's sweet and sour opakapaka, page 110; Daniel Delbrel's steamed onaga, page 105; and Gerard Reversade's roasted opakapaka, page 86, would all be excellent), and lomi lomi. Fresh fruit, pokes (see pages 16, 36, and 50), chicken long rice, laulau (see page 37), and coconut cake are all traditional. Fruit punch is the drink of choice.

Chicken Long Rice

Serves 12

The "long rice" is bean thread noodles broken into short lengths. There are as many variations of chicken long rice as there are families; don't be afraid to add your own touches.

8 ounces bean thread noodles, broken into 2- to 3-inch pieces
4 cups chicken stock (page 199)
2 pounds chicken pieces, skinned, bones, and cut into 1-inch cubes
One 2-inch piece of ginger, crushed
2 large carrots, peeled and cut into julienne
6 stalks celery, thinly sliced
1 large onion, thinly sliced
1 pound mushrooms, sliced

Soak the noodles in warm water to cover for 1 hour. In a soup pot, combine the chicken stock, chicken, and ginger. Bring to a boil, reduce heat to low, and simmer for 5 minutes. Add the carrots, celery, onion, and mushrooms and simmer for 4 minutes. Drain the noodles and add to the chicken mixture. Cover and cook for 5 minutes, or until the noodles are translucent.

It's all self-serve at the luau table. Sam Choy's son Christopher shows he knows how to carry on a family tradition.

Lomi Lomi

Serves 12

Start the night before. Lomi lomi is very simple to make, but the salmon needs to marinate in salt water for at least 8 hours.

3 pounds salmon
1¼ tablespoons sea salt
6 tomatoes, stemmed and chopped
5 green onions, minced
2 Hawaiian or Thai chilies, minced
6 cups crushed ice

Debone the salmon. Chop into quarter-inch dice and sprinkle with salt. Put the salmon in a shallow baking dish filled with 4 cups of the crushed ice, cover, and refrigerate for at least 8 hours.

Drain the salmon, place in a large bowl, and toss with chopped tomatoes and green onions. Toss with the remaining 2 cups crushed ice just before serving.

Five-Spice Smoked Rack of Lamb with Poha Berry and Ginger Butter; Katsuo Sugiura (Chef Suki), Ihilani Resort & Spa, Kapolei, Oahu

Pairing Wine with Pacific Flavors

Forget the buttery Chardonnays and oaky Cabernets. You're smack dab in the middle of the Pacific now, and it's a whole new ballgame.

There are those of you who will opt for a beer rather than tread into such unfamiliar territory. But if you like wine, and enjoy serving it with dinner, here are some suggestions. The rest is up to you and your tastebuds.

Pacific flavors are bold and exotic, like the salty flavors of soy sauce and black bean sauce, the hot spice of Hawaiian chilies, ginger, and Thai chili paste, and the sweetness of mango and passion fruit.

Most wine lovers prefer high-quality, dry wines with lots of oak and high alcohol content, considering sweet wines to be for neophytes. Sweeter wines, however, work best with Pacific flavors, helping to balance the heat and spice of the food.

Some of the chefs in this book use classic European cooking styles that incorporate island products, while others are almost totally influenced by Asia. A good way to select a wine is to look at what is in the recipe itself. For instance, a recipe that has strong Mediterranean flavors, such as olive oil, tomatoes, garlic, and basil, will most likely pair well with the dry white wines and rosés of Southern France or Italy. California also produces rosés of a similar style, such as Vin Gris, as well as white and red wines made from the indigenous grapes of Southern France and Italy.

Dishes with an Asian influence, using ingredients such as kaffir lime leaves, ginger, curry, wasabi, lemongrass, chilies, and hoisin sauce, would be complemented by a Riesling, a Vouvray, a Gewürztraminer, a Chenin Blanc, or a white Zinfandel. The contrast is like biting into a cold mango, to soothe and cool the palate, says master sommelier Chuck Furuya, who judges international wine events and conducts training and public tastings throughout Hawaii.

You're on a culinary adventure, so have a good time. Try lots of different wines with the dishes in this book — and, in the end, drink what you like.

Crispy Sea Scallops Wrapped in Shredded Phyllo; Corey Waite, Coast Grill, Hapuna Beach Prince Hotel, Mauna Kea Resort, Kamuela, Hawaii

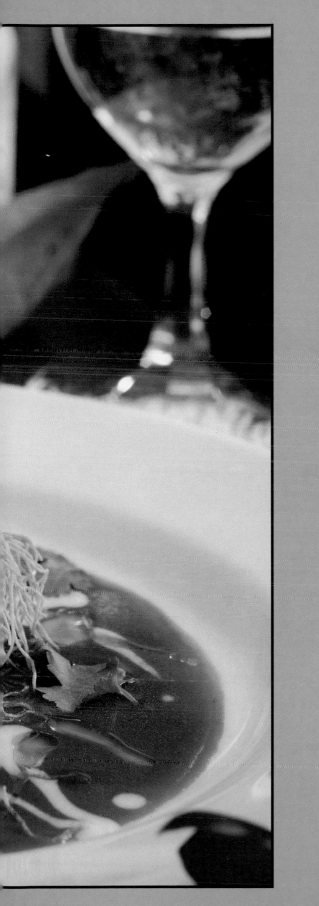

Basic Recipes
and Techniques

Many of the basic recipes and techniques in this chapter
are classic elements of American and European cooking,
such as chicken stock, and roasting and peeling bell peppers. But a variety of tropical recipes and techniques are
also included. Husking coconuts, making chili pepper
water, and cutting pineapple with the dexterity of a professional are some of the key steps in preparing island cuisine you'll find here.

Brown Sauce

Makes 4 cups

This versatile Asian-style brown sauce can be used as a braising sauce for nearly any meat or vegetable. Chilled, it gels and can be used as a garnish for savories and salads.

2 tablespoons vegetable oil
2 whole green onions, finely chopped
2 tablespoons minced peeled fresh ginger root
4 garlic cloves, minced
1 teaspoon Sichuan peppercorns
3 star anise pods
½ cup beef stock (page 200)
1 cup soy sauce
½ cup sake
1 tablespoon sugar
1 teaspoon salt

In a large stockpot over medium-high heat, heat the oil and sauté the onions, ginger, garlic, peppercorns, and star anise until the onions are translucent and the mixture is fragrant, about 2 minutes. Add the stock, soy sauce, sake, sugar, and salt. Raise heat to high and boil for 10 to 12 minutes. Use immediately, or cover and refrigerate for up to 3 days, or freeze for up to 3 months.

Butter

Clarified Butter Melt butter over low heat, then cover and refrigerate it. Once the fat has hardened, scoop it off, being careful to leave the bottom layer of milk solids. Cover the clarified butter and refrigerate for up to 2 weeks.

If you don't have time to let the butter chill, melt the butter gently so that the milk solids settle on the bottom of the pan, forming a creamy white sediment. Carefully pour off the clear yellow butter, and discard the milk solids or add them to soup or sauce.

Herb Butter

Makes 2 cups
⅛ teaspoon garlic powder
1 teaspoon minced fresh parsley
1 teaspoon minced fresh basil
1 teaspoon minced fresh shallots
1 teaspoon minced fresh watercress
Juice of 1 lemon
1 pound (4 sticks) salted butter

In the bowl of a food processor or mixer, combine all ingredients. Beat until smooth, about 4 minutes. Pack into molds or a glass container with a lid, and refrigerate. Keeps up to 1 week.

Citrus-Herb Butter

Makes 2 cups

Juice of ½ lemon
Juice of ½ orange
Juice of ½ lime
1 pounds (4 sticks) salted butter
1 tablespoon dried tarragon leaves
1 tablespoon dried basil leaves
Pinch of freshly ground black pepper
½ teaspoon salt (optional)
½ teaspoon sugar (optional)

In the bowl of a food processor or mixer, combine all ingredients. Beat until smooth, about 4 minutes. Add salt and sugar to taste. Pack into molds or a glass container with a lid, and refrigerate. Keeps up to 1 week.

Garlic Butter
Makes 2 cups

1 tablespoon garlic powder
3 minced fresh garlic cloves
Juice of 1 lemon
1 pound (4 sticks) salted butter

In the bowl of a food processor or mixer, combine all ingredients. Beat until smooth, about 4 minutes. Pack into molds or a glass container with a lid, and refrigerate. Keeps up to 1 week.

Garlic–Herb Butter
Makes 2 cups

1 tablespoon garlic powder
1 minced fresh garlic clove
1 teaspoon minced fresh parsley
1 teaspoon minced fresh basil
1 teaspoon minced fresh shallots
1 teaspoon minced fresh watercress
Juice of 1 lemon
1 pound (4 sticks) salted butter

In the bowl of a food processor or mixer, combine all ingredients. Beat until smooth, about 4 minutes. Pack into molds or a glass container with a lid, and refrigerate. Keeps up to 1 week.

Caramel Sauce
Makes 2 cups

This thick caramel sauce is enriched with butter and cream.

1½ cups sugar
½ cup water
3 tablespoons butter
1 cup heavy (whipping) cream, heated
½ teaspoon vanilla extract

In a heavy, medium saucepan, combine the sugar and water and bring to a simmer over medium heat, swirling occasionally. Cover, raise the heat to medium high, and cook for 2 minutes, or until the liquid gives off large, thick bubbles. Uncover and cook, swirling the syrup, until it turns golden brown.

Remove from heat and stir in the butter with a wooden spoon. Add the cream, stirring constantly, then add the vanilla. Return the pan to low heat and stir constantly until any lumps have melted and the syrup is smooth. Serve warm over ice cream or cake, or pour into a jar, cover, and refrigerate for up to 1 week.

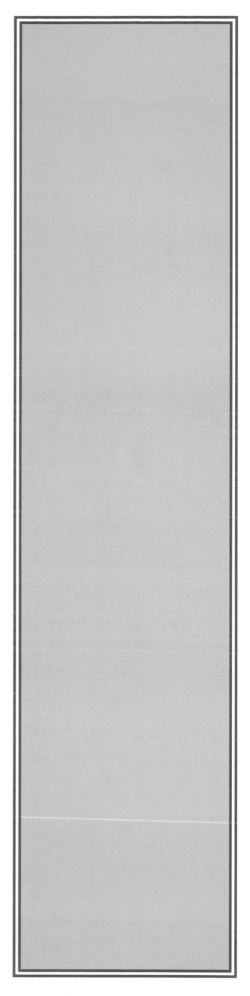

Chili Oil
Makes 1 cup

In a medium bowl, combine 4 Hawaiian or Thai peppers with 1 cup of olive oil. Cover and let sit for a minimum of 48 hours. Pour through a fine-meshed sieve into a glass jar or bottle and cover.

Chocolate

Ganache

1 cup heavy (whipping) cream
1 pound semisweet chocolate, chopped

In a heavy pan, bring the cream to a boil over medium-high heat. Remove from heat. Add the chocolate and stir until melted. Let cool thoroughly.

Chocolate Sauce
Makes 4 cups

1 cup sugar
2 cups half-and-half
8 ounces bittersweet or semisweet chocolate, chopped
8 ounces unsweetened chocolate, chopped

In a heavy, large saucepan, combine the sugar and half-and-half and heat over medium-low heat until hot but not boiling. Add the chocolate and stir until the chocolate is melted and the mixture is smooth. Serve warm, or pour into a jar, cover, and refrigerate for up to 1 week.

To melt chocolate: Melt chopped chocolate in a double boiler over barely simmering water. Stir until smooth.

To pipe chocolate: Place melted chocolate in a small pastry bag fitted with a very fine tip. Use as you would any piping. For larger lines, put the chocolate in a squeeze bottle. For small amounts of melted chocolate for piping narrow lines or small dots to affix other decorations, place the chocolate in a small zip-top plastic bag. Melt the chocolate in the bag in a double boiler over barely simmering water. When the chocolate has liquified, snip a tiny opening in one corner of the plastic bag and use the bag as your "pastry bag" for piping.

To temper chocolate: Tempering is used to prepare chocolate for coating and molding. Heating and then cooling the chocolate to precise temperatures makes the chocolate shiny. In the top of a double boiler over not-quite-simmering water, melt chopped chocolate and heat to 100°F. Do not let any water come in contact with the chocolate. Remove the pan from the hot water bath let cool to 90°F. Set the pan on a heating pad set on low to maintain the temperature at 90°F.

Chocolate Garnishes
Hawaiian Vintage Chocolate is the only chocolate grown in the United States. Hawaiian chefs frequently use beautiful chocolate garnishes to complete masterpiece desserts. Chocolate can be very tricky, "seizing" (stiffening) instantly if a drop of water accidentally falls into the pan, "breaking" (separating) if heat is applied incorrectly, and requiring a "tempering" process for coating and molding work. Yet sculpted flowers, leaves, geometric pieces and filigree designs are worth the effort of learning to work with this tempermental ingredient.

The recipe which follows gives steps for forming garnishes used with desserts in this book, and the quantity will make at least enough of any one type to garnish four dessert plates. At any time while you are working chocolate, you can warm it just slightly with a heat lamp or blow dryer to keep it flexible. Any excess chocolate at any step can be scraped back into the pan and allowed to remelt. Chocolate garnishes can be held in the refrigerator or freezer until ready to use.

To make chocolate curls: Melt 2 ounces chopped bittersweet chocolate in a double boiler and heat to 100°F. Let cool to 90°F. Pour the chocolate out on a baking sheet and spread it into a smooth layer ⅛-inch thick. When cool, scrape up narrow strips of chocolate with the back of your nail or a narrow spatula, creating small curls.

To make flat chocolate shapes: Place a heavy flexible plastic sheet on a work surface. Melt chopped bittersweet chocolate in a double boiler and heat to 100°F. Let cool to 90°F. Pour the chocolate out on the plastic and spread it out into a smooth layer of the desired thickness, usually just over ⅛ inch thick. Let cool to room temperature and use molds, cookie cutters, or the tip of a sharp knife to cut out the desired shapes. Pull the excess chocolate from around the shapes and place the designs in the refrigerator to set.

To make plain chocolate wings: Melt 4 ounces of bittersweet chocolate and spread out as described above. Cut into 4 freeform wing shapes when cooled.

To make chocolate discs: Melt 4 ounces of bittersweet chocolate and spread out as described above. Cut into eight 4-inch discs when cooled.

Striped Chocolate

This recipe makes dark chocolate striped with white chocolate. To create dark lines on a white background, simply use the dark chocolate first. Striped chocolate is used in the Chocolate-Macadamia Nut Torte (page 164) and the Unforgettable Torte (page 170).

Makes one 12 by 16 inch sheet

4 ounces white chocolate, chopped
8 ounces bittersweet chocolate, chopped

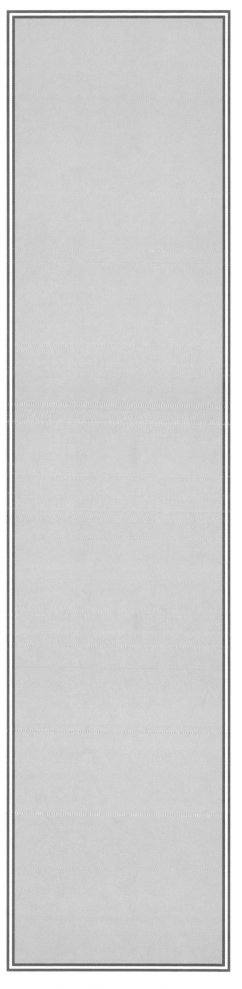

You will need a sheet of heavy flexible plastic, a long thin spatula, and a masonry comb. Melt chopped white chocolate in a double boiler and heat to 100°F. Let cool to 90°F. Pour the white chocolate out onto the plastic. With the spatula, spread the chocolate out to a thin layer of less than ⅛ inch. Using the masonry comb, scrape through the chocolate down to the plastic to create straight lines in the chocolate. Refrigerate for about 5 minutes, or until set.

Melt chopped bittersweet chocolate in a double boiler and heat to 100°F. Let cool to 90°F. Remove the white chocolate lines from the refrigerator. With a clean spatula, spread the dark chocolate over the back of the stripes. Be careful not to disturb the stripes. Refrigerate for 5 minutes.

Striped chocolate wings: After the chocolate has set slightly, cut through the chocolate and plastic with a sharp knife and drape it across a curved surface, plastic-side down. Refrigerate until set. Peel away the plastic to expose the shiny striped surface. Makes 8 wings.

Striped chocolate tulip petals: Let the chocolate set at room temperature and use a cookie cutter to stamp out the desired shapes. Pull the excess chocolate from around the cut shapes. Put the shapes, still on the plastic, in the refrigerator to firm completely, and peel the plastic from the designs. Makes 24 chocolate tulip petals.

An alternative method of making striped chocolate is to pour and smooth a thin layer of chocolate, then pipe stripes of the same color or contrasting color chocolate on top of the smooth layer.

Dark Chocolate Lattice Leaves Place a heavy flexible plastic sheet on a work surface. Melt 2 ounces chopped bittersweet chocolate in a double boiler and heat to 100°F. Let cool to 90°F. Drizzle the chocolate onto the plastic in a thin stream from the tip of a spoon, crisscrossing the strands of chocolate. When set, cut the lattice into leaf shapes and dust with cocoa powder.

Chocolate filigree: Draw a design to follow. Lay the design on the work surface and place a sheet of heavy flexible clear plastic on top of it. Melt 2 ounces chopped bittersweet chocolate in a double boiler and heat to 100°F. Let cool to 90°F. Place the melted chocolate in a pastry bag fitted with a fine writing tip and pipe the chocolate over the design, following the lines. Lift the plastic and place it on a flat sheet pan or, if a curved design is desired, lay it across a curved surface. Refrigerate to set.

Coconuts

Shelling a Coconut: Puncture one of the "eyes" of a husked coconut with an icepick. Pour out the coconut water, reserving it if desired, then crack the coconut by hitting it with a heavy hammer in the middle where the shell is the widest. Continue rapping around the coconut until you have cracked the shell in a circle and can separate the two halves. Pry the coconut meat out of the shell with a sharp, heavy knife. Or, heat the coconut in a preheated 350°F oven for 15 minutes, remove, and let cool. Wrap the coconut in a kitchen towel and crack into pieces with a hammer.

Grating Fresh Coconut Meat: Break the shelled fresh meat into small pieces. With a sharp, heavy knife, peel off the brown outer skin. Grate the meat with the large holes of a grater or with a vegetable peeler. Coconut can also be grated in a food processor with the shredding disc, or chopped finely with the steel blade.

Toasting Coconut: Preheat the oven to 350°F. Cut the peeled coconut meat into thin strips with a sharp paring knife. Spread the coconut strips in a single layer on a baking sheet and toast in the oven for 15 to 20 minutes, until golden. If the coconut has been dried already, reduce the toasting time to 5 to 7 minutes.

Making Coconut Milk: Place the freshly grated coconut meat from 1 coconut in a square of cheesecloth. Bring the edges of the cheesecloth together and tie with a piece of string. Place the cheesecloth bundle in a large pot. Bring enough water to cover the bundle to a boil in a separate pot, and pour over the coconut bundle. Let cool. When the water and coconut are cool enough to handle, with your hands, squeeze the coconut milk out through the cheesecloth into the pot. Use immediately or refrigerate for up to 2 days.

Cream Puffs
Makes about 15 2-inch puffs

½ cup milk
½ cup water
½ cup (1 stick) unsalted butter
1 cup unbleached all-purpose flour
2 tablespoons sugar
4 eggs

Preheat oven to 400°F. Line 2 baking sheets with parchment paper or grease them. In a medium saucepan, combine the milk, water, and butter and bring to a boil over medium-high heat. Add the flour and sugar all at once and stir the mixture until it forms a ball and comes away from the side of the pan, about 2 or 3 minutes. Add the eggs one at a time, stirring until each is blended. Remove from heat and let stand for 5 minutes.

Place the mixture in a pastry bag fitted with a 1-inch plain tip. Pipe 1½-inch-diameter portions 2 inches apart on the prepared pans. Bake for 10 minutes, then reduce heat to 350°F and bake for 10 to 15 minutes, or until light brown.

Crème Anglaise
Makes 2 cups

4 egg yolks
⅓ cup sugar
1½ cups milk, heated
1 vanilla bean, halved lengthwise, or 2 teaspoons vanilla extract
1 tablespoon unsalted butter at room temperature (optional)

In a heavy, medium saucepan, whisk the egg yolks over low heat until they are pale in color. Whisk in the sugar 1 tablespoon at a time, then whisk until the mixture reaches the consistency of cake batter.

Whisk in the milk and vanilla bean, if using, then stir continuously with a wooden spoon until the custard coats the spoon and a line drawn down the back of the spoon remains visible. Remove from heat and stir in the vanilla extract. Strain through a fine-meshed sieve.

If the custard is to be chilled, press a sheet of plastic wrap directly onto the surface to prevent a skin from forming, or dot the top with bits of butter. Chill the custard for up to 2 days.

__Note:__ If the custard begins to overheat and the egg yolks are forming lumps, remove it immediately from the heat and whisk briskly to cool the mixture. Push the custard through a fine-meshed sieve with the back of a spoon to remove the lumps. If it has not sufficiently thickened, return it to heat to complete cooking.

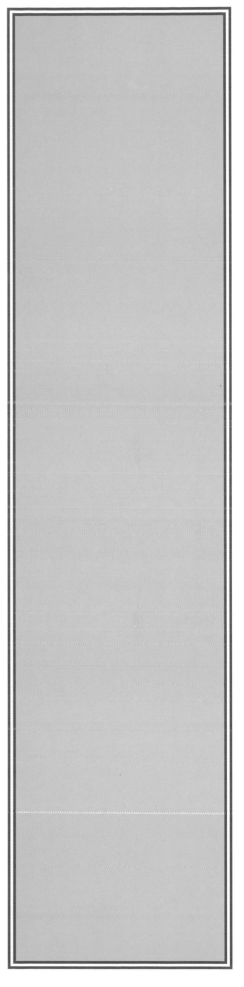

Croutons

Preheat the oven to 300°F. Cut the crusts from 5 or 6 slices of day-old or leftover bread. Slice the bread into 1/2-inch dice. In a sauté pan or skillet over high heat, melt 2 tablespoons of butter and 2 tablespoons of olive oil. Add the bread cubes and stir until coated on all sides. Spread the cubes over the prepared sheet pan in a single layer and bake until crisp and light brown in color. Cool; store in a sealed container up to 2 days, or in the freezer. To make garlic or herb croutons, use one of the flavored butters, page 186-187, and proceed as directed.

To "French " a lamb chop: Hold a rack of lamb so that the bones extend away from you. Using a sharp knife, scrape and cut away the meat from the bones. Press the chop meat back toward the chops between each bone, leaving the bones clean. Butchers will usually perform this task for you.

Fruit

Lilikoi (Passion Fruit): To use, cut the fruit in half and peel. For juice, press the fruit through a sieve and discard the pulp.

Mango: Lay the mango on its flattest side on a cutting board. With a small sharp knife, cut a thick slice off the top, avoiding the stone. Flip the fruit over and repeat the process on the other side. Cut away any flesh still clinging to the stone and discard the pit. Score the flesh inside the large halves, and, using your fingers, bend the skin backwards until it is almost inside out, which spreads the chunks apart. Cut them away from the skin and proceed to puree or use as desired.

Papaya: With a sharp knife, remove the skin, scoop out the seeds, and slice the meat. Many chefs reserve a few of the seeds, wash them, and use them as a garnish. Papaya contains an enzyme that breaks down protein; rinse and add papaya as close to serving time as possible when using in dishes containing gelatin.

Pineapple: Protect your hands with a small towel and twist or cut the top off a fresh pineapple. With a small sharp knife, cut the stem and bottom ends off the fruit. Stand the fruit upright on a cutting board and use the knife to slice off the tough, prickly outer peel from top to bottom. When the yellow core is exposed, cut out and discard any "eyes" left. The eyes lie in spirals around the fruit; making a V-shaped cut along the spiral line will quickly remove a whole row of eyes. Repeat until all eyes are removed. Fresh pineapple contains an enzyme which will break down protein; rinse well and add as close to serving time as possible when using in dishes containing gelatin.

Sapote: With a sharp knife, peel the skin from the fruit and cut the flesh into pieces.

Juice and reduced juice: Automatic juicers take the effort out of pressing the juice from fruit, but the process is easily done with a simple glass or ceramic juicer as well. Cut the fruit in half and press onto the center cone of the juicer. Or, peel the fruit, cut into 1-inch pieces, and press through a fine sieve with the back of a spoon, collecting the juice in a bowl. Squeeze citrus fruits before cutting to make extracting the juice easier. Strain juice through a fine-meshed sieve to remove any pulp, if desired.

The flavor of fruit juice can be intensified by reducing the juice: In a small saucepan over medium-high heat, bring the juice to a low boil and cook until the volume is reduced by half.

Pulp: Pulp is unsweetened, uncooked fruit. For pulp, pare, pit, and cut large fruit into small pieces and mash or press through a fine sieve until the pulp is a uniform texture. Berries can simply be mashed. Strain through a fine-meshed sieve to remove the seeds.

Uncooked Fruit Puree (Coulis)
Makes about 2 cups

4 cups fresh berries, or 1 pound fresh fruit, peeled and cut into ½-inch dice
2 tablespoons sugar or more to taste
1 teaspoon fresh lemon juice (optional)

Place the fruit in a food processor or blender and puree until smooth. Strain the puree through a fine-meshed sieve. Stir in sugar and lemon juice, adjusting to taste. Cover and refrigerate until needed. This puree may be used as an ingredient in another recipe, or by itself as a sauce.

Cooked Berry Puree or Sauce
Makes about 2 cups

4 cups fresh berries
¼ cup sugar, or more to taste
¼ cup water
2 tablespoons raspberry liqueur or eau-de-vie (optional)
1 tablespoon fresh lemon juice, or more to taste
½ teaspoon ground cinnamon. or more to taste

Put the berries in a large sauté pan or skillet with the ¼ cup sugar, water, and optional liqueur or eau-de-vie. Cook over medium heat for 15 minutes, or until the fruit is soft enough to mash with a spoon and most of the liquid has evaporated. Add the lemon juice and cinnamon, then taste and adjust the flavor with additional sugar, lemon juice, or cinnamon as needed.

Transfer the mixture to a blender or food processor and puree until smooth. Strain the fruit through a fine-meshed sieve, cover, and refrigerate until cold, about 2 hours; this should be a very thick puree. It may be used as an ingredient in another recipe, or by itself as a sauce.

Blackberry Sauce
Makes 2 cups

Zest and juice of ½ orange
Zest and juice of ½ lemon
3 tablespoons raspberry liqueur
3 tablespoons crème de cassis
1 tablespoon Pernod or other anise-flavored liqueur
¼ cup sugar
1½ cups fresh blackberries
1 vanilla bean, halved lengthwise

Combine all of the ingredients except ½ cup of the blackberries and the vanilla bean in a saucepan and heat over medium heat. Scrape the seeds from the vanilla bean and add the seeds and the pod to the pan. Bring to a boil and cook for 3 minutes. Strain through a fine-meshed sieve. Add the remaining whole blackberries.

Ice Creams and Sorbets

Vanilla Ice Cream
Makes 1½ pints

2 cups heavy (whipping) cream
½ cup half-and-half
1 vanilla bean, halved lengthwise, or 1 tablespoon vanilla extract
8 egg yolks
1 cup sugar

In a heavy medium saucepan, combine the cream, half-and-half, and vanilla bean, if using. Bring to a boil over medium-high heat. Meanwhile, beat the egg yolks with the sugar in a medium bowl until light and fluffy. Slowly whisk some of the hot cream mixture into the egg yolks, then add the egg yolks to the hot cream mixture and cook over low heat, stirring constantly, until the mixture is thick enough to coat the spoon. Remove from heat and remove the vanilla bean or stir in the vanilla extract. Cover and chill for at least 2 to 3 hours.

Freeze in an ice cream maker according to the manufacturer's instructions, or see page 195 if you do not have an ice cream freezer.

Fruit Ice Cream: Delete the vanilla bean or extract. Stir 1 cup fruit puree into the chilled ice cream base and freeze in an ice cream maker according to the manufacturer's instructions Makes 1 quart.

Macadamia Nut Ice Cream: Freeze the ice cream in an ice cream maker according to the manufacturer's instructions until partially frozen. Blend in ½ cup caramel sauce (page 187) and 1 cup chopped macadamia nuts. Return to the ice cream maker until frozen. Makes 1 quart.

Green Tea Ice Cream: Prepare the ice cream base, placing 5 Earl Grey tea bags in the cream before it is heated. Bring the cream to a boil, remove from the heat, and let sit for 5 minutes. Remove the tea bags and proceed with the ice cream base as above.

Fruit Sorbet

Sorbet, also called sherbet or ice, is made from fruit puree, fruit juice, and sugar syrup. The length of time the syrup cooks affects the texture of the sorbet: French sorbets are usually made with a very light syrup and are slightly grainy while Italian *sorbettos* are made with heavier syrup and are smoother.

2 pounds fresh fruit, peeled, seeded, and diced
1 cup simple syrup (page 202)
Juice of ½ lemon

In a blender or food processor, combine the syrup and fruit and puree until smooth. Strain through a fine-meshed sieve if necessary to remove seeds. Freeze in an ice cream maker according to the manufacturer's instructions.

Making Ice Cream Without a Machine

While there are a number of inexpensive ice cream makers on the market, it is possible to make ice creams and sorbets without any sort of machine. Here are two methods:

Blender or food processor method: Freeze the mixture in ice cube trays for 45 minutes to 1 hour, or until the cubes are almost frozen. Empty the ice cube trays into a blender or food processor and process, using on-and-off pulsing motions, until the mixture is smooth. Return to the ice cube trays and freeze for another 30 minutes. Process again and scrape the ice cream into a plastic container or mixing bowl. Freeze again until solid. When you are ready to serve, let stand at room temperature for several minutes to soften slightly.

Electric mixer method: Freeze the mixture in a mixing bowl until the outer 2 to 3 inches is frozen. Remove from the freezer and beat with an electric mixer until smooth. Repeat 2 more times, then allow to freeze completely. When you are ready to serve, let stand at room temperature for several minutes to soften slightly.

Mayonnaise

Makes 1½ cups

1 teaspoon Dijon mustard
2 egg yolks
Salt and white pepper to taste
2 cups peanut or other vegetable oil
2 tablespoons white wine vinegar or fresh lemon juice

Using a whisk or an electric blender, beat the mustard, egg yolks, salt, and pepper in a medium bowl until thick. Gradually whisk the oil into the egg mixture, starting with 1 drop at a time; when 2 or 3 tablespoons or the oils have been whisked into the eggs, you can pour in the rest of the oil in a fine stream while whisking constantly. Add the vinegar or lemon juice to the mixture 1 teaspoon at a time, whisking constantly until smooth. Cover and refrigerate up to 1 week.

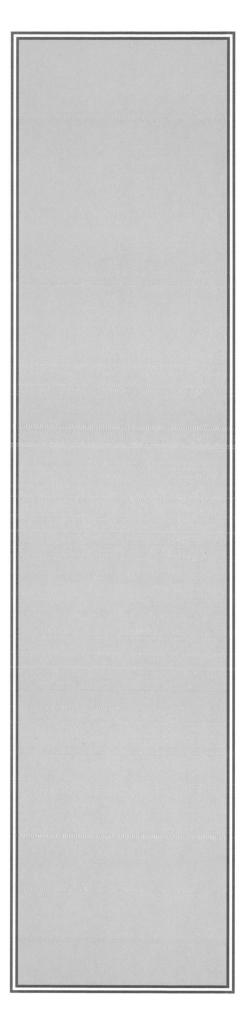

Nuts

Shelling Macadamia Nuts

Macadamia nuts are round and extremely hard, making them very difficult to crack. They are readily available already shelled, but if you wish to do the job yourself, preheat the oven to 150°F. Spread the nuts in a single layer on a baking sheet and roast for 2 hours (very large nuts may roast for up to 4 hours). Let cool. Place a nut in the indent of a chopping block (or even a crack in the sidewalk) and rap it sharply with a small hammer. The nuts will almost always come out whole. Macadamia nuts in the shell can be husked and kept in a basket in a dry place up to 6 months. Unshelled macadamias may be frozen and used as needed. To salt them, sauté the nuts in a little butter or oil. Lightly salt them, then cool and place in an airtight jar. Or, soak the nuts in salted water overnight, then place in a single layer on a baking sheet and dry for 1 hour at 150°F.

Toasting Nuts

Preheat the oven to 350°F. Spread the nuts in a single layer in a shallow pan. Bake, shaking the pan occasionally to toss the nuts, until golden, 5 to 12 minutes. Let cool.

Toasting Sesame Seeds

Spread the seeds in a small dry sauté pan or skillet over high heat. Stir and toss the sesame seeds until nutty brown and fragrant, about 3 to 5 minutes.

Glazed Nuts

Makes 2 cups

2 cups peeled unsalted nuts
2 cups water
1 cup sugar

In a heavy saucepan, stir the water and sugar over low heat just until the sugar dissolves. Increase heat to medium-high and continue to cook, brushing away the crystals which form on the sides of the pan with a damp brush. Do not stir the sugar mixture. Let the mixture boil until the sugar begins to color and turns golden brown. Remove from heat immediately and gently place the pan in a bowl of ice to stop the cooking process. When the caramel has cooled slightly, dip the prepared nuts in the caramel to glaze, and set aside on aluminum foil or waxed paper. If the caramel thickens too much before use, warm it gently to melt.

Peppers

Bell peppers now come in a rainbow of colors, and there are literally hundreds of varieties of chilies. Here are some general procedures common to all:

Handling fresh chilies: Precautions should be exercised in handling fresh chilies, since they contain potent oils. Either wear rubber gloves, or wash your hands thoroughly with soap and hot water after handling chilies. Never touch your skin until you've washed your hands. Also, wash the knife and cutting board in hot soapy water. Do not handle hot chilies under running water, since that spreads the oil vapors upward to your eyes.

Seeding and deribbing: Either cut out the ribs and seeds with a paring knife, or cut away the flesh, leaving a skeleton of ribs and seeds to discard. For the second method, cut a slice off the bottom of the pepper or chili so that it will stand up on the cutting board. Holding the pepper or chili with your free hand, slice its natural curvature in sections. You will be left with all the flesh and none of the seeds and ribs. The flesh may now be cut as indicated in the recipe.

Roasting and peeling: Cut a small slit near the stem end of each whole pepper or chili to ensure that it will not explode. Roast the peppers or chilies in one of the following ways:

- For a large number of peppers or chilies, and to retain the most texture, lower them gently into 375°F (almost smoking) oil and fry until the skin blisters. Turn them with tongs when one side is blistered, since they will float to the surface of the oil. This method is also the most effective if the vegetables are not perfectly shaped, since it is difficult to get the heat from the broiler into the folds of peppers and some chilies.
- Preheat the broiler. Cut the peppers or chilies into quarters lengthwise and place them on a broiler or rack 6 inches from the heat source, turning them with tongs until all surfaces are charred.
- Put the peppers or chilies on the cooking rack of a hot charcoal or gas grill and turn them until the skin is charred.
- Place a wire cake rack over a gas or electric burner set at the highest temperature and turn the peppers or chilies with tongs until all surfaces are charred.

Cool the peppers or chilies by one of the following methods:

- Put them in ice water. This stops the cooking action immediately and cools them enough to peel them within 1 minute. The peppers or chilies will stay relatively firm.
- Put the peppers or chilies in a paper bag, close it, and let them cool. This also effectively separates the flesh from the skin, but it will be about 20 minutes before they are cool enough to handle, and they will soften somewhat during that time.

Finally, pull the skin off and remove the seeds.

Chili Pepper Water
Makes 3 cups

Bottles of homemade chili pepper water are a staple on Hawaiian tables. At its most basic, chili pepper water consists of fresh chilies, rice vinegar, and garlic, bottled and aged for 2 to 3 weeks. This version shows its Asian influence with ginger. Chili pepper water can be purchased at markets in Hawaii and through mail order services.

2½ cups boiling water
¾ cup cold water
2 tablespoons distilled white vinegar
1 garlic clove, minced
1 tablespoon chopped fresh ginger
14 Hawaiian or Thai chilies

In a blender or food processor, combine all ingredients and puree until smooth, about 1 minute. Pour into hot sterilized bottles, cover, and refrigerate.

Rice

Steamed rice: Place the rice in a large saucepan. Cover with water and rinse twice. Drain. Add water to cover the rice by one inch. Cover the saucepan and bring to a boil over medium-high heat. Boil 1 minute. Reduce the heat to low and steam 10 minutes. Reduce heat to very low and steam for 10 minutes more. Or, line the basket of a bamboo steamer with 2 layers of cheesecloth. Place the rinsed rice in the lined basket, cover the basket, and place over boiling water, making sure the steaming basket does not touch the water. Steam for 20 minutes, or until the rice is tender to the bite. One cup of dry rice will serve 4 people when cooked.

Steamed Jasmine Rice: Jasmine rice is a long-grained variety with a slight jasmine scent. Steam as above.

Steamed Sticky Rice: Use glutinous rice, a short-grained variety frequently used in Asian dishes. Place the rice in a large bowl and cover with cold water. Rub the rice between your hands and drain off the water. Cover the rice with clean water and repeat until the water runs clear. Cover the rice with water and soak overnight, or, soak the rice in hot water for 3 hours before steaming. Drain the rice. Place in a cheesecloth-lined steaming basket or a steamer. Place over boiling water, making sure the steaming basket does not touch the water. Cover and steam 30 minutes. Three cups of glutinous rice will serve 4 people when cooked.

Roasting Garlic

With a sharp knife, cut the top quarter off a head of unpeeled garlic. Rub the head with olive oil. Place in a baking dish in a 350°F oven and roast for 1 hour. Let cool to the touch. Separate the cloves from the head and squeeze the roasted garlic pulp or puree from each.

Rendering Duck Fat

Pull the yellow fat away from the skin and meat of the duck and put it in a heavy, medium sauté pan or skillet. Cook slowly over low heat, letting the fat melt. When all the fat has drained away from the tissue and the tissue is brown and crisp, strain the fat through a fine-meshed sieve or cheesecloth into a small heat-proof bowl. Use immediately, or, let the fat cool, cover, and refrigerate.

Scallion-Infused Oil

In a medium bowl, combine 2 minced whole scallions with 1 cup extra-virgin olive oil. Cover and let sit for at least 48 hours. Strain through a fine-meshed sieve into a glass jar or bottle; cover.

Seafood

Select the freshest fish available. Look for fish with bulging, not sunken, eyes, and a sweet fresh smell (shark, squid, and skates, exceptions to the rule, will have a slightly ammoniated smell when fresh). Store fresh fish in the coldest part of the refrigerator, wrapping in plastic wrap and placing on ice chips if necessary. Lean fish keeps longer than fatty fish, but in no case keep it longer than 2 days. Freeze fish immediately to keep it longer. Do not freeze fish that has already been frozen.

Cleaning Squid: Press the body from the top end toward the tentacles to squeeze out the entrails and quill. Discard the quill. Rinse under cold water, cut off the tentacles just above the eyes, and squeeze the tentacles to eject the horny beak. Discard the beak. Pull the skin from the body with your fingers. Pull the wings from the sides and skin them also. Chop the tentacles into rings if desired.

Peeling and Deveining Shrimp: Rinse under cold water and break the head portion from the body and tail. Pull off the legs on the underside. With your fingers or a small knife, split the shell on the underside and peel it back over the shrimp. You can pull off the small tail at this time, or break the shell away from the tail and leave the small tail attached. With a small sharp knife, split the top of the back of the shrimp and lift out the black strip.

Smoking

Arrange your smoker or charcoal grill for smoking: You want indirect heat and a low fire with barely enough oxygen to burn. In a charcoal grill, place the charcoal to one side of the grill, ignite it and let it burn until white ash forms on the briquettes. Add selected wood for smoke flavor (hickory, mesquite, apple, etc.). Only a few small pieces are needed; about the equivalent of 4 charcoal briquets. Wood shavings or a small amount of sawdust work well. Place a rack over the fire area. In a gas grill, light the gas, turn to low flame, and place the wood chips over the fire area. Place the food to be smoked on the opposite side of the grill from the fire. Cover, open the air vents in the bottom of the grill, and nearly close the vents in the top of the grill.

Stocks

Chicken Stock
Makes 12 cups

6 quarts water
5 pounds bony chicken parts, skin, and trimmings
2 carrots, peeled and cut into chunks
1 large onion, halved
3 garlic cloves, halved
3 celery stalks, halved
3 fresh thyme sprigs, or 1 teaspoon dried thyme
6 fresh parsley sprigs
3 bay leaves
12 black peppercorns

In a large stockpot, combine the water and the chicken parts, skin, and trimmings. Bring to a boil, then reduce heat to a simmer, skimming off the foam that rises for the first 10 to 15 minutes. Cook for 1 hour, then add the remaining ingredients. Bring to a boil, reduce heat to low, and simmer the stock for 3 hours.

Strain the stock through a fine-meshed sieve and let cool to room temperature, then refrigerate. Remove and discard the congealed layer of fat on the surface. Store in the refrigerator up to 3 days. To keep longer, bring the stock to a boil every 3 days, or freeze it for up to 3 months.

To clarify the stock: Let the stock cool until it is lukewarm. Blend 3 egg whites together and pour into the warm stock; as the whites coagulate and rise they will trap bits still floating in the stock. When the egg whites have risen to the top and the stock is clear, skim the eggs off the top with a slotted spoon. You can repeat the process if necessary to obtain clear stock.

Veal or Beef Stock
Makes 12 cups

8 pounds veal or beef bones and trimmings
2 onions, halved
2 carrots, peeled and cut into chunks
2 celery stalks, halved
3 garlic cloves, halved
8 quarts water
3 fresh thyme sprigs, or 1 teaspoon dried thyme
6 fresh parsley sprigs
2 bay leaves
12 black peppercorns

Preheat the oven to 400°F. Put the bones and trimmings in a roasting pan and roast about 45 minutes, turning occasionally. Add the vegetables to the pan and roast for 20 minutes, or until the vegetables are browned.

Place the bones and vegetables in a large stockpot, pouring off any fat. Add 1 quart of the water to the pan and place on the stove over high heat. Stir to scrape up the brown bits clinging to the bottom of the pan. Pour this liquid into the stockpot with the remaining 7 quarts water and the herbs and spices. Bring to a boil, then reduce heat to a simmer, skimming off the foam that rises for the first 10 to 15 minutes. Simmer for 5 to 6 hours.

Strain the stock through a fine-meshed sieve and discard the solids. Let cool, then refrigerate. Remove and discard the congealed layer of fat on the surface. Store in the refrigerator up to 3 days. To keep longer, bring the stock to a boil every 3 days, or freeze it for up to 3 months.

Fish Stock
Makes 12 cups

4 quarts water
1 cup dry white wine
4 pounds fish trimmings such as skin, bones, and heads
2 tablespoons fresh lemon juice
1 onion, halved
2 celery stalks, halved
4 fresh parsley sprigs
2 fresh thyme sprigs, or 1 teaspoon dried thyme
2 bay leaves
6 black peppercorns

In a large stockpot, bring the water and wine to a boil. Rinse all the fish trimming, under cold running water, add to the stockpot, and return to a boil. Reduce heat to a simmer, skimming off the foam that rises for the first 10 to 15 minutes. Simmer for 1 hour.

Add the remaining ingredients to the pot. Bring the mixture to a boil, then reduce heat to a simmer and cool for 1½ to 2 hours. Strain the stock through a fine-meshed sieve, pressing on the solids with the back of a large spoon. Discard the solids. Let cool, then cover and refrigerate up to 3 days. To keep longer, bring the stock to a boil every 3 days, or freeze it for up to 3 months.

Duck Stock
Makes 12 cups

3 pounds duck trimmings (bones, skin, fat, and/or anything else you can trim
 away) and meat
4 quarts water
1 onion, halved
1 carrot, peeled and halved
2 celery stalks, including leaves, cut into sections
3 fresh thyme sprigs, or 1 teaspoon dried thyme
3 fresh parsley sprigs
6 black peppercorns

Preheat the oven to 450°F. Put the trimmings and meat in a shallow roasting
pan and roast for 30 minutes, or until browned. Bring the water to a boil over high
heat. Add the trimmings and meat to the water and reduce heat to medium. When
the water returns to a boil, skim frequently until the foam stops rising, then add
the remaining ingredients and simmer, uncovered, for at least 6 hours. Add additional water if the stock level falls below the level of the ingredients.

Strain the stock and discard the solids. Let the stock cool to room temperature, then refrigerate. Remove and discard the congealed fat layer from the top.
Store in the refrigerator for up to 3 days. To keep longer, bring to a boil every 3
days, or refrigerate for up to 3 months.

Veal or Beef Demi-Glace
Makes 2 cups

Demi-glace is unsalted meat stock that has been degreased and then reduced over
medium-low heat until it becomes rich and syrupy. The concentrated flavor adds
richness and depth to sauces and stews. Traditional demi-glace is thickened with
flour and must simmer gently with much tending, but this quick version is lighter
and can be made more quickly because it is thickened at the end with arrowroot
or cornstarch.

2 tablespoons vegetable oil
1 large onion, diced
2 celery stalks, diced
1 carrot, peeled and sliced
½ cup diced ham
3 tablespoons tomato paste
1 fresh thyme sprig
1 bay leaf
6 peppercorns
10 cups veal or beef stock (page 200)
½ cup Madeira
2 to 3 teaspoons arrowroot or cornstarch mixed with 2 tablespoons cold water
Salt and freshly ground black pepper to taste
1 tablespoon unsalted butter

Heat the oil in a large saucepan over medium heat. Stir in the onion, celery,
carrot, and ham. Cover and cook over low heat for 10 minutes. Uncover the pan
and stir in the tomato paste, thyme, bay leaf, and peppercorns. Whisk in the stock
and Madeira, and bring to a boil over high heat.

Once the mixture has started to boil, reduce heat to medium high and cook
the sauce to reduce to 2 cups. Depending on the rate at which the liquid is
boiling, this may take anywhere from 30 minutes to 1 hour. Strain the liquid
through a fine-meshed sieve into a 2-cup measuring cup. If it has not reduced
enough, pour the liquid back into the pan and keep boiling. If it has reduced too
much, add enough water to make 2 cups.

Pour the liquid back into the pan and bring it back to a simmer. Whisk in the
arrowroot or cornstarch mixture 1 teaspoon at a time, returning the sauce to a
simmer after each addition, until the sauce reaches the desired consistency. Add

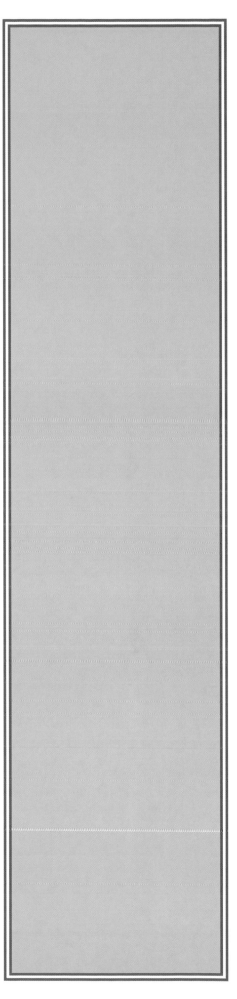

salt and pepper. If using the sauce immediately, swirl in the butter. If not serving immediately, do not whisk in the butter, but remove the pan from heat and place dots of butter on the surface of the sauce to prevent a skin from forming. Whisk in the butter when reheating the sauce. To store, cover and refrigerate for up to 5 days or freeze for up to 3 months.

Sugar

Simple Syrup
Makes 3 cups

2 cups sugar
1 cup water

In a heavy, medium saucepan, combine the sugar and water and cook over high heat until the sugar dissolves and the mixture reaches a full boil, about 3 minutes. Remove from heat, let cool, and store in a covered container in the refrigerator for up to 3 weeks.

Pulled Sugar
Pulled sugar is definitely in the "advanced" category of confectionery. Yet it makes spectacular garnishes, and, once pulled and worked into a shiny mass, it can be kept for months if you place it on a piece of clean limestone in an airtight container. Keep it workable by placing it under a heat lamp until warm, soft, and pliable.

4 pounds sugar
2 cups water
1 teaspoon cream of tartar
Food coloring, if desired

In a heavy, medium saucepan, combine the sugar, water, and cream of tartar and bring to a boil over medium heat. Cook until the syrup reaches 160°F. Do not stir the syrup during this time. When the temperature has reached 160°F, remove the pan from heat and set it in a pan of ice water to stop the cooking. The syrup will still be colorless.

When the syrup has cooled slightly, pour it out onto a marble slab or a baking sheet. Let it continue to cool. If desired, drop 4 or 5 large drops of food coloring randomly over the surface of the syrup as it cools. Brown coloring will result in a golden color; all colors will lighten considerably as the sugar is worked. When it appears to have thickened, put on heavy rubber gloves and lift the edges of the syrup; the syrup will pull away from slab and fold back on itself. Use the palm of your hand to roll the edges in over the remainder of the syrup. Continue to lift the syrup over itself again and again, working slowly at first, then faster as the sugar cools. As it becomes cool enough to pull, it will hold its shape. When it is cool enough to handle, grasp the lump with both hands, lift it, and quickly pull your hands apart, stretching the sugar. Let the center of the strip rest on the work surface and fold the ends across, folding the sugar strip in thirds. Lift again with both hands and twist as if you are wringing it. Repeat the pulling, folding, and twisting motions about 45 times, or until the sugar develops a deep shine (overpulling the sugar will kill the shine). It will look like mother of pearl. The wringing action helps distribute the color evenly throughout the mass; if you prefer the effect of fine straight lines of color, do not wring between foldings. Place the sugar mass under a heat lamp to keep it pliable.

• **To make leaves or petals:** Using scissors, cut off a small piece of the sugar and press it into a leaf mold or other form. If creating flowers, press several of these "petals" together to form the flower.
• **To make spirals:** Working under the heat lamp, pull a piece of sugar from the lump and press it against a wooden dowel or spoon handle. Holding the sugar in place with your thumb, twist the dowel, pulling it away from the sugar to draw a thin twisting strand from the mass, until the desired length is reached. Pinch off

the end from the lump, remove from the lamp area to let cool, and slide the finished spiral off the dowel.

• **To make ribbons:** Working under the heat lamp, grasp a piece of sugar and pull a long thin strip from the lump. Pinch or cut it off, stretch it as thin as desired, and twist and ruffle as desired. Remove from the lamp area and let cool.

Tomatoes

Smoked Tomatoes

Arrange your smoker or charcoal grill for smoking (see page 198). Cut plum (Roma) tomatoes in half lengthwise, sprinkle with salt, and place on the rack cut-side up on the side away from the fire. Cover, open the air vents in the bottom of the grill, and nearly close the vents in the top of the grill. Smoke until the tomatoes are almost dry and have absorbed the smoky flavor, 45 to 60 minutes.

To peel and seed tomatoes: Cut out the core of the tomato. With a knife, make an X on the bottom of th tomato. Plunge the tomato into boiling water for exactly 10 seconds. Remove with a slotted spoon and plunge into a bowl of cold water, then drain. Peel off the skin. Cut the tomato in half crosswise. Squeeze and shake the tomato gently over a bowl or sink to remove the seeds. Any clinging seeds may be removed with the tip of a paring knife or your finger.

Preparing Ti Leaves

With a sharp knife, remove the stiff back of the leaf rib, starting at the tip. Do not cut the leaf itself. With the rib removed, the leaf will be pliable enough to wrap food in packages tied with the removed rib or kitchen string.

Vegetable Curls

To curl carrots, beets, and radishes for garnish, grate or pare the cleaned vegetable in long thin strips and immediately place the strips in ice water. To curl green onions (scallions), with a small sharp knife, cut in half lengthwise through the bulb. Trim the stems 4 to 5 inches above the bulb. Cut the green stems into lengthwise strips, leaving attached at the bulb, and place in ice water.

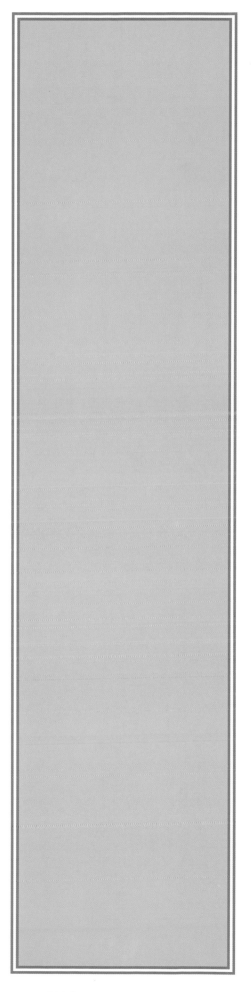

Lemongrass-grilled Mako Shark with Sticky Rice and Roasted Banana–Mint Sauce; Jacqueline Lau, Roy's Nicolina, Kahana, Maui

Glossary of Ingredients

The ingredients used in Hawaiian recipes come from all over the world. It is a challenge to find the perfect ingredient, but nearly all, no matter how exotic, can be located—or a suitable alternative can be located. This extensive glossary will help you understand the international lexicon of Hawaiian ingredients. The mail order section which follows will help you obtain the most unusual items

A

Ahi:
The Hawaiian name for both yellowfin and bigeye tuna. Often served in the islands as sashimi (Japanese-style raw fish).

Aku:
The Hawaiian name for skipjack tuna. Deep red in color and stronger tasting than ahi. Good broiled, or grilled, or used raw in poke.

Amaranth:
A slightly sweet vegetable with small dark green leaves and a red stem. An ancient Chinese food and a symbol of immortality. Also called Chinese spinach, the leaves have a watercresslike flavor and are used throughout Asia.

Anaheim Chili:
Long green narrow chili used often in Southwest cuisines.

Ancho Chili:
The dried poblano chili, dark red and usually 4 to 6 inches long.

Asian sesame oil:
A strong-flavored oil made from toasted sesame seeds and used in most Asian cuisines. Only a small amount is needed for flavoring. Sesame oil burns at a lower heat than most oils. Refrigerate after opening.

Au:
The Hawaiian name for swordfish, or marlin.

Azuki beans:
Reddish beans used in Chinese and Japanese cuisine, often in sweet pastries. Look for them in an Asian grocery.

B

Baby corn:
Miniature ears of corn 2 or 3 inches long. Also called young corn. If fresh baby corn is not available it can be found canned in most Asian markets.

Bamboo shoots:
Young, cone-shaped shoots sold fresh or in cans in Asian groceries.

Bean sprouts:
Mung beans that have sprouted. Available fresh or canned.

Bean thread noodles:
Also called cellophane noodles, glass noodles, or Chinese long rice, these noodles are reconstituted in water before using.

Black Sesame Seeds:
Also called goma. Available in bottles or packages in Asian markets.

Bok choy:
A Chinese cabbage with a white stem and dark green leaves. You can substitute napa cabbage if not available.

Breadfruit:
A bland, starchy vegetable widely used in the Pacific, but difficult to get on the U.S. mainland. Potatoes are a good substitute.

C

Cajun spice mix:
A hot dry spice of black pepper, paprika, cayenne, and other spices. Available bottled in most markets.

Char Siu:
Pork or beef that has been marinated in a sweet-spicy red sauce and dried. Used in small amounts to flavor noodle dishes or as a side dish.

Chili oil:
An Asian oil seasoned with hot chili peppers. Substitute any hot sauce.

Chili paste:
A thick chili sauce produced and used in many Asian cuisines such as Thai, Vietnamese, Indonesian, and Filipino. It is made of chilis, onions, sugar, and tamarind.

Chili pepper water:
A hot mixture of small red chilies, salt, vinegar, and garlic. It may be purchased in bottle form, or see the recipe on page 197.

Chinese broccoli:
See choi sum.

Chinese cabbage:
See won bok.

Chinese fermented black beans:
Salted fermented black beans. They can be purchased bottled or in cans in Asian markets, and should be rinsed and chopped to release their flavor.

Chinese five spice powder:
A spice mix of anise, cinnamon, cloves, fennel, and star anise. Available in Asian markets.

Chinese long rice:
See bean thread noodles.

Chinese mustard cabbage:
Also known as gai choy; mustard greens may be substituted.

Chinese parsley:
See cilantro

Chinese peas:
Also known as snow peas

Choi sum:
Chinese broccoli. If not available, substitute napa cabbage or regular broccoli.

Cilantro:
A pungent flat-leaf herb resembling parsley; also called fresh coriander or Chinese parsley.

Coconut milk:
A liquid extracted from shredded coconut meat by soaking it with hot water and straining. Available in cans from Southeast Asia, or see the recipe on page 191.

Curry (kari) leaves:
Small, shiny fragrant leaves resembling bay leaves used prominently in Sri Lankan cooking. Used fresh or dried. The fresh leaves are pulverized and fried in oil to release a currylike flavor. Available in Asian markets. Substitute a pinch of curry powder.

D

Daikon:
Japanese name for a white, crisp radish. Turnips can be substituted.

Dashi:
Commercially available powdered Japanese soup stock. Available in Asian markets.

Date palm sugar:
A rich, brown, sugar made of ground dried dates, often made into flat bars, or added to soy sauce to make a sweet sauce. Available in Asian markets.

E

Edible flowers:
Flowers add a beautiful touch to dishes, and many flowers are edible. Make sure they are free of pesticides: your own garden is your surest supplier. Among edible blooms are pansies, violas, and violets; roses, apple, peach, and plum blooms; geraniums; orange and lemon blossoms; nasturtiums; lavender, jasmine, daises, daylilies, dianthus, marigolds, and squash blooms.

F

Fiddlehead ferns:
Known as pohole, or warabi, or hoio fern in Hawaii. Available in specialty markets. Substitute haricots verts or baby Blue Lake green beans.

Fish sauce:
Also called nam pla in Thai cuisine or nuoc mam in Vietnamese cuisine. Very salty and pungent. Made from fermented small fish and shrimp. Available in Asian markets.

Furikake:
A spicy Japanese seaweed-based seasoning mix.

G

Galangal:
Also called Thai ginger or galangha. A large, juicy rhyzome with a thin pinkish-brown skin. Substitute fresh ginger.

Ginger:
Fresh ginger is a brown, fibrous, knobby rhizome. It keeps for long periods of time. To use, peel the brown outside skin and slice, chop, or puree. It will keep indefinitely placed in a jar with sherry and refrigerated.

Goma:
See black sesame seeds.

Green curry paste:
A blend of chilies and other seasonings, including lime and coriander, used in Thai cuisine and available packaged or in jars. Substitute curry powder.

Green papaya:
The unripe form of the papaya, usually shredded and used in salads and stir-fries in Southeast Asian cuisines.

Guava:
A round tropical fruit with a yellow skin and pink inner flesh and many seeds. Grown commercially in Hawaii. The puree or juice is available as a frozen concentrate. Guava can also be made into jams, jellies and sauces.

Gyoza:
A Japanese dumpling, also known as a pot sticker.

H

Haha:
The Hawaiian word for the stem of the taro plant. See taro.

Hajikami:
Pickled ginger sprouts, used in Japanese cooking as a garnish. Available bottled in Japanese markets.

Haupia:
Traditional Hawaiian pudding made of coconut milk, sugar, and cornstarch.

Hawaiian Chili:
Small, hot red chili pepper. Substitute Thai chilies or red pepper flakes.

Hawaiian salt:
A coarse sea salt gathered in tidal pools after a storm or high tide. Hawaiians sometimes mix it with a red clay to make alae salt. Substitute kosher salt.

Hearts of palm:
Tender palm shoots, sometimes available fresh, but most often found in cans in Asian markets. Used mostly in salads and stir-fries.

Hoio fern:
See fiddlehead ferns.

Hoisin sauce:
A thick, brownish sweet sauce made from soybean paste, sugar, and spices. Can be purchased bottled.

I

Ichimi:

See togarishi.

Imu:

A firepit, or underground oven of hot volcanic stones, used in Hawaiian cooking to steam food.

Inamona sauce:

A traditional Hawaiian seasoning paste of kukui nuts, salt, and chilies.

J

Japanese eggplant:

A long, narrow purple, eggplant. Substitute Italian eggplant.

Japanese plum wine:

Wine made from the Japanese plum, or ume, and available in Asian and specialty foods stores.

Jasmine rice:

A fragrant and delicate Asian rice. Substitute white long-grained rice.

Jícama:

A bulbous, turniplike root used raw in salads or cooked as a vegetable. Available in Asian and Latino markets.

K

Kaffir lime leaves:

Citrus-flavored leaves sold in Asian markets. Used widely in Southeast Asian dishes. Sold fresh or dried. Reconstitute dried leaves by soaking in warm water. Substitute grated lime zest.

Kahuku prawns:

- Farm-raised, freshwater prawns that are slightly sweeter than shrimp. Jumbo shrimp may be substituted.

Kaiware sprouts:

A sharp-flavored sprout used in Japanese dishes.

Kajiki:

The Japanese name for Pacific blue marlin. Substitute swordfish or shark.

Kalo:

The Hawaiian word for taro root. See taro.

Kalua pig:

Shredded pork that has been cooked in a traditional underground pit, or imu.

Ka'u orange:

A variety of orange grown on the island of Hawaii. The outer skin is ugly and blackened, but the inside is especially sweet and juicy. Substitute Valencia oranges.

Keahole baby lobster:

Small freshwater farmed lobsters grown in the Kona district of the island of Hawaii. Substitute spiny lobsters or jumbo prawns.

Kecap manis:

A thick dark Indonesian soy sauce sweetened with palm sugar. Available in Asian markets.

Kiawe tree:

The Hawaiian name for a the mesquite tree, a source of excellent charcoal.

Kiwi:

Kiwis hide their sweet green flesh in a fuzzy brown skin. Select fruit with few imperfections in the skin, and no very soft bruised spots. Peel the kiwi and slice; the seeds are edible.

Kukui nuts:

A native Hawaiian nut very high in oil. Used roasted, salted, or pounded in traditional Hawaiian cooking.

Kulolo:

A traditional Hawaiian pudding made with taro and brown sugar.

Kumu:

A reef fish and a member of the goatfish family. Its meat is mild and delicate. Substitute any white meat fish with a high fat content, such as flounder or halibut.

L

Lauae fern:

A shiny, smooth fern used as a border in Hawaiian gardens, and as decorations for parties.

Laulau:

A bundle of meat, fish, and taro leaves wrapped in ti leaves and steamed. A traditional Hawaiian dish.

Lemon-scented basil:

A leafy aromatic herb used in Southeast Asian cooking.

Lemongrass:

Long greenish stalks with a pungent lemony flavor. Also called citronella. Substitute grated lemon zest.

Lilikoi:

The Hawaiian name for passion fruit, which is a small yellow, purple, or brown oval fruit of the passion fruit vine. The "passion" in passion fruit comes from the fact that its flower resembles a Maltese cross and refers to Christ's crucifixion, not to aphrodesiac qualities. The flavor is delicate but somewhat sharp, and perfume-like. Passion fruit is a natural substitute for lemon juice. Passion fruit concentrate can be found in the frozen juice section of many markets. Substitute oranges.

Limu:

The Hawaiian word for seaweed, of which they use as many as twenty-five varieties. Japanese ogo is a type of seaweed. Much ogo today is farm raised.

Lingham chili sauce:

A hot sweet sauce from Malaysia, made from chilies, onions, sugar, and spices. Substitute any sweet hot chili sauce or paste.

Lomi lomi salmon:

A fresh-tasting Hawaiian salad of salt-cured salmon, onion, and tomato.

Lotus root:

The root of the Chinese water lily. Available fresh or canned in Chinese markets.

Luau:

A traditional Hawaiian feast that usually includes foods prepared in an imu, or underground oven. See page 177.

Luau Leaves:

The young, green tops of the taro root. Substitute fresh spinach.

Lumpia wrappers:

Thin rectangular noodle sheets used to make lumpia, the Filipino version of pot stickers. Substitute eggroll skins.

Lundberg rice mix:

A packaged mix of wild and premium brown rices produced by the Lundberg family of California. Available in specialty foods stores. Substitute any wild and brown rice mix.

Lychee:

A small fruit with white meat and a hard shell Available fresh and canned in Asian markets.

M

Macadamia nuts:

A rich, oily nut grown mostly on the Big Island of Hawaii. Native to Australia. They're good, but expensive, canned.

Macadamia nut oil:

A premium cooking and salad oil produced in Hawaii from macadamia nuts. It has a high heat threshold for burning.

Mahimahi:
Also called dolphinfish, with a firm pink flesh. Best fresh, but often available frozen. A standard in island restaurants and markets. Substitute snapper, catfish, or halibut.

Mango:
Gold and green tropical fruit available in many supermarkets. Available fresh June through September in Hawaii. Substitute fresh peaches.

Maui onion:
A very sweet, juicy, large round onion similiar to the Vidalia or Walla Walla onion. Often available on the West Coast, but expensive. Substitute any sweet white onion.

Mirin:
A sweet Japanese rice wine found in Asian markets. Substitute sweet sherry.

Miso:
A soybean paste made by salting and fermenting soybeans and rice. Shiro miso, or white miso, is the mildest of several different types. Available shrink-wrapped, and in cans and jars, in Asian markets. Can be stored for months in a refrigerator.

Mizuna:
Japanese cabbage. Available in Asian markets and natural foods stores. Substitute fresh spinach.

Moana:
Also called moano; a member of the goatfish family with delicate, white meat. Substitute any white meat fish with lots of fat content.

Mochiko sweet rice flour:
Japanese glutinous rice flour used in making pastries and some sauces.

Molokai sweet potatoes:
Grown in small quantities on the island of Molokai. Substitute any sweet potato.

Momiji chili sauce:
A sauce of grated daikon and red pepper. Available in Asian markets.

N

Nam pla:
See fish sauce.

Napa cabbage:
See won bok.

Noodles:
Bean thread noodles: Also called glass noodles, cellophane noodles, and long rice, these extremely fine, transparent noodles are made from mung bean starch and sold in skeins. They are soaked in water for a few seconds before cooking, and are used in salad, stir-fry, and soup.

Chinese egg noodles: Made of wheat flour and egg, these noodles come in several widths and can be bought fresh or dried. They are eaten warm or cold, or cooked, made into noodle cakes, and fried.

Rice stick noodles: Thin rice noodles usually sold coiled in the package. When dropped into hot oil they puff up into cruchy sticks.

Soba Japanese buckwheat flour noodles: Soba noodles are light brown and thin. They are eaten warm or cold.

Somen: Japanese wheat flour noodles, white in color and very thin. Somen noodles are usually eaten cold.

Nori:
Sheets of dried and compressed seaweed used in making rolled sushi. Available in Asian markets.

O

Ogo:
The Japanese name for seaweed.

Okinawan sweet potato:
A sweet potato with purple flesh. Substitute any yam or sweet potato.

Onaga:
The Japanese name for red snapper. Best steamed, baked or sautéed. Substitute monkfish or orange roughy.

Ono:
A mackerel with white firm flesh. Also known as wahoo. Substitute tuna, swordfish, or shark.

Opah:
A very large moonfish. Substitute swordfish.

Opakapaka:
A pink snapper with a delicate flavor. Good poached, baked or sautéed. Substitute any red snapper, sea bass, or monkfish.

Opal basil:
A purple-tinged basil used in Asian cooking.

Opihi:
A small limpet gathered from the rocks along the Hawaiian coast. Most often eaten raw, but sometimes grilled. Similar to a snail in texture and an oyster in flavor. Because of the difficulty in gathering opihi, they are considered a rare delicacy.

Oyster Sauce:
A concentrated sauce made from oyster juice and salt, used in many Chinese and other Asian dishes. Keeps a long time in the refrigerator.

P

Panko:
A crispy large-flaked Japanese bread crumb that adds more texture than ordinary bread crumbs. Found in Asian markets.

Papaya:
The most common papaya used in Hawaii is the solo papaya, a tropical fruit with a yellow flesh, black seeds, and a perfumey scent. Other types are larger, and may have pink flesh; all are suitable for island recipes. Also see green papaya.

Passion fruit:
See lilikoi. Passion fruit juice concentrate can be found in the frozen juice section of some markets. Substitute orange juice concentrate.

Patis fish sauce:
A strong-flavored seasoning sauce used in Southeast Asian cuisines. Tiparos is one brand name.

Persimmon:
Tart, red-orange fruit of the persimmon tree. Fuyu and Hachiqa are the most common varieties found in markets. Fuyu persimmons are small, resembling tomatoes, and may be eaten when still firm. Hachiqa are larger, the size of peaches, and must be fully ripe before being used. Persimmons are fall fruit, but may also be found dried in natural foods stores and Asian markets.

Pickled ginger:
Thinly sliced ginger preserved in rice wine vinegar.

Pineapple:
Fresh pineapples are covered with a prickly brown skin, and topped with sharp, pointed leaves. To select a fresh ripe pineapple, give the tiny center leaves at the top a light tug:

The leaves will easily pluck out of a ripe pineapple. Fresh pineapple contains an enzyme which will break down protein; rinse well and add as close to serving time as possible when using in dishes containing gelatin.

Pipikaula:
The Hawaiian version of beef jerky.

Plum sauce:
Also called Chinese plum sauce. A sweet and sour sauce available in most Asian markets.

Plum wine:
See Japanese plum wine.

Poha:
The Hawaiian name for cape gooseberries, marble-sized tart berries encased in a papery husk.

Pohole fern:
See fiddlehead ferns.

Poke:
A traditional Hawaiian dish made of raw fish, Hawaiian salt, seaweed, and chilies.

Poi:
A starchy paste made by pounding the taro root with water until it reaches a smooth consistency. A staple in the traditional Hawaiian diet.

Portuguese sausage:
Linguiça, a pork sausage spiced with chili. Substitute hot Italian sausages.

Pot Sticker Wrappers:
Thin round pastry skins made from flour and water. Used to make Chinese dim sum.

Puna goat cheese:
A fresh white goat cheese produced in the Puna district of the island of Hawaii. It is made in the traditional French way. Substitute any fresh white goat cheese.

Purple potatoes:
See Okinawan sweet potatoes.

R

Rice noodles:
Also called rice vermicelli. When they are deep-fried they expand immediately to several times their size. They can also be soaked and served as soft noodles. Packages of the dry noodles are in Asian markets.

Rice paper:
Thin sheets of noodles made from rice flour and water. Soften the sheets in water before wrapping food with them.

Rice wine vinegar:
A light vinegar made from fermented rice.

S

Sake:
Clear Japanese rice wine. Other strong clear liquors, such as tequila or vodka, can be substituted.

Sambal olek:
A chunky red chili paste used in Indonesia and Malaysia. Any Asian hot chili paste can be substituted.

Sansho peppercorns:
An expensive bottled peppercorn found in Japanese markets. Substitute any fine quality peppercorn, or Sichuan peppercorns.

Sapote:
The sapote is large, the size of an avocado, with a rough brown skin. Look for unblemished skin and a slight softness under the skin when pressed gently.

Sesame seeds:
Small flat oval white or black seeds used to flavor or garnish main dishes and desserts.

Shichimi:

A Japanese spice blend of chilies, sesame seeds, orange peel, seaweed, and poppy seeds. Substitute Cajun spice mix.

Shiitake mushrooms:

The second most widely cultivated mushroom in the world, medium to large with umbrella-shaped, flopped tan to dark brown caps with edges that tend to roll under. Shiitakes have a woodsy, smoky flavor. Can be purchased fresh or dried in Asian groceries. To reconstitute the dried variety, soak in warm water for 30 minutes before using. Stem both fresh and dried shiitakes.

Shiso leaf:

Also called the beefsteak leaf, the 2- to 3-inch aromatic red-and-green leaf is very popular in Japanese cuisine. Substitute fresh basil or mint.

Shoyu:

The Japanese and Hawaiian name for soy sauce.

Shutome:

The Hawaiian broadbill swordfish. Substitute any swordfish.

Soba noodles:

Thin brown noodles made from buckwheat and wheat flour. They cook quickly and can be served hot or cold.

Solo papaya:

A small yellow papaya with orange flesh and black seeds. The most common variety found in Hawaii.

Soy Sauce:

A dark salty liquid made from soybeans, flour, salt, and water. Dark soy sauce is stronger than light soy sauce. A staple in most Asian cuisines.

Spicy tobiko:

Japanese caviar seasoned with wasabi.

Sprouts:

Bean, daikon, pea, sunflower, and radish are all types of sprouts used in salads and vegetable dishes in Hawaii. Most can be found in Asian or natural foods stores.

Star Anise:

Brownish seeds with eight points that taste like licorice.

Star fruit:

A waxy, light green fruit; also called carambola. Cut in cross section, it reveals a five-pointed star shape. Trim the points off the stars if the points are too dark for your taste.

Sticky Rice:

A glutinous short-grain white rice used in Thai cuisine. Sticky rice is steamed in baskets and is often used in Thai desserts.

Strawberry papaya:

A small papaya with pinkish flesh and black seeds.

Sweet chili sauce:

See Thai chili paste.

Szechuan chili paste:

A Northern Chinese spicy chili paste using chilies, garlic, oil, and salt.

T

Tako:

The Japanese name for Hawaiian octopus. A popular appetizer prepared as poke or smoked.

Takuan:

A yellow pickled daikon radish available bottled in Japanese markets.

Tamarind:

A brown, bean-shaped pod from the tamarind tree. The fruit is sweet-sour, and is made into sauces, candy, and pastes.

Tapa cloth:

A feltlike fabric made from the pounded bark of the wauke, or mulberry, tree. Traditionally used by the Hawaiians for clothing, bedding, and canoe sails.

Taro:

A starchy root of the taro, called kalo, is pounded to make poi. Its flavor is similar to artichokes or chestnuts. The leaves (luau) and stems (haha) are also used in cooking. Taro contains an irritating substance and must be cooked before any part of the plant can be eaten.

Taro leaves:

See luau leaves.

Thai basil:

A green and red variety of basil. Substitute fresh sweet basil.

Thai chili paste:

A slightly sweet, thick, hot bottled-paste of garlic, vinegar, and chilies. Sriracha is a brand name.

Thai curry paste:

Yellow, red, and green curry pastes used in many Thai and Southeast Asian sauces. Yellow is generally the mildest and green the hottest.

Thai ginger:

See galangal.

Tiger shrimp:

A large saltwater shrimp with a striped shell.

Tiparos fish sauce:

A brand of bottled Filipino fish sauce used to season many Asian dishes.

Ti leaf:

The leaves of the ti plant. Used to steam and bake fish and vegetables. Often called "Hawaiian aluminum foil." Substitute banana leaves, grape leaves, or even corn husks. Available at wholesale florist shops.

Tobiko:

The orange roe of the flying fish. Similar to caviar, it has a mild flavor and slight crunch. It is available in red, black, and green in Japanese markets.

Tofu:

The Japanese name for soybean curd. Available fresh in Asian markets.

Togarashi:

Japanese red pepper flakes, also called ichimi. Substitute red pepper flakes.

V

Venison:

Island deer are hunted primarily on the islands of Lanai, Molokai, and Hawaii. Because it has so little fat, venison is usually marinated or cooked slowly in liquid. Venison is a favorite meat for pipikaula, a version of beef jerky.

Vietnamese chili paste:

An extremely spicy paste of garlic, vinegar and chilies.

W

Wana:

A purple sea urchin considered a delicacy by Hawaiians and Japanese.

Warabi:

See fiddlehead ferns.

Wasabi:

The Japanese name for a root that resembles horseradish. It is most often sold in cans as powder or paste.

Won bok:

Cabbagelike vegetable, also called napa or Chinese cabbage.

Wonton wrappers:

Thin sheets of noodle dough used to wrap food for frying or steaming.

Mail-Order Sources

Aloha Shoyu Company

96-1205 Waihona St.
Pearl City HI 96782
Telephone (808)-456-5929
FAX (808) 456-5093

A producer of specialty cooking sauces, with distributors on the West Coast. Call for information on an outlet near you.

Aquaculture Development Program

Department of Land and Natural
*   Resources*
State of Hawaii
335 Merchant St., Room 348
Honolulu HI 96813
Telephone (808) 587-0030
FAX (808) 587-0033

This department acts as a clearinghouse of information for Hawaiian aquaculture products and can put you in touch with a wholesaler or farm, as well as direct you to a store in your area. Fresh products are available mostly on the West Coast.

Chickory Farms

723 Hillary Street
New Orleans LA 70118
Telephone 1-800-605-4550

All manner of mushrooms, both cultivated and wild.

D'Artagnon

399-419 St. Paul Avenue
Jersey City NJ 07306
Telephone 1-800-327-8246

Fresh foie gras, plus sausages, ducks and duck fat, and other specialty items.

Fresh Island Fish

RR#1, P.O. Box 373-B
Wailuku, Maui HI 96793
Telephone 1-800-628-3329 or
*   (808) 244-9633*
FAX (808) 244-9421

A wholesaler of ocean-caught or aquacultured fresh Hawaiian fish for export to mainland restaurants and distributors. They specialize in snappr, sashimi-grade ahi, mahimahi, ono, and swordfish. They will retail directly to the consumer, but it can be expensive.

Hana Herbs

P.O. Box 323
Hana HI 96713
Telephone and FAX (808) 248-7407

A wholesaler of Hawaiian herbs such as lemongrass and Thai basil. Will ship by Federal Express to professional chefs and distributors.

Hawaii Marine Enterprises

P.O. Box 301
Kahuku HI 96731
Telephone 1-800-542-4459 or
*   (808) 293-1230*

A grower and wholesaler of Hawaiian edible seaweeds such as ogo. Call for information on a supplier in your area.

Hawaiian Fruit Specialties, Ltd.

P.O. Box 637
Kalaheo HI 96741
Telephone (808) 332-9333
FAX (808) 332-7650

This retail supplier will mail island jams, jellies, mango chutney, and syrups.

Hawaiian Vintage Chocolate Company

4614 Kilauea Avenue, Ste. 435
Honolulu HI 96816
Telephone (808) 735-8494

High-quality white, semisweet, and dark chocolate produced on the Big Island of Hawaii. Available both wholesale and retail.

Kitchen Crafts, Inc.

2410 W. 79th Street
Merrillville IN 46307

Confectionary and bakery supplies and tools.

Langenstein Farms

84-4956 Mamalahoa Highway
Captain Cook HI 96704
Telephone 1-800-621-5365
FAX and message, 800-328-8356

A top-quality grower of sun-dried, air-roasted 100 percent Kona estate coffee available in several roasts. Brochure and order form available.

MacFarms of Hawaii

3615 Harding Avenue, No. 207
Honolulu HI 96816
Telephone (808) 737-0645
FAX (808) 734-4675

Unsalted dry-roasted macadamia nuts and other macadamia products by mail.

Mauna Loa Macadamia Nuts

HC01, P.O. Box 3
Hilo, Hawaii HI 96720
Telephone (808) 966-8619

Macadamia nut products and Kona coffee.

Oils of Aloha

P.O. Box 685
Waialua HI 96791
Telephone 1-800 367-6010 or
* (808) 637-5620*
FAX (808) 637-6194

Producers of macadamia nut oil. A mail-order catalogue is available.

Orchid Isle Chève

Kuokoa Farm
P.O. Box 452
Kurtistown HI 96760
Telephone (808) 966-7792

Producer of high-quality goat cheese. They make fresh chèvre, chèvre in olive oil, and feta on the Big Island of Hawaii. Mail order available.

Penzeys Ltd.

Merchants of Quality Spices
P.O. Box 1448
Waukesha WI 53187
Telephone (414) 574-0277
FAX (414) 574-0278

A wonderful source of spices and herbs by mail. A mail-order catalogue is available.

Rooster Farms Coffee Company

P.O. Box 471
Honaunau HI 96726
Telephone (808) 328-9173
FAX (808) 328-9378

Producer of sun-dried handpicked 100 percent Kona coffee. Both regular and organically grown coffees are available. A mail-order brochure is available.

Sweet Celebrations

P.O. Box 39426
Edina MN 55439
Telephone 1-800-328-6722
FAX (612) 943-1688

A complete catalogue of confectioners' supplies including chocolate and other ingredients, and equipment.

Take Home Maui, Inc.

121 Dickenson Street
Lahaina HI 96761
Telephone (808) 661-8067
FAX (808) 661-1550

A mail-order source for Maui onions, fresh pineapple and papaya, and macadamia nut products.

The Oriental Pantry

423 Great Road
Acton MA 01720
Telephone (508) 264-4576
FAX (617) 275-4506

An extensive and helpful mail-order source for Asian cooking utensils and foods ranging from Thai chili paste to lemongrass and hoisin sauce. Call for mail-order catalogue.

Albert Uster Imports, Inc.

9211 Gaither Road
Gaithersburg MD 20877
Telephone 1-800-231-8154

A professional source for confectionary and bakery supplies and tools, including edible gold dust.

Wilton Enterprises, Inc.

2240 West 75th Street
Woodridge IL 60515
Telephone (708) 963-7100, ext. 320

Pastry and cake decorating supplies, paste food colors, and icing ingredients.

Great Chefs® of HAWAII
Credits

Book

Publisher	Great Chefs® Publishing
	John Shoup
Author	Kaui Philpotts
Editor	Carolyn Miller
Photography	Eric Futran
Book Design	Larry Escudier
	Dwain Richard Jr.
Production Services	Mimi Luebbermann
	Linda Anne Nix
Culinary Advisor	Carolyn Buster
Recipe Testing	Calabash Occasions
	Judy Furtado
Indexing Services	Frances Bowles
Public Relations	Linda Anne Nix

Home Video — **Great Chefs® Video**

Design	Escudier & Richard
Duplication	Bowling Green Associates

CD/Music — **Leisure Jazz**

Music	Kapono Beamer
	The Charlie Byrd Trios
Distributor	Leisure Jazz
Design	Escudier & Richard

Television Series — **Great Chefs® Television**

Producer/Writer/Director	John Beyer
Presenter	Mary Lou Conroy
Announcer	Andres Calandria
Camera/Lighting	Dave Landry
Editor/Animation	George Matulik
Assistant Editor	Maria D. Estevez
Post Production Audio	Andres Calandria
Theme Music	Composed and performed by
	Kapono Beamer
Original Music	The Charlie Byrd Trios
Transportation Captian	Rex Johnson
Location Manager	Capt. Jerome Judd
Additional Footage	Hawaii Vistors' Bureau
	Ackerman-Black Productions
Offical Hotel	Aston Hotels & Resorts
Executive Administrative	
Assistant to the Executive Producer	Cybil W. Curtis
Executive Producer	John Shoup

HAWAII™

Aston at the Waikiki Shore

More choices, more islands, more value make Aston Hawaii's leading hotel and condominium resort operator.

Aston Kauai Beach Villas (beachfront unit)

More Choices: Choose from over 30 hotels and condominium resorts located right in Waikiki, and on Maui, Kauai, and the Big Island of Hawaii. High-rises or low-rises, quiet or active, elegant or business-like, ocean views, mountain views—at Aston the choice is yours.

More Value: Enjoy more room for your money without paying more money for your room. In Hawaii, the word for value is Aston. Mix 7 discounts 20-25% off regular rates for stays of 7 or more consecutive nights. Sun Club offers seniors discounts of up to 25%. And, "astonishing deals" coupon books worth hundreds of dollars of discounts on dining, shopping, golf, and car rentals.

More Fun: Most Aston hotels and condominium resorts are beachfront with swimming pools, jet spas, tennis courts, barbecue grills, nearby championship golf, shopping, and more!

The Shores at Waikoloa

ASTON®
Hotels & Resorts
Relax and enjoy the value.™

Call your travel agent or 800-922-7866, continental U.S. & Canada.

Great Chefs® of HAWAII
The Television Series

Program Number	Appetizer	Entree	Dessert
1	Crispy Sea Scallops Wrapped in Shredded Phyllo *Corey Waite,* *Coast Grill,* *Hapuna Beach Prince Hotel,* *Kamuela, Hawaii*	Opakapaka with Sesame-Chili Sauce *OnJin Kim,* *Hanatei Bistro,* *Honolulu, Oahu,*	Kathleen's Low-Fat Chocolate Chip Ice Cream Sandwich *Kathleen Daelemans,* *Grand Wailea Resort,* *Wailea, Maui*
2	Puna Goat Cheese and Vegetable Torte *Beverly Gannon,* *Halimaile General Store,* *Halimaile, Maui*	Roast Rack of Lamb with Sun-dried Tomato and Apple-smoked Bacon *Edwin Goto,* *The Lodge at Koele,* *Lanai City, Lanai*	Warm Pineapple Tart with Coconut Sauce *Jeff Walters,* *La Mer,* *Halekulani Hotel,* *Honolulu, Oahu*
3	Cassoulet of Island Opihi in Pineapple Cream with Okinawan Sweet Potatoes and Crispy Ogo *Ronald Nasuti,* *Roy's Poipu Bar & Grill* *Poipu Kauai*	Sautéed Shrimp and Penne with Rice Cream Sauce *Alan Wong,* *Alan Wong's Restaurant,* *Honolulu, Oahu*	Kona Coffee–Chocolate Cheesecake with Macadamia Nut Crust *Mark Hetzel,* *Four Seasons Resort Maui,* *Wailea, Maui*
4	Caramelized Maui Onion Soup *David Paul Johnson,* *David Paul's Lahaina Grill,* *Lahaina, Maui*	Beef Tenderloin and Poached Oysters with Essence of Pinot Noir and Chervil Sauce *George Mavrothalassitis,* *La Mer,* *Halekulani Hotel,* *Honolulu, Oahu*	Honey and Hawaiian Vintage Chocolate Ganache with Gold-dusted Chocolate Leaves and Poha Berry Sauce *Philippe Padovani,* *The Manele Bay Hotel,* *Lanai City, Lanai*
5	Spicy Thai Beef Salad with Lemongrass-Mint Vinaigrette with Toasted Macadamia Nuts *Roy Yamaguchi, Roy's* *Restaurant,* *Honolulu, Oahu*	Seared Mahimahi with Garlic-Sesame Crust and Lime-Ginger Sauce *Jean-Marie Josselin,* *A Pacific Café* *Kapaa, Kauai*	Caramel Miranda *Mark Ellman,* *Avalon Restaurant & Bar* *Lahaina, Maui*
6	Kalua Ducklings with Mango-Tomato Relish and Chili Pepper Cream *Gary Strehl,* *Hawaii Prince Hotel Waikiki,* *Honolulu, Oahu*	Crispy Thai-style Chicken *Amy Ferguson-Ota,* *The Dining Room,* *The Ritz-Carlton Mauna Lani,* *Kohala Coast, Hawaii*	Chocolate Cake *Kathleen Daelemans,* *Cafe Kula,* *Grand Wailea Resort,* *Wailea Maui*
7	Nalo Green Salad with Crispy Wontons and Tangerine Vinaigrette *Gerard Kaleohano,* *Mid-Pacific Country Club,* *Lanikai, Oahu*	Roasted Opakapaka Orange-Ginger Butter Sauce *Gerard Reversade,* *Gerard's at the Plantation Inn,* *Lahaina, Maui*	White Chocolate–Mango Mousse *Manuel Garcia,* *La Cascata,* *Princeville Hotel,* *Princeville, Kaui*
8	Fried Poke with Keahole Ahi Nori *Sam Choy,* *Sam Choy's Restaurants* *of Hawaii,* *Kailua Kona, Hawaii*	Roasted Rack of Lamb with Macadamia Honey, Minted Papaya and Star Fruit Salsa, and Cabernet Sauce *Daniel Delbrel,* *La Cascata,* *Princeville Hotel,* *Princeville, Kaui*	Molokai Sweet Bread Pudding *Derek Langlois,* *The Plantation House Reastaurant,* *Kapalua, Maui*

Program Number	Appetizer	Entree	Dessert
9	Oahu Rock Shrimp with Sprout Slaw and Asian Cocktail Sauce *Steve Amaral, Kea Lani Hotel Suites & Villas, Wailea, Maui*	Nanakuli Chicken Breasts with Shiitake Mushrooms and Steamed Baby Vegetables *Dominique Jamain, The Maile Restaurant, Kahala Hilton, Honolulu, Oahu*	Oheloberry Dessert in Tulip Cookies *Peter Chilla, Coast Grill, Hapuna Beach Prince Hotel, Mauna Kea Resort, Kamuela, Hawaii*
10	Crisp Nori-wrapped Shrimp and Wasabi Aïoli and Sweet Shoyu Glaze *Mako Segawa-Gonzales, Roy's Poipu Bar & Grill, Poipu, Kauai*	Wok Lobster with Lehua Honey and Black Bean Sauce *Patrick Callarec, The Dining Room, The Ritz-Carlton Kapalua, Kapalua, Maui*	Chilled White Nougat with Candied Fruit and Guava Coulis *Jeff Walters, La Mer, Halekulani Hotel, Honolulu, Oahu*
11	Nori-wrapped Peppercorn-crusted Tuna with Mizuna, Enoki, and Wasabi *Kelly Degala, Gordon Biersch Brewery Restaurant, Honolulu, Oahu*	Macadamia Nut-crusted Hawaiian Shutome and Vegetable Lumpia with Black Bean and Orange Shrimp Butter Sauces *Tod Kawachi, Roy's Kahana Bar & Grill, Kahana, Maui*	Five Spoons of Crème Brûlée *Mark Okumura, Alan Wong's Restaurant, Honolulu, Oahu*
12	Grilled Shrimp and Star Fruit Salad *Peter Merriman, Merriman's Restaurant, Waimea, Hawaii*	Ginger Sake Breast of Duck and Duck Adobo *Thomas B.H. Wong, The Surf Room, Royal Hawaiian Waikiki Sheraton, Honolulu, Oahu*	Papaya and Cheese Charlotte with Coconut Vanilla Sauce *Gerard Reversade, Gerard's at the Plantation Inn, Lahaina, Maui*
13	Seared Lanai Venison Carpaccio with Crisp Herb Salad *Edwin Goto, The Lodge at Koele, Lanai City, Lanai*	Papillotte of Kumu with Basil, Seaweed, and Shittake Mushrooms *George Mavrothalassitis, La Mer, Halekulani Hotel, Honolulu, Oahu*	Lilikoi Custard Tart *Beverly Gannon, Haliimaile General Store, Haliimaile, Maui*
14	Ono Poke with Crisp Wontons and Ogo Vinaigrette *Alex Stanislaw, The Plantation House Restaurant Kapalua, Maui*	Jasmine Tea-steamed Fillet of Opakapaka with Coriander Butter Sauce *Russell Siu, 3660 on the Rise, Honolulu, Oahu*	Banana Split *Kathleen Daelemans, Cafe Kula, Grand Wailea Resort and Spa, Wailea, Maui*
15	Puna Goat Cheese and Vegetable Terrine *Amy Ferguson-Ota, The Dining Room, The Ritz-Carlton Mauna Lani, Kohala Coast, Hawaii*	Seared Opakapaka with Crab Rolls *Jean-Marie Josselin, A Pacific Cafe, Kapaa, Kauai*	Chocolate-Macadamia Nut Toffee Torte *Rodney Weddle, The Dining Room, The Ritz-Carlton Kapalua, Kapalua, Maui*
16	Charred Sichimi Ahi Coated with Japanese Spices in Lilikoi-Soy Sauce *OnJin Kim Hanatei Bistro, Honolulu, Oahu*	Opah Baked in Pistachio Crust with Ginger Essence *Corey Waite, Coast Grill, Hapuna Beach Prince Hotel, Kamuela, Hawaii*	Banana Lumpia with Macadamia-Sapote Ice Cream *Gerard Kaleohano, Mid-Pacific Country Club, Lanikai, Oahu*

Program Number	Appetizer	Entree	Dessert
17	Red and White Sashimi Sald *Alan Wong* *Alan Wong's Restaurant,* *Honolulu, Oahu*	Indonesian Grilled Lamb Chops with Ginger Cream *Mark Ellman,* *Avalon Restaurant & Bar,* *Lahaina Maui*	Pineapple Tart *Dominique Jamain,* *The Maile Restaurant,* *Kahala Hilton,* *Honolulu, Oahu*
18	Wok-charred Ahi *Peter Merriman,* *Merriman's Restaurant,* *Waimea, Hawaii*	Lemongrass-grilled Mako Shark with Sticky Rice and Roasted Banana-Mint Sauce *Jacqueline Lau,* *Roy's Nicolina* *Kahana, Maui*	Black Sesame Nougatines with Green Tea Mousse and Glazed Chestnuts *Katsuo Sugiura (Chef Suki),* *Ihilani Resort & Spa,* *Kapolei, Oahu*
19	Venison Pipikaula with Kau Orange Vinaigrette *Thomas B.H. Wong,* *The Surf Room,* *Royal Hawaiian Waikiki Sheraton,* *Honolulu, Oahu*	Kalua Duck with Plum Sauce and Lundberg Rice *David Paul Johnson,* *David Paul's Lahaina Grill,* *Maui*	Big Island Vintage Chocolate Suprise *Jeff Walters,* *La Mer,* *Halekulani Hotel,* *Honolulu, Oahu*
20	Ahi Carpaccio with White Truffle Vinaigrette *Jean-Marie Josselin,* *A Pacific Cafe,* *Kapaa, Kauai*	Togarashi-seared Kumu with Pohole Fern Salad and Sesame Dressing *Amy Ferguson-Ota,* *The Dining Room,* *The Ritz-Carlton Mauna Lani,* *Kohala Coast, Hawaii*	Bittersheet Chocolate Pie *Kathleen Daelemans,* *Cafe Kula,* *Grand Wailea Resort,* *Wailea, Maui*
21	Spicy Island Ahi Poke with Tobiko Caviar on Seared Furikaki Rice Cakes *Mako Segawa-Gonzales,* *Roy's Poipu Bar& Grill,* *Poipu, Kauai*	Blackened Jawaiian Spicy Chicken Breasts with Banana-Rum Sauce and Chili Corn Cakes *Beverly Gannon,* *Haliimaile General Store,* *Halaiimaile, Maui*	Sam Choy's Pineapple Cheesecake *Robert Eng,* *Sam Choy's Diamond Head Restaurant,* *Honolulu, Oahu*
22	Seared Spicy Ahi with Ogo-Wasabi Sauce and Fiddlehead Fern Sald *Daniel Delbrel,* *La Cascata,* *Princeville Hotel,* *Princeville, Kauai*	Pan-seared Onaga Fillet with Pumpkin and Curry Sauce *Steave Amaral,* *Kea Lani Hotel Suites & Villas,* *Wailea, Maui*	Panna Cotta and Exotic Fruit in Lilikoi-Apricot Sauce *Philippe Padovani,* *The Manele Bay Hotel,* *Lanai City, Lanai*
23	Ahi and Taro Salad *Mark Ellman,* *Avalon Restaurant & Bar,* *Lahaina, Maui*	Opakapaka CanoeHouse *Alan Wong,* *Alan Wong's Restaurant,* *Honolulu, Oahu*	Hawaiian Sweet Potato Cakes with Pineapple Ice Cream and Coconut Crème Fraîche *Mark Hetzel,* *Four Seasons Resort Maui,* *Wailea, Maui*
24	Seared Smoked Ahi with Lychee Salsa and Ogo-Wasabi Sauce *Gary Strehl,* *Hawaii Prince Hotel Waikiki,* *Honolulu, Oahu*	Salmon and Shrimp Gyoza with Sweet Chili Vinaigrette and Sweet Chili Beurre Blanc *Jean-Marie Josselin,* *A Pacific Cafe,* *Kapaa, Kauai*	Tropical Fruits with Passion Fruit Sabayon and Balsamic Syrup *Jeff Cabiles,* *Kea Lani Hotel Suites & Villas,* *Wailea, Maui*
25	Grilled Kahuku Prawn Relleno with Puna Goat Cheese and Smoky Tomato Salsa *Jacqueline Lau,* *Roy's Nicolina,* *Kahana, Maui*	Grilled Kajiki and Okinawan Sweet Potatoes with Peppercorn-Wasabi Vinaigrette *Gordon Hopkins,* *Roy's Restaurant,* *Honolulu, Oahu*	Fresh Fruit in Vanilla-infused Balsamic Vinegar *Heather Carlin,* *David Paul's Lahaina Grill,* *Lahaina, Maui*

Program Number	Appetizer	Entree	Dessert
26	Ahi Cake *Alan Wong* *Alan Wong's Restaurant,* *Honolulu, Oahu*	Rich Forest *Alex Stanislaw,* *The Plantation House* *Restaurant,* *Lahaina, Maui*	Cold Tapioca with Coconut Milk, Mango, and Berries *Daniel Delbrel,* *La Cascata,* *Princeville Hotel,* *Princeville, Kauai*
27	Ahi and Onaga Poke with Green Papaya Salad and Lime Vinaigrette *Philippe Padovani,* *The Manele Bay Hotel,* *Lanai City, Lanai*	Wok-fried Opakapaka with Spicy Black Bean Sauce *Mark Ellman,* *Avalon Restaurant & Bar* *Lahaina Maui*	Floating Island *Jeff Walters,* *La Mer;* *Halekulani Hotel,* *Honolulu, Oahu*
28	Nori-seared Ahi with Citrus-Garlic Miso Sauce and Shiitake "Chopsticks" *Tod Kawachi,* *Roy's Kahana Bar & Grill,* *Kahana, Maui*	Wok-seared Opakapaka with Amaranth, Hearts of Palm and Okinawan Sweet Potatoes *Kelly Degala,* *Gordon Biersch Brewery* *Restaurant,* *Honolulu, Oahu*	Flourless Macadamia Nut–Chocolate Cake *Gerard Reversade,* *Gerard's at the Plantation Inn,* *Lahaina, Maui*
29	Peking-Style Squab with Foie Gras and Pineapple Tatin with Persimmon Sauce *Bradley Montgomery,* *The Dining Room,* *The Ritz-Carlton Kapalua,* *Kapalua, Maui*	Steamed Onaga *Daniel Delbrel,* *La Cascata,* *Princeville Hotel,* *Princeville Kauai*	Lilikoi Truffle *Mark Hetzel,* *Four Seasons Resort Maui,* *Wailea, Maui*
30	Tempura of Keahole Baby Lobster *Corey Waite,* *Coast Grill,* *Hapuna Beach Prince Hotel,* *Kamuela, Hawaii*	Portuguese Steamed Clams *Beverly Gannon,* *Haliimaile General Store,* *Haliimaile, Maui*	Hot Lilikoi Soufflés *Amy Ferguson-Ota* *The Dining Room,* *The Ritz-Carlton Mauna Lani,* *Kohala Coast, Hawaii*

Index

Note: Page numbers in boldface type indicate chefs' biographies.

Notes